Llandaff Cathedral

This book is dedicated to our subscribers

Mrs D T James
Canon S Kirk
Mrs D M Lambert
Sir Norman Lloyd Edwards
Mr J Morgan
Mr K Morris
Mrs P Philips
Sir Donald Walters

Llandaff Cathedral

edited by
Nick Lambert

SEREN

Seren is the book imprint of
Poetry Wales Press Ltd
Nolton Street, Bridgend, Wales
www.serenbooks.com

ISBN 978-1-85411-499-0

A CIP record for this title is available from
the British Library

The publisher works with the financial assistance
of the Welsh Books Council

Printed by the Gutenberg Press, Malta

Contents

Preface 6

Introduction 7

Llandaff from its Earliest days until the Reformation – Nick Lambert 9

Three Centuries: Three Restorations – Nevil James 52

The Art of Llandaff Cathedral – Pat Aithie 117

The Stained Glass of Llandaff Cathedral – Nevil James 171

The Bells of Llandaff Cathedral – Nevil James 199

Music at Llandaff Cathedral – Graham Holcombe 215

Bibliography 232

List of Bichops, Deans and Organists 234

Image Acknowledgements 236

Index 237

Preface

This book celebrates the long and varied history of our beloved Cathedral at Llandaff. Since tradition accords it a foundation around 546 and the present building has stood on this site since 1120, we may claim justifiably that Llandaff Cathedral is a monument to 1500 years of Christian worship in South Wales.

The Cathedral has seen so many changes and such turbulent times! From the arrival of the Normans to Owain Glyndwr's fight for independence, from the Reformation to the turmoil of the Civil War, from the extraordinary reconstruction of a ruined building by the Victorians to the aerial destruction wrought during World War II, Llandaff has been restored again and again, thanks to the dedication of its clergy and people.

During my time as Dean, I have been privileged to oversee the installation of our award-winning lighting and the building of our great new organ. Its towering pipes in the arches of the chancel provide a twenty-first century counterpoint to the superb arch of Bishop Urban's Norman church, John Prichard's majestic spire and Jacob Epstein's humbling masterpiece, Christ in Majesty. The organ embodies the musical tradition of Llandaff and the continuation of our worship in this building.

I hope that this book will be read and enjoyed by members of our Cathedral and Parish and the wider Diocese and will help to spread Llandaff's name to more distant places. Every year we welcome visitors from every part of the world and they come away full of praise for the Cathedral's art and architecture. Though its physical dimensions may be relatively modest, Llandaff is a truly great Cathedral that embodies the Christian aspirations of its ancient patrons St Dyfrig, St Teilo and St Euddogwy.

The Very Reverend John T. Lewis
Dean of Llandaff

Introduction

The suggestion for a new book about Llandaff's architecture was made almost forty years ago when Nick James proposed reprinting and updating J.H. James's classic *A History and Survey of the Cathedral Church of SS Peter, Paul, Dubritius, Teilo and Oudoceus Llandaff*. First published in 1898, this volume featured many beautiful scale drawings of the restored Victorian Cathedral and was reprinted again in 1929. By 1970, however, the Cathedral's structure had been significantly altered by rebuilding after World War II and James's book was long out of date.

The idea lay dormant until 1990 when the recently appointed Honorary Cathedral Archivists received a telephone call from Miss J Hamlett in Barry. She told them that, in clearing her grandfather's house in Llandaff, she had discovered a collection of his drawings of the Cathedral that might be of interest. When she added that her grandfather's name was John H. James, the archivists arranged to meet her that same day.

The meticulous architectural drawings, in Indian ink on heavy cartridge paper, were indeed the originals from James's handsome volume. Miss Hamlett very generously offered the total collection of the drawings to the Cathedral Archive and they accompanied the overjoyed archivists back to Llandaff where they now form a valued part of the collection.

In 2007, Nick James again suggested that a new volume should be written about the Cathedral's art and architecture, including the James drawings. A team was formed by Nick Lambert, including Nevil James, Patricia Aithie and Canon Graham Holcombe writing on different aspects of the building. Our aim was to examine the history of Llandaff in the light of new research on its origins, and to understand its more recent restorations in the 1860s and 1950s. Hitherto, much of Llandaff's history has been written up in the Friends Report, in historical journals, and mentioned in other books. We made a concerted effort to pull together these disparate sources and to unearth many rare images of the Cathedral throughout its development.

We were very fortunate in receiving the support of eight subscribers without whom this project could not have gone forward. Special mention must be made of Mr Keith Morris who sadly passed away before this book was published.

We would like to thank the Dean and Chapter for allowing access to the archives and the Cathedral Archivists, Mr John Bethel and Mr Eric Treharne, for patiently guiding us to new sources in the collection.

It is our hope that this book will create a new awareness of Llandaff's unique history and its position as a gem amongst the Welsh cathedrals.

The cathedral, viewed from the meadows in the late nineteenth century

Llandaff from its Earliest Days until the Reformation

Introduction

Llandaff Cathedral rises like a sculpted outcrop on the banks of the Taff. It is at its most dramatic when the spire is viewed from a distance, piercing the Cardiff skyline in the midst of the plain. Seen at close range, the spire helps to offset the Cathedral's location in a hollow beneath the village of Llandaff. Victorian architect John Prichard's decision to ennoble the Cathedral with a spire was a departure from the simpler towers of the medieval structure. In doing so Prichard created the distinctive silhouette that establishes the Cathedral's presence for miles around.

Cardiff was raised to city status in 1905 and Llandaff became part of the city in 1922. Modern Cardiff grew rapidly from a sleepy borough town into a cosmopolitan port city due to the prosperity generated by the Industrial Revolution in South Wales. The same economic and social forces revitalized the Cathedral itself and turned Llandaff into a genteel Victorian suburb. But for most of its existence, Llandaff Cathedral stood in near isolation in a semi-rural locale, surrounded for the most part by a few farmhouses and a small medieval settlement whose only other notable building was the Bishop's Castle at the top of the High Street.

The Cathedral's pre-industrial locale can be seen at its best in the drawings and paintings made by Romantic artists at the start of the nineteenth century. The decayed fabric of the medieval building lent itself to atmospheric depictions that showed a structure not dissimilar to Tintern Abbey, standing aloof in fields going down to the Taff. Though its form is familiar, only the west front and Jasper Tower were intact; the southern tower and much of the walls had collapsed, leaving only the incongruous structure of John Wood's 'Italianate Temple' propping up the eastern end of the building. Most of the Romantic paintings of Llandaff deliberately ignore the Wood temple, observing from angles that conceal it in favour of the broken Gothic shell where sheep graze amidst the fallen pillars of the nave.

Some sense of the old village of Llandaff can be gained from mid-Victorian photographs of tightly-packed houses typical of Glamorganshire and Monmouthshire, before they were demolished in the 1850s to make way for the grander dwellings created by John Prichard, Iwan Christian and George Halliday. These Gothic Revival architects recreated the whole of Llandaff as a unit, ensuring that the cathedral and village fitted together as parts of a larger design. In the main, this plan has survived the developments of the twentieth century. Llandaff retains a certain coherence and although this book focuses on the Cathedral itself, the village must not be forgotten.

Despite being surrounded by the modern city, in some ways Llandaff Cathedral retains its seclusion. Unlike most English cathedrals, it does not impress by vastness but by the use of its space, both interior and exterior, and in the way that quite dissimilar periods of architecture have been fused together into a relatively harmonious whole. Llandaff wears its history for all to see and this is one of its greatest assets both as a building and a place of worship.

The Cathedral has an extraordinary capacity to rejuvenate itself. Perhaps it is the inherent sanctity of the site or its romantic setting. Something about Llandaff has inspired several profoundly influential figures to rebuild and remake it over the centuries. A succession of churches have risen and fallen on this site. The fortunes of Llandaff Cathedral might be said to mirror those of South Wales as a whole, and Glamorgan in particular. And like the old kingdoms of Glamorgan and Gwent that arose after the Romans, the earliest history of Llandaff Cathedral and its Bishops is shrouded in the obscurity of the early medieval period popularly known as the Dark Ages. Traditions preserved in a number of places, combined with recent archaeological discoveries and historical deductions, make it possible to glimpse something of what led to the establishment of a cathedral see at Llandaff before the arrival of the Normans in around 1081.

Whilst the visible architectural history of the building begins with the Normans, we must first look at the earlier period to understand why the site became so important. This chapter attempts to cover a span of 1200 years from the semi-legendary foundation stories of around 540 AD to the downfall of the medieval structure in the 1700s. Nearly half of this period, up to the first Norman building at Llandaff, has left almost no material traces; yet it is crucial to understanding why Llandaff exists where it does and why its origins are so hotly disputed.

Llandaff from the Early Welsh Kingdoms to the Coming of the Normans

Llandaff is located by a ford in the Taff and at the junction of two ancient roads, one running to the west via the highest crossing point of the tidal Taff, the other leading northwards from Cardiff's Roman fortress to Llantrisant. Originally the Taff passed much closer to the Cathedral than today and its valley-bottom site resembles that of Llancarfan[1]. The Roman connection and the distance from

Cardiff's later Norman castle both argue in favour of an early date for Llandaff's site. Its location in a river valley below a ridge is characteristic of the post-Roman era and is comparable to St Davids[2].

The medieval diocese of Llandaff encompassed the counties of Glamorgan and Monmouthshire. Seen on the map, Llandaff is towards the centre of this area and nearly equidistant from the western extremity at Neath and the easternmost edge at Chepstow on the English border. There were significant manors held by Llandaff at Bishopston (Llandeilo Ferwallt) on the Gower, and at Mathern in the Gwent levels.

Sitting on the edge of the fertile Vale of Glamorgan, Llandaff's name indicates its position beside the long river Taff that travels from deep in the heart of the South Wales valleys. This was important at a time when river routes were more easily navigable than many roads and Llandaff is also close to the sea port at Cardiff. The ridge of hills beyond Cardiff mark the edge of the coastal plain and the whole area is divided quite sharply between upland and lowland settlements.

The written history of this area begins around 55 AD when the Romans established a fortress at Usk. They subdued the local Celtic tribe, the Silures, and built their great legionary fortress at Caerleon. Cardiff was the location of another Roman fort whose walls survived long into the medieval period, which was partly why the Normans built their town there. Caerleon became the site for King Arthur's legendary court in Geoffrey of Monmouth's imaginative *History of the Kings of Britain* that gave rise to the Arthurian romances of the Middle Ages.

Llandaff has yielded few traces of the Roman period, unlike nearby Ely which we now know was the site of a villa. However the remains of a Roman road running north towards Llantrisant out of Cardiff were excavated on the

Llandaff Green in the 1850s, with farmhouses

grounds of the Cathedral School in 1987.[3] This would seem to confirm that the main road of Llandaff originally ran through the Green, past the Bishop's Castle and down to Mill Lane (see photograph, p.11). The building of Llandaff Court (the present-day Cathedral School) in the eighteenth century re-routed this road and what is now Cardiff Road developed into the main thoroughfare.

After the arrival of the Romans, the Silures became heavily Romanised and developed a town at Caerwent, whose Latin name Venta Silurum later gave its name to the kingdom of Gwent. The town's impressive fortifications and towers, defending against raiders from across the Irish Sea, survive to this day and Venta has also yielded a plethora of Romano-British archaeological remains. This is one of several continuities between Roman rule and the later Welsh kingdoms that developed when the Roman state of Britannia collapsed in the late fifth century. Post-Roman South Wales inherited some organisations (including the Church) from the Roman administrative area of Britannia Prima, which extended from Oxfordshire through the south west of Britain and included the cities of Gloucester, Bath, and Dorchester amongst others. Its regional capital was at Cirencester and it survived as a patchwork of tribal kingdoms, based around the old Roman towns and also hillforts like Cadbury Castle in Somerset, until the 570s when the Saxons finally captured Bath after the battle of Dyrham. This drove a wedge between the Welsh and the 'West Welsh', the Celts of Devon and Cornwall, who were gradually conquered over the next two centuries.

Christianity came to South Wales around the third century when the Roman converts Julius and Aaron were martyred at Caerleon in 304 AD, leaving behind a saintly cult that persisted through the Middle Ages. Later traces of the new religion include the possible remains of a Christian shrine at Caerwent. In late Roman times, the Church was primarily an urban organisation that spread outwards into the countryside via the road network.

In the sub-Roman period, churches and monasteries often flourished near villas and estates as the region's power structure became more rural again. Near Cardiff, both Llandough (Juxta Penarth) and Llantwit Major were significant monastic bases that appeared near villas and were also strategically close to the Roman road. Further east, some Roman towns still served local populations: Caerwent and Caerleon survived in various forms, though greatly reduced from Roman times. All these locations would contribute to the development of Llandaff's later diocese.

The Cardiff area was part of the regional kingdom of Glwysing, later Morgannwg, associated with the princely settlement at the hillfort of Dinas Powys. The area's rulers favoured these defensible sites and Roman-style urban living largely disappeared. Yet archaeological finds at this fort show that sea trade with the Mediterranean continued into the sixth century AD and the sea routes were always important to the post-Roman kingdoms.

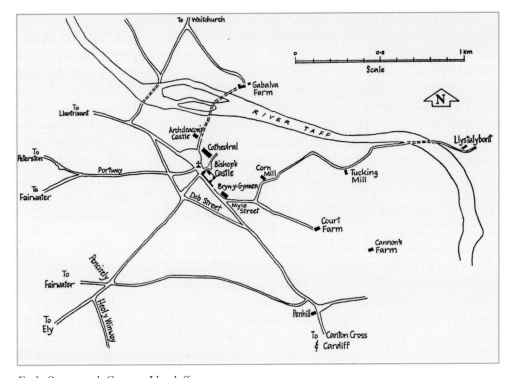

Early Seventeenth Century Llandaff

South Wales remained closely linked to Somerset, Devon and Cornwall (Celtic Dumnonia), and beyond that to Britanny (Armorica), which was culturally part of the British sphere. It is not a coincidence that the early development of Christianity across all these areas was continuous from the Roman period, and remained distinct from other areas of Britain for a long time, a crucial fact in understanding the early history of Llandaff and its locality.

Scant archaeological remains from the crucial period of 450-600 AD make it difficult to understand the dynamics of the early Welsh kingdoms and their religious establishments. However, there is an intriguing continuity between Roman villas and later monastic communities. This happens at Llantwit Major, site of the major monastic settlement of St Illtud, and at Llandough, where an early Christian cross and suggestions of villa buildings were found below the church. Such developments are consistent with the more rural character of Celtic Christianity, which tended to focus on monastic communities instead of towns, and where abbots often had equal status to bishops. In the Celtic world, judging from the later *Lives* written about the saints, these abbots and bishops were peripatetic and roamed across large areas; though some advised specific kings and princes too.

Welsh Christian organisations were based around 'mother churches' called a *clas* church or *monasterium* connected with specific saints and local kingdoms. The saints themselves were often part of local royal families. Families of clerics held hereditary positions at these major sites and the influence of the *clasau* strengthened or weakened according to the local ruler's power. Though these churches were headed by bishops or abbots they did not have a diocese in the modern sense. This structure was modernised by the Normans and the *claswyr*, or clerics who lived at the church, became styled as canons[4]. Their influence was absorbed by later monasteries and true dioceses such as St Davids and Llandaff.

Teilo's foundation and the *Book of Llandaff*

Llandaff is traditionally said to have been founded around 546 AD by St Teilo, whose tomb in the medieval Cathedral was the focal point for an important pilgrimage route. The story of Teilo's foundation of the church by the Taff has been retold countless times since the Middle Ages; it remains as important to the Cathedral's sense of self today as it was then. However, the description of Teilo as the first Bishop of Llandaff is a medieval re-writing of history to justify the creation of a diocese around Llandaff, and the truth is far more complex. In some respects, the history of the bishopric must be disentangled from the site at Llandaff.

Teilo's associations with Llandaff extend to Teilo's Well, which is an ancient appellation; and the Celtic cross that now stands in the south aisle was tradition-ally called *Croes Deilo*. His feast day on the 9th February was observed with great celebration in medieval Llandaff and he featured on the personal seals of Llandaff Bishops alongside Saints Peter and Paul. Teilo also has an association with Brittany that is typical of several Welsh and Breton saints, as the two regions enjoyed close connections in the early Middle Ages.

One of the principal monuments to Llandaff's history is not fashioned from stone or wood but is made of parchment. The *Liber Landavensis*, or Book of Llandaff, was compiled between 1120 and 1140 by Bishop Urban to justify his territorial claims to what he perceived as the historic area covered by Llandaff's diocese. Many of the Teilo traditions were established by the *Liber Landavensis*. Although its medieval origins are interesting in themselves, it is the fact that it contains the text of much older documents which makes it especially valuable. Only in the past thirty years, especially since Wendy Davies published her landmark study, has this more ancient material been properly considered in relation to the post-Roman and early medieval history of South Wales[5].

The very survival of the copy of the *Book of Llandaff* at the National Library of Wales is itself an historical accident, as it was lent by Bishop Theophilus Field

A page from the Book of Llandaff

to the antiquarian John Selden in the early seventeenth century before being acquired by Robert Davies of Llanerch and Gwysaney in Flintshire in the late 1600s. He rebound it and preserved it at his house, where it remained until it was loaned to the National Library of Wales in the 1940s, and purchased by them in 1959.

The text was transcribed and published by J. Gwenogvryn Evans in 1893 and can now be found online at the National Library of Wales website. The book is being rebound for preservation and eventual display and the previous page shows some of the writing from NLW MS 17110E.f.3.v. This medieval compendium provides a fogged lens through which we can perceive something of Llandaff's truly ancient history; the question is how much might be distorted fact or clerical confabulation.

The *Life of St Teilo* is at the heart of the *Liber Landavensis* but its veracity has been debated by scholars since its translation in the early nineteenth century. John Reuben Davies sums up the historical accuracy of the *Life of Teilo* and other saints' *Lives* contained in the *Book of Llandaff*:

> The *Lives* of the founding saints and the charters were all copied into the book by one scribe in the early twelfth century. As history, the saints' *Lives* are impossible. The charters purport to record grants from the sixth to late eleventh century but are, in general, manifestly not what they claim to be. The one consistent position of these texts – that there has been a diocese of Llandaf since the fifth century – is demonstrably untrue. [...] Nevertheless there may be some earlier material buried somewhere in these texts.[6]

Professor Wendy Davies has long argued that the *Book of Llandaff* contains a wealth of detail which comes from earlier periods. Though these records and land grants were heavily edited and reworked in the twelfth century, Davies finds plenty of evidence of earlier material worked into the text. Ancient names and phrases that had no significance to the Norman compilers are included, enabling one to build a fragmentary picture of church activity in the early Welsh kingdoms of Glamorgan, Gwent and Ergyng. According to Davies, the *Book of Llandaff* contains the fragmentary record of post-Roman Christian and civil activity in South Wales, including the existence of territorial Bishops associated with the different royal courts of the region and grants made to them by their various rulers.

Even if the continuous succession of 'Bishops of Llandaff' is fictitious, the presence of a monastery or *clas* church beside the Taff is indicated by a reference to "Tavi urbis... princeps" from 680 AD. The name *Menechi* (modern Mynachdy) is associated with a piece of monastic land near Gabalfa and is recorded both in the *Book of Llandaff* and the *Llancarfan Cartulary*, another medieval compilation about St Cadoc. This monastic land by the Taff seems to have belonged to a disciple of St Cadoc and demonstrates that there was early ecclesiastical activity in this area. The Medievalist A.W. Wade-Evans thought it might actually be the ancient name for Llandaff itself. It may well be that this monastery had some affiliation with St Teilo but the original home of his saintly cult was indisputably located at Llandeilo Fawr, far to the west, until his relics were translated to Llandaff.

Looking at the names of the oldest Welsh churches, it is obvious that most of the Teilo church dedications are in West Wales along with his principal monastery at Llandeilo Fawr. There are only a few in Glamorgan and Monmouthshire, scattered in the Gower and near Abergavenny. The main saints of the Glamorganshire coast were Illtud, Cadoc and Dochau who all have specific monasteries identified with them; Gwent had St Gwynllyw (St Woolos) and St Tewdrig at Mathern; and further east St Dyfrig (Dubricius) worked in the border region of Ergyng. One salient fact about these early Welsh saints is that they were closely associated with the regional kingdoms and their spheres of influence corresponded with tribal and political boundaries. This makes it unlikely that the West Wales St Teilo would have been active in Glamorgan, or made it his principal residence when Llandeilo Fawr has such a strong claim to his name.

In his lecture, the Reverend Fenn speculated that St Euddogwy (Oudoceus) moved the see from Llandeilo to Llandaff because of the curious story in the *Liber Landavensis* about him taking Saint Teilo's relics from his old monastery.[7] This could not have happened until much later because Llandeilo was flourishing until at least the tenth century, and Llantwit Major, Llancarfan and Llandough were too strong to admit a competing claim to be the principal ecclesiastical centre of Glamorgan. Yet at some stage between the tenth and eleventh centuries, Llandaff eclipsed the original Teilo shrine at Llandeilo.

The Bishopric of Ergyng

Another patron saint of Llandaff, St Dyfrig, is also claimed as a 'Bishop of Llandaff' by the *Liber Landavensis*. In fact he was the first Bishop of Ergyng, the easternmost Welsh kingdom that bordered Gwent and Herefordshire. It arose around the Roman town of Arriconium (modern day Weston-under-Pennard) and remained independent until the ninth century, when it was absorbed into Mercia, at one stage the most powerful English kingdom. King Offa of Mercia had previously fixed the border along his famous Dyke and established Hereford as a significant city with a cathedral. The Diocese of Hereford's western edge included ancient British churches with communities that remained Welsh-speaking into the seventeenth century. Ergyng was eventually anglicized into 'Archenfield'.

It was in Ergyng that St Dyfrig, or Dubricius, established a line of bishops that continued until the area was mostly incorporated into Herefordshire. It was long remembered that Dyfrig was active in this border region and therefore the Bishops of Ergyng are incorporated into the Llandaff lists. They were often embroiled in the cross-border conflicts that afflicted the region, not only between Welsh and English forces but also between rival Welsh princes. The

Vikings too were a constant threat and in 918 AD the Bishop of Ergyng, Cyfeiliog, was seized by Vikings. King Edward ransomed him for forty pounds, a considerable sum[8].

This shows that English influence was increasing in the tenth century, and various Kings of Gwent and Glwysing had sworn fealty to the Saxon monarchs. This did not prevent eruptions of violence along the border, such as the sacking of Hereford by Gruffydd ap Llywelyn in 1056, but this dispute, like many others, was carried out within a web of dynastic ambitions, in support of certain Saxon factions.

Bishop Joseph and the beginning of the Llandaff Diocese

The kingdom of Glwysing/Morgannwg was less affected by English incursions than nearby Gwent, though Vikings and pirates were a constant threat. There is evidence to suggest a Bishop in the Glamorgan area from an early period. It has been proposed that an itinerant bishopric moved between the triad of communities at Llantwit Major (founded by Illtyd), Llancarfan (St Cadoc's monastery) and Llandough (St Dochau). These were the most notable churches in Glamorgan, with Llantwit Major in particular acting as a royal burial ground with many fine crosses from the ninth and tenth centuries. The historian Mark Redknap contrasts the numerous royal burial slabs and other monuments at Llantwit Major, dating from the eighth to tenth centuries, with the paucity of such monuments at Llandaff predating the Celtic pillar-cross. Evidently Llandaff did not have comparable status in that period, otherwise it would surely have more remnants. This could then explain why the pre-Norman building on the Llandaff site, the 'little minster', was so unimposing. At around 8.5m by 4.6m and 6.1m high, it must have served a small monastic community and would have been overshadowed by the greater monasteries around the Glamorganshire coast.

The first bishop who was indisputably based at Llandaff was Bishop Joseph who died in 1040. Many historians now believe that Joseph began bringing together a number of formerly disparate Bishops' territories into a modern diocesan formation. As the diocese grew to take in the old regions of Gwent and the border state of Ergyng as well as Glamorgan, it seems that Llandaff gave a better connection to this larger area because it was located beside a major river and road junction.

The monastery at Llandough, overlooking the Bristol Channel, was the closest large church and Jeremy Knight contends that its parish boundary and Llandaff's indicate they were once part of the same unit. Llandough, like Llantwit Major, shows excellent evidence of Roman and post-Roman continuity: being close to a previous Roman villa and then becoming a significant

The Celtic cross discovered at Llandaff in 1870

monastic site, with a ninth century pillar cross in the graveyard. The pillar cross is especially interesting because its head is missing and the decoration is very reminiscent of the Celtic cross found at Llandaff in 1870. One theory suggests the Llandaff cross is a fragment of Llandough's, so its presence near the newly established cathedral cannot be an accident. Most likely it represents a transfer of authority around the eleventh century. Certainly Llandough's decline and Llandaff's rise are remarkably coincidental[9].

The pillar-cross set up in the south aisle at Llandaff was first noticed built into a wall by the dairy well in Llandaff Court. After standing on a pedestal in the bishop's garden for nearly seventy years, it was placed in the Cathedral in

1939. It is made of Sutton stone with a bulbous cross-head with roll-mouldings and a shaft decorated with Stafford and triquetra knots. Researchers have linked it with the 'moulded pillar-crosses' of Breconshire, dating from the late tenth or eleventh century, and the type of interlacing also links it with the Irbic cross at Llandough and an unfinished section of a similar shaft at Llancarfan. These crosses are similar enough to suggest the work of the same craftsman, and the fact they use the Sutton stone from Ogmore-by-Sea suggests a deliberate effort to locate a durable source of monumental stone for carving. This cross remains the most striking piece of pre-Norman sculpture on display at Llandaff and serves as a visual reminder of the cathedral site's links to Celtic Christianity.

Although this is by far the most impressive early remnant from pre-Norman Llandaff, two other small grave markers in the form of six-armed crosses survive in the lancets of the west front and the west gallery of the building. They consist of multi-armed crosses set in discs and are dated to the eleventh or twelfth century, late in Herewald's episcopacy or early in Urban's time.

Moving St Teilo to Llandaff

The emerging diocese of Llandaff supplanted St Teilo's former centre at Llandeilo Fawr to become the focus of his saintly cult. It is indisputable that Teilo's tomb and reputation were relocated to Llandaff before Urban built his Norman cathedral, and it is at this point that the bishopric of Glamorgan was founded. In the 1060s, Bishop Herewald was granted lands beyond the River Tywi by King Gruffudd of Morgannwg, including 'Lann Teilaumaur' as possessions of Llandaff. Bishop Urban continued the claim to these lands at the western edge of the diocese but eventually they fell under the sphere of St Davids.

Llandaff succeeded in becoming the principal Teilo church and henceforth the Bishops of Teilo became Bishops of Llandaff. Bishops until the eleventh century used the title 'Bishop of Teilo' (*episcopus Teiliau*) rather than Bishop of Llandaff and the 'family of Teilo' denoted the clerics closely linked with the bishopric. Because of this, the *Book of Llandaff* lists Bishops such as Nobis, who was based at Llandeilo Fawr, as Llandaff Bishops though this is a distortion of history. Llandeilo's rise and fall preceded the Normans and reflects the changing fortunes of the native Welsh kingdoms. When Llandeilo's local protectors lost their power, the religious community also suffered, to the extent that their famous *Teilo Gospels* ended up at Lichfield Cathedral and their ornate stone crosses were buried in the churchyard, to be recovered only in the nineteenth century[10]. The story about St Euddogwy moving Teilo's relics found its way into the *Liber Landavensis* as the memory of a later event when the monastery at Llandeilo fell on hard times and lost both its influence and its relics of Teilo himself.

Bishop Joseph commemorated by a large inscribed stone at Llandaff. The antiquary Edward Lhuyd recorded it as being set in the middle of a street in Llandaff, but originally placed inside the Cathedral. The inscription read 'EPISCOPI IOSEPH' and must have marked the tomb of Bishop Joseph. Its squared letterforms suggest a similarity to inscriptions at Llancarfan and Llanddewi Ystradenni in Radnorshire, which suggests an eleventh or early twelfth century date. This would agree with the dates of Bishop Joseph's death (either 1033 or 1040) and he appears to have been buried at Llandaff[11]. Unfortunately the stone has disappeared since Lhuyd saw it in the early 1700s, but there is a chance it was incorporated into a building and may yet reappear. It is the only unambiguous record of a pre-Norman Bishop at the Llandaff site.

Under the episcopacy of Bishop Joseph a unified diocese began to emerge in Glamorgan and Gwent. His successor, Bishop Herewald, continued the process as Bishop of Glamorgan. It is possible that Joseph or Herewald erected the original church building that was demolished by Bishop Urban to make way for the present cathedral.

The Norman Period

The signal event in the history of medieval Glamorgan was the arrival of the Normans around 1081. In this year, the last Welsh king of Morgannwg, Caradog ap Gruffudd, was murdered by his local enemies and William I marched all the way across South Wales to reach St Davids where he made pilgrimage at the shrine of David. The Normans seem to have founded commercial centres across the Severn estuary as they advanced, and Cardiff was also the site of a large Roman fortress which they reoccupied, later building Cardiff Castle. The *Margam Annals* record that Cardiff was founded as a villa in 1081, meaning that Cardiff was built to be the principal town for the new Norman polity of Glamorgan. There is also a theory that Cardiff, like Bristol, might have been the site of a Viking trading settlement before the Normans came.

Robert fitz Hamon, a favourite of William Rufus, received the lordship of Cardiff in around 1093 as the Normans pushed back the Welsh princes from the lowlands of Glamorgan. He made considerable grants of churches and lands to Tewkesbury Abbey, including the ancient church of Llandough which David Crouch identifies as "the original ecclesiastical centre of the Cardiff region". The proceeds from the manor of this former mother church went to Tewkesbury, and although it survived as a parish church, its role shifted to the new priory church of St Mary, close to Cardiff Castle. This church was later abandoned in the seventeenth century as it was continually inundated by floods from the Taff and its mantle of principal town church passed to St John's.

The town of Cardiff was mainly made up of English immigrants, though some Welsh names are recorded from the 1200s onwards. David Crouch notes that it served as a way-station for the Norman invasion of Ireland and sometimes played a significant part in Anglo-Norman politics, for instance in 1172 when Henry II and his court returned from Ireland and passed through the town. However Cardiff ceased expanding in the early thirteenth century due to a changing political climate, as the descendents of fitz Hamon had died out by 1183 and their successors as Lords of Cardiff had interests elsewhere. It settled into the status of a small county town and continued in this mode until the dawn of the Industrial Revolution brought it a new vitality in the 1800s[12].

At the time of the Norman invasion, the Bishop of Glamorgan was Herewald who was continuing to amalgamate the new see from the old territorial bishoprics. It is notable that Herewald dedicated a number of churches in Ergyng to St Dyfrig, on the English border and in a region later claimed by the Diocese of Hereford. Perhaps he was already establishing a boundary line and staking his claim to the ancient lands of the Bishops of Ergyng. Although very long-lived – Herewald died in 1107 at the age of one hundred – his later years were overshadowed by the Norman ascendancy and the incursions of the Norman lords into Llandaff's lands. Like his predecessor, Herewald must have understood the necessity of creating a modern, centralised diocese to ensure its survival. It is also important to note that one of his archdeacons was the future Bishop Urban, who succeeded him after his death. Herewald is consequently a transitional figure but is likely also to have been a strong influence on Urban's career and achievements.

Bishop Urban's Achievements

When the Normans eventually conquered Gwent and established themselves in Glamorgan, the territory was mainly divided between the lowlands and the highland areas, which largely remained under Welsh control. In this context, the Norman Marcher lords established a chain of castles, including Cardiff and Caerphilly, and also a number of monasteries, priories and abbeys, like Margam and Ewenny. Llandaff's proximity to Cardiff and the main roads into the Vale, as well as the Taff itself, made it ideal as a cathedral site. It is no coincidence that Llandaff also retains a small castle, very likely a fortified residence for the Bishop, which might be seen as a link in the chain from Cardiff to Caerphilly via Castell Coch. The castle is a prominent feature of the Green to this day.

Urban, who was appointed Bishop in 1107 was a Welshman, Gwrgan, who reaffirmed Llandaff's allegiance to Canterbury. Brought up in the new realities of Norman South Wales, and educated at Worcester Cathedral where he served his early years as a priest, he was responsible for building the first true cathedral at Llandaff.

Initially styled as the Bishop of Glamorgan, and also Bishop of Teilo, Urban replaced the previous church at Llandaff with a Norman structure. Simultaneously, he sought to put the diocese on a firm foundation by establishing its assumed ancient boundaries. Using a range of ancient land grants to various local saints and bishops by kings from the sixth century onwards, he and his clerics developed a narrative around the *Life of St Teilo* and other important figures. The aims were to see off rival claims from Llancarfan, to claim certain lands from Hereford and, most importantly, to build a western bulwark against the diocese of St Davids. Urban also attempted to prevent the Marcher Lords from interfering in Llandaff's designated territories; as Bishop of Llandaff he was also a Lord and thus wielded some secular power.

Bishop Urban's letter to Pope Calixtus II in 1119 produced immediate results, as the Pope issued a solemn privilege which confirmed Llandaff's protection by the apostolic see and confirmed forty-eight possessions. Further letters from Rome enjoined the clergy and lay people of the diocese to recognise Urban as their Bishop and assist him to recover the goods and land that had been taken from Llandaff. Later the Pope commanded the Marcher barons and their servants to restore titles and goods to the diocese, and instructed the Archbishop of Canterbury to ensure justice was done. Not only had the Normans seized many church lands, but they had later granted some of them to abbeys in England and even further afield. As a late insertion into the *Liber Landavensis* shows, Bishop Urban and Robert, earl of Gloucester eventually reached a 'solemn compromise' to bring this Norman spoliation to an end. In principle, this involved the creation of a lordship of Llandaff in the vicinity of the Cathedral along with specific rights for the Bishop, in return for him relinquishing claims to other ecclesiastical lands in Robert's control.

John Reuben Davies poses an interesting question: does this apparently cordial agreement between the Bishop and the Lord of Glamorgan provide a clue to Urban's success in building Llandaff Cathedral? Despite having a fragmentary diocese beset with problems, and land-hungry neighbours like St Davids and Hereford, Urban was still able to create a fine Norman church, collect the relics of his patron saints, and launch a major lawsuit at Rome. This suggests that Urban had a major source of funding behind him, and Robert of Gloucester would be an obvious sponsor. He would have gained much prestige from being associated with an ancient cathedral and pilgrimage site, and the Glamorgan diocese closely matched the secular county the Normans were creating. However, Urban still faced a major problem with the ruling families of the Gower, Kidwelly and border areas like Ewyas, and the dioceses of St Davids and Hereford[13].

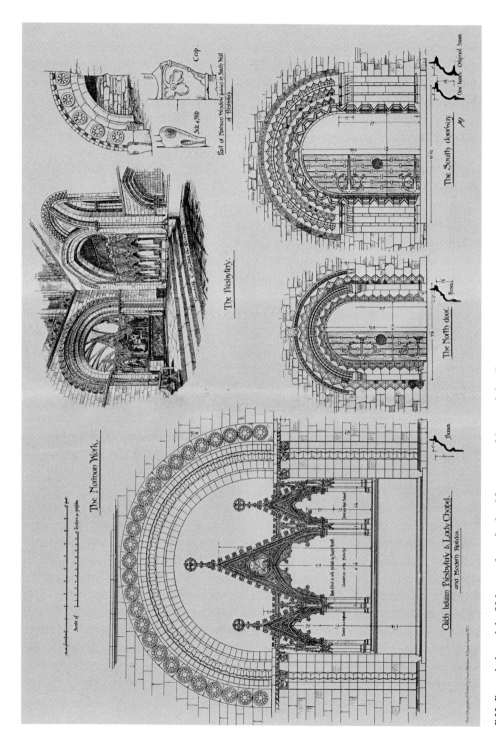

J.H. James' plan of the Urban arch and other Norman architectural details

Urban's clerks compiled the *Liber Landavensis* from a vast range of sources to support his claims for the diocese. On the basis of this cartulary, he took his claims to Rome and continued battling for an enlarged Llandaff diocese until his death in 1130. He also brought about the establishment of the Teilo shrine at Llandaff, which became the focus for the lucrative pilgrimage trade, and the translation in May 1120 of St Dyfrig's remains from Bardsey Island to a new tomb on the north side of the high altar in the Cathedral – the traditional place for the interment of the Founder.

The Norman Cathedral at Llandaff

Bishop Urban replaced the small monastic church with something much greater on its site. In 1120 he constructed a Romanesque building of which the sanctuary arch survives, along with a portion of the arches near the present high altar. This was shorter than the later cathedral and featured a tower near the site of the present Chapter House. The style has been linked with Gloucester Cathedral and other Norman churches in the Welsh Marches. Having trained at Worcester Urban would have been exposed to the ecclesiastical architecture of the English church; indeed he drew on masons who were already working in the Marches. As the outcome of a Welsh bishop associated with the Norman rulers of Glamorgan, Llandaff could be said to be a Cambro-Norman creation. Urban's work took place in the context of a wide-ranging Norman building programme that not only produced a chain of great castles through the Marches (Chepstow and Cardiff for instance) but also erected major churches and abbeys. Margam Abbey and the priories at Ewenny and Chepstow showed the scale which could be achieved.

The surviving arch was the centrepiece of the original building and remains one of its most distinctive features. It has four decorated sections superimposed upon each other, resting on four capitals that vary from rich foliated decoration to a plain square section. These are connected by a band of beaded cable that extends to the edge of the wall on each side of the arch. The medallions that follow the span of the arch are unusual, but they are repeated in the fragmentary surviving presbytery windows, behind the south presbytery arch, the capitals of which also resemble those of the main arch. This demonstrates that the same decorative pattern was carried on around the walls of the Norman cathedral.[14]

Malcolm Thurlby points to similarities with the decoration of several major churches in the Marches, especially Hereford Cathedral and St Peter's Abbey, now Gloucester Cathedral. There is an arch at Hereford with similar paired shafts and Gloucester also has a chevron pattern on its surviving Romanesque arches. The foliate decoration on the columns is paralleled by similar work at St

The presbytery and Urban arch

Mary's Wootton, on the outskirts of Gloucester, whilst the medallions occur at Sarum Cathedral, which was commissioned by Roger, the Bishop of Salisbury, during his episcopacy from 1102-34, and in profusion in the abbey at Malmesbury. The suggestion is that masons who had worked on Sarum, or at least were familiar with it, later worked at Llandaff; the connection is reinforced by Roger's construction of a church and castle at Kidwelly, 1106-14, where he held the lordship.

Apart from the arch and windows, nothing further remains of the earliest fabric, but the size of Urban's cathedral has been estimated by comparing it to the reconstructed Romanesque plan of Ewenny Priory (built 1111-26). Here the nave is twice as long as the presbytery, and if this scheme was applied to Llandaff, the west front of Urban's building would have stood in line with the fourth pair of arches in the later Gothic cathedral.

When Urban undertook to build his cathedral at Llandaff, it was significant in a number of ways. Firstly it represented a far more impressive feat of building than the 'little minster' that preceded it; secondly it made concrete the claims that Urban was advancing to represent the ancient Christian heritage of the Welsh saints in Glamorgan and Gwent; and thirdly it was somewhat detached from the Norman castle at Cardiff, emphasising the Bishop of Llandaff's independent power within the Welsh Marches. This last point was important in that it showed how the Church and clerics could act as a counterbalance to secular military rulers. In his disputes with St Davids and Hereford, Urban demonstrated his astuteness by going beyond the political confines of Norman England and making direct appeals to Rome.

Though unquestionably part of the Norman power-structure, the Church was also the agent of an international body whose local officials could call kings to account, if necessary. The Church was such a pervasive part of life that even if those kings defied the Church, they almost inevitably had to do penance. The dispute between Thomas a Beckett and Henry II is an extreme example: not only did Henry do ample penance for Beckett's murder, but Canterbury gained a martyr whose cult enriched the cathedral and gave it the status of an international site of pilgrimage.

In a less dramatic way, Urban's translation of the relics of St Dyfrig from Bardsey (with the acquiescence of the powerful Welsh prince, Rhys ap Gruffydd) and centralising of Teilo's tomb at Llandaff had a similar result. It was not just the matter of receiving the revenues of pilgrims to Llandaff; the relics ensured the continued spiritual protection of the site's founders and gave a symbolic centrality to Llandaff. Urban skilfully incorporated a variety of older traditions within a contemporary religious framework, thereby ensuring their continuity. The cathedral he built to house Dyfrig and Teilo's remains was simultaneously a statement of ecclesiastical power and of Norman ascendancy in South Wales. It

Remnants of a Norman arch in the south presbytery wall

consequently ensured the preservation of a distinctive regional religious identity.

Urban's episcopy was followed by a succession of Cambro-Norman and English Bishops who extended the cathedral building eastwards. This is why the surviving remnants of Urban's church centre on the superb arch behind the high altar. By the early thirteenth century, building styles had evolved into the Early English form that elongated and elevated the previously squat rounded arches of

The excavation of the Norman apse in the early 1930s

the Norman period. The two excellent Norman doorways (probably by Urban's successor, Bishop William Saltmarsh) may have been moved to serve the newer part of the building which ends in the west front.

The Cathedral was surrounded by a close and various prebends' houses were built on the flat ground to the east, under the shadow of the hill. At some point in the late twelfth or early thirteenth century, the so-called Bishop's Castle was

The Norman South and North doors

built on this promontory and a smaller Archdeacon's Castle also existed closer to the Cathedral itself. A ruined campanile on the southwest ridge above the Cathedral was the original belltower, perhaps in a similar manner to the Porth y Twr fortified belltower at St Davids. Indeed, the geography and setting of Llandaff closely reflect those of its westerly rival. In the village of Llandaff there were a range of farmhouses and permission was granted for an annual fair, an important economic concession in the medieval era. In fact the Lordship of Llandaff was a relatively wealthy one and remained under the Bishop's control until the sixteenth century when it was sold off to the Mathew family.

The Early Gothic Cathedral

The first major additions to Urban's cathedral came under Bishop William Saltmarsh (1186-91). Malcolm Thurlby sees strong resemblances between the decoration of Llandaff's north and south doorways and the gatehouse of St Augustine's Cathedral in Bristol, where Saltmarsh had been the chamberlain, as it was at that time an abbey church. The grander exterior of the south door has four orders of decorated chevrons, occurring singly in the second and fourth row, and as a double lattice in the third. Around the hood of the door runs a 'greek key' border. The smaller north door has three orders of wider-spaced chevrons and a dog-tooth motif around its hood, with the head of a bishop at the apex of the arch.

The positioning of the doorways suggests that Saltmarsh intended to extend the existing structure, perhaps to compete with St Davids which had recently been extensively rebuilt. However, Newman speculates that they might have formed part of the twelfth century west front before the church was extended in the early thirteenth century; and that they were moved to their present positions because they were still quite new. This might account for their slightly asymmetric positioning.[15]

Bishop Henry of Abergavenny (1193-1218) extended the cathedral to its current size, with the west front being his signal contribution to the modern building. That this survived intact through all the vicissitudes of Llandaff's history is nothing short of amazing. It was originally supported by two symmetrical towers, one of which survives in part as the stairway on the southern side of the west front up to the bell-chamber level, although the main structure of the southern tower collapsed in the eighteenth century. The other, northern, tower was heavily rebuilt in the late fifteenth century. During the phases of construction, architectural styles developed into Early English and the westernmost end of the cathedral clearly shows this transformation. In many respects the building is mid-way between a true cathedral and a large monastic church: it is only two storeys high and has no transepts. Even so, it provided a distinct focus for the diocese of Llandaff and for a time it was a prosperous medieval bishopric.

Henry's work marks an architectural shift to a newer and grander style of Early Gothic, inspired by the two great examples of West Country gothic architecture: Glastonbury Abbey and Wells Cathedral. It is quite likely that his masons were recruited from these relatively local sources and their works, including the decorative motifs, the heads of the capitals and the figure sculptures, make the strong connections with West Country work evident. Bishop Henry's revised building style drew on the latest developments in Gothic architecture and was likely a response to the rebuilding of St Davids Cathedral that had begun in 1182.

It was Bishop Henry who also constituted the Chapter at Llandaff and brought together several benefices to the cathedral. The grant of an annual fair to Llandaff on the four days of Whitsun week and a Sunday market was approved by King John and was probably associated with the cathedral's building programme, as it was contemporaneous with the work. Bishop Henry's successor, William Goldcliff, may have completed the building during his episcopacy (1219-29).

Numerous commentators since E.A. Freeman in 1850 have linked this phase of Llandaff's architecture with contemporary features at Wells, Glastonbury,

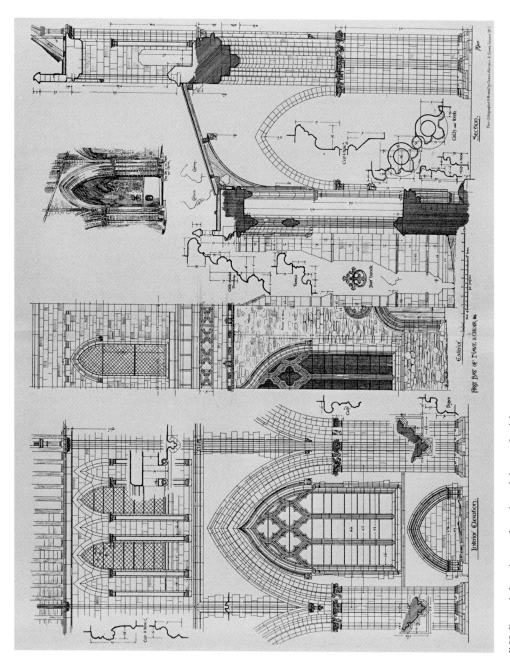

J.H. James' elevation and section of the south aisle

Dore Abbey, Llanthony Priory, and St Davids. In particular, the connections between Glastonbury and Llandaff seem strong, with evidence that the foliage on the capitals of the western nave pillars at Llandaff has similarities to the east transepts at Wells and Glastonbury. The west front at Llandaff also has similarities with that of Wells. The building of the Gothic extension took place in two phases of four bays each but it is unclear which part came first.

The Gothic section runs west from the Romanesque presbytery. It consists of a two-bay choir separated from the side aisle by a wall, then a six-bay nave. A single row of clerestory windows, reconstructed by John Prichard in the mid-nineteenth century after the surviving examples in the ruined nave, runs above the nave arches but ends in a solid wall at the westernmost bay. Here the arches are reinforced to support the western towers. Slightly east of the entrance to the Chapter House is the sole vaulted bay of this fabric, and Thurlby suggests this vaulting marked out a chapel with a separate altar. Looking west back down the aisle, one can see the remnants of a larger and broader arch that must have supported a tower on the south side, near the Chapter House. This was probably removed in the fourteenth century during a rebuilding of the aisle wall.[16]

Westwards from the choir, the first three bays of the nave arcades share the same design of three alternating orders in the arches. Their octagonal plan is also found in piers in the nave of St Davids Cathedral, and the western bays of the choir at Christ Church Cathedral, Dublin. The next three western piers share aspects of this design but are larger and more richly decorated. The change in design suggests that the western end was constructed first, to enable the original cathedral building to be used for as long as possible before the Romanesque nave had to be pulled down to allow the rest of the Gothic nave to be built. This section resembles the nave piers of Llanthony Priory, built between 1171 and 1205; and both it and Llandaff share features of the Great Church of Glastonbury Abbey, suggesting the same master masons worked on all three buildings. The capitals of the arches, in particular, are very reminiscent of Glastonbury. However, details of capitals and the piers are closely linked to examples at Wells Cathedral, whose west front includes similar pillars to those on Llandaff's western facade. In summary, Thurlby says:

> The Llandaff master clearly had a detailed knowledge of Glastonbury and the eastern arcades of the transepts and other parts of Wells. [...] So, for dating Llandaff we must consider closely the dates of Glastonbury and Wells.[17]

Based on the reconstruction of Glastonbury after its great fire in 1184, which proceeded rapidly until the death of Henry II in 1189, Thurlby considers that Llandaff's early Gothic building began around 1193.

From the outside, the most striking impression of the early Gothic fabric is

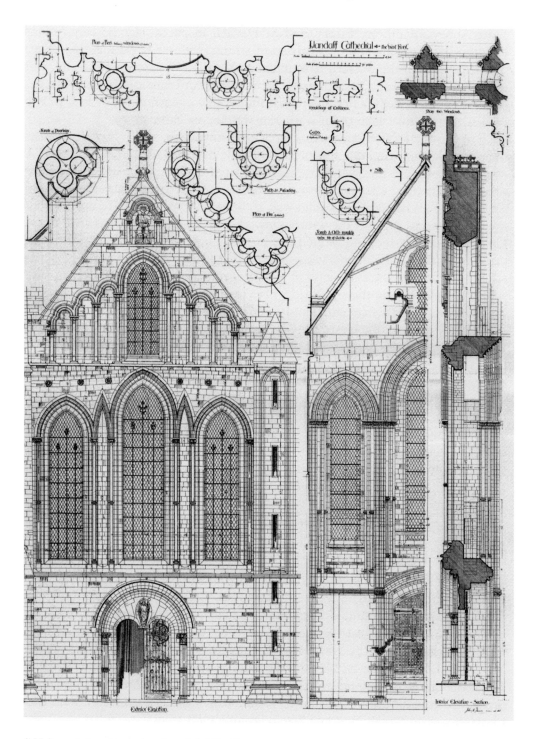

J.H. James' elevation and section of the West Front

provided by the elegantly proportioned west front. It is framed by two later additions: the fifteenth century Jasper Tower and the nineteenth century spire, which replaces the southern tower that fell in the eighteenth century. The lowest section of the west front has a central round-headed doorway of three alternating orders set in a plain wall. The innermost order curves downwards in the centre of the door to provide a niche for the figure of a bishop within a vesica (p. 118). Carved birds and a cross-legged figure can be seen in the capitals of the columns. Immediately above the doorway are three lancet windows, with two thin blind lancets framing the central window, creating an effect somewhat like a triptych. To accentuate the west front's height, another window is set over the central lancet, lower and rounder in form and flanked by six blind lancets that rise inwards. Finally, a niche at the top crowns the composition, and the eroded figure that once occupied this lofty position now sits in the David Chapel by the processional way. The steep pitch of the roof draws the eye upwards to the cross on the top.

The Lady Chapel

In the late thirteenth century, the final extension of the Cathedral was initiated by Bishop de Braose in the form of the Lady Chapel, perhaps the most unified (and certainly least altered) section of the building. This replaced the apse of the Norman church, traces of which were discovered during excavations in the early 1930s Throughout the building's chequered career, it was the Lady Chapel that remained in constant use apart from a brief interlude in the period after the bombing of 1941.

William de Braose was a descendent of a Norman Marcher Lord who held the lordships of Gower, Brecon and Abergavenny, and possibly a nephew of Giles de Braose, Bishop of Hereford (d. 1235). He was elected Bishop in 1265, whilst still a young man, and died in 1286 or 1287. At the time of his enthronement much of the Cathedral as we know it had been built and the west front had existed for at least fifty years. However the east end had been only slightly remodelled since Urban's time; if Williamson is correct, a square east end was built to allow processions to go behind the high altar, replacing the previous Norman apse.

Bishop de Braose followed a new development in English cathedrals during the thirteenth century: the creation of large lady chapels at the eastern end of the building, as the cultus of the Virgin Mary grew more important. By the time he came to build the Lady Chapel at Llandaff, the English Gothic style had developed into a distinct form with clean lines and high vaulted ceilings. Williamson speculates that the side windows in the Chapel owe something to Westminster Abbey and decorations on the buttresses resemble those at Salisbury. An early

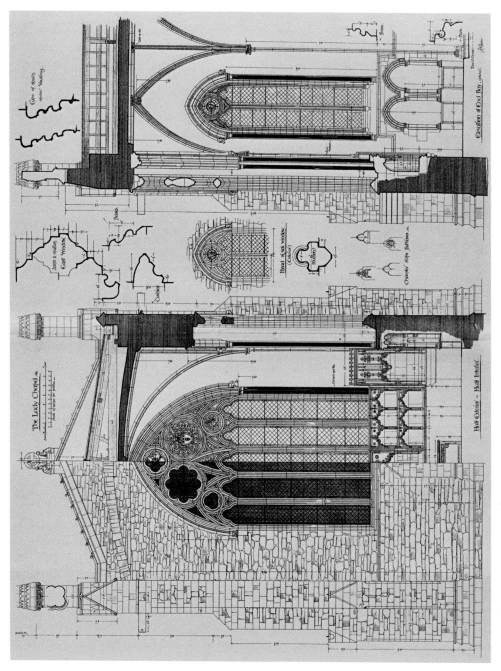

J.H. James' elevation and section of the Lady Chapel east end

The restored Webb ceiling in the Lady Chapel, c. 1988

visitor, John Carter, who saw it in 1804 when the rest of the Cathedral was ruined or encased in pseudo-Classical plaster, wrote:

> Here every line affords that complete satisfaction which our ancient architecture ever inspires. The elevation lofty, the groins airy, the embellishments light, though simple in their application; and it may be observed that, upon the whole, the design conveys much instruction in the search after the knowledge of what is termed the sublime and beautiful. The altar-screen is an elegant performance.[18]

Because it is the least changed part of the Cathedral, the Lady Chapel can be appreciated as a unified space, and its builders' intentions most clearly seen. The tall windows lead the eye up to the vaulted roof and endow it with a simple grace. Perhaps the painted tracery detracts from its lines though we should remember that cathedrals were once richly endowed with murals and polychrome statues. The whole design is focused on the great east window, now occupied by Webb's florid Tree of Jesse stained glass. However the medieval structure was gradually blocked up, as can be seen in John Buckler's drawing of 1815 and John Prichard rebuilt it to his own design, based on the windows of the Chapter House at York Minster.

The reredos deserves a special mention because, despite now being recognised as fine medieval work, it was removed during the 1908 restoration and replaced with a painted wall. It then languished in Clarke's builders yard until Sir Charles Nicholson heard about it and resolved to put it back. The stone which the builders rejected has now resumed its rightful place. Appropriately, Bishop de Braose's effigy lies in his own chapel, and both John of Monmouth and John Paschall (1347-61) were buried there. Additionally, it seems to have held a shrine of St Teilo until the Reformation.

John of Monmouth

John of Monmouth was one of the most significant medieval Bishops of Llandaff, whose long episcopacy marked a period of stability and security for the diocese (1297-1323). His appointment came at a time when the power of the Marcher lords, the de Braose family, was being checked by King Edward I after his Welsh conquests. The previous appointee to the Llandaff bishopric had been blocked by the Chancellor, Bogo de Clare, who wanted a bishop approved by the de Clare family instead. There followed some wrangling between them and the King, and finally the Pope appointed a Dominican monk who had recently become Archbishop of Dublin. However, he demurred and the Pope handed the matter to the Archbishop of Canterbury, Robert Winchelsey. He appointed John of Monmouth, who spoke Welsh although he was English, and was apparently loved by the Welsh people. He may well have come from Monmouth itself or the Marches, as this would fit the profile of an Englishman who also knew Welsh. He had a significant scholarly profile, gaining first an MA then a doctorate in theology at Oxford, and retained these connections during his twenty-five year episcopacy at Llandaff. Indeed, he was appointed to reform the University of Oxford whilst he was bishop, and also tried to gather a group of scholars around him at Llandaff. He was one of the few bishops who seemed able to balance his duties at the Court, and his external interests at Oxford, with the requirements of the Llandaff diocese as well. He certainly enjoyed a better reputation than some of the other medieval incumbents, who were in the main English appointees who spent varying amounts of time in the diocese.

As Glanmor Williams remarks, John's time as bishop occurred on the cusp of the fourteenth century, the turning point between the relative stability of the previous two centuries and the mounting tensions of the next two hundred years. In the 1300s, the Catholic Church was split by schism, the Black Death entered Western Europe, and a devastating series of continental wars began that embroiled the English state.

Territorial conflicts between the Marcher lands in South Wales and the formerly independent principalities of the North culminated in the rebellion initiated by Owain Glyndwr in 1400. Inevitably, Llandaff was caught up in the turmoil of the rebellion around 1401 and the account of Adam of Usk suggests it was sacked several times, including by anti-Glyndwr forces dispatched from Bristol:

> Owen, seizing his chance, emerged with his manikins from the caves and the woods and marched with a great host right across Wales as far as the Severn sea; those who resisted him he either drove across the sea – where, being Welsh, they were persecuted by the local people – or forced with fire and sword into surrender; nor did he spare even the churches, which ultimately was to lead to his downfall. Then, taking enormous quantities of booty with him, he returned to the safety of the mountains of Snowdonia in the north of Wales, the source of all the evils in Wales, while the people silently cursed his flagrant barbarities. The men of Bristol, captained by the esquires James Clifford and William Rye, took an armed fleet and raided Glamorgan, plundering the church of Llandaff, but through a miracle of St Teilo they were defeated by the local people and driven off in confusion, with considerable loss.[19]

There are reasons to doubt this account but in any case the Cathedral entered a period of slow decline. The bishops decamped to a manor house at Mathern, near Chepstow, and the affairs of the Cathedral were increasingly left

The gateway of the Bishop's Castle, c. thirteenth century

in the hands of its Canons. The Llandaff area suffered economically like the whole of Wales, and in 1428 the Bishop complained about the Cathedral's state.

The Later Middle Ages

At this point, bishops were appointed by the Pope's *fiat* and tended to be ambitious figures who quickly advanced elsewhere, or abbots who were rewarded with a bishopric. A bishop also had to be present in London and active in various aspects of government, and a pattern of non-residency began to develop. The day-to-day running of the Cathedral and diocese were handled by the Archdeacon and the Canons in the main.

However, towards the end of the fifteenth century, the economic situation in Wales improved and it is notable that the majority of surviving Welsh medieval churches date from this period. Llandaff benefited from this more prosperous

The Mathern palace

and stable period, too, and the Cathedral was consolidated by Bishop Marshall (1478-96), who strengthened the building's structure and left the Marshall throne painting as his most lasting memorial. The most obvious architectural addition is the mighty Jasper Tower, funded by Jasper Tudor, Duke of Bedford, to become the cathedral's main belltower when the structure on the Green became inadequate. Marshall also rebuilt the church of St Tewdric at Mathern and he and his successors enlarged the Bishop's Palace there.

Llandaff also received the patronage of the powerful Mathew family, who sided with the Yorkist cause in the Wars of the Roses. They had helped defend this part of Glamorgan during Glyndwr's uprising. Their ornate tombs testify to their significance and the Mathews remained closely linked with the Llandaff area until the late eighteenth century. Their late medieval memorials, explored most recently by Dr Madeleine Gray, are a testament to their integral role in the life of the Cathedral.[20]

By the late 1400s, the Cathedral itself had achieved the form shown in the

The tomb of Sir William Mathew and his wife Lady Jenette

engraving by Browne Willis, c.1707 (see p.44), which is the best surviving record of the medieval building when it was reasonably intact. Apart from the double towers, the Cathedral's arrangement is quite familiar to the modern eye because in the main the Victorian reconstruction followed the lines of these older plans, excepting the polygonal roof of the Chapter House, the removal of the consistory court (on the south side) and the pitch of the Lady Chapel roofline. The depiction of the building in Speed's 1610 map and the other seventeenth century engravings also bear this out. The west front and the double towers remain its most distinctive feature.

The Reformation and Afterwards

Although the Reformation brought rapid and often unwelcome changes, there is evidence that Llandaff suffered before this, following the stability it enjoyed under Bishop Marshall. The most extreme example of the trend towards non-resident bishops was the appointment of the Spaniard George de Athequa in 1517. He was Queen Katharine of Aragon's confessor and spent most of his time away from the diocese, but sold off some important manors. From this time onwards, through the episcopacy of Bishop Robert Holgate (1537-1545, later Archbishop of York) there was an ongoing dispersal of the Cathedral's lands and revenues. The Bishops' use of the Mathern Palace in preference to Llandaff itself ensured there was no central authority at the Cathedral, especially since the office of Dean had been discontinued since the thirteenth century.

Much of the blame has been laid upon the timeserving Bishop Anthony Kitchin (1545-66) who "spoiled the good meat of Llandaff" according to a later pun. He was a former monk who was rewarded for overseeing the dissolution of his own monastery during Henry VIII's seizure of monastic properties. Because of this and his remarkable survival of the turbulent reigns of Edward VI and Queen Mary, Kitchin was singled out as the cause for Llandaff's impoverishment, not least by his immediate successors.

However, the accounts of the time show a more widespread looting of the Cathedral's treasures by its own officers: the Canons were especially blameworthy, both for enthusiastically desecrating Teilo's tomb and other valuables, and for letting the fabric of cathedral and village fall into disrepair. The records of the Commissioners who supervised the appropriation of Church wealth for the Crown demonstrate the Canons' larcenous efforts. Additionally, the Cathedral's lands were increasingly dispersed amongst secular landowners, who also acquired territories from defunct monasteries. Major local dignitaries such as Miles Mathew and William Herbert became Commissioners appointed to oversee the removal of the Cathedral's wealth, demonstrating their loyalty to the new order

South elevation of the cathedral, c.1717

established by Henry VIII. The power of the Church was permanently eclipsed:

> Until the time of the Bishops Jones and Blethin, the bishops and clergy did nothing for the Reformation. Attica (Athequa) was a cypher; Holgate and Kitchin were time-servers. Both Holgate and Kitchin had surrendered their abbeys to the King without demur, and were elected to episcopal office because of their known subserviency to the sovereign's will. Holgate was non-resident and took little interest in Llandaff, Kitchin held the episcopal office with composure under four Tudors, and so impoverished the See at the end of his term of office that it was difficult to obtain a successor. [...] His episcopacy was a tragedy. It crippled the old and paralyzed the new movement. It was sheer ruin. On the death of Kitchin a new day was dawning upon Llandaff. The new Archbishop [Parker] showed a deep concern for the welfare of the Welsh Church and eventually a Welsh-speaking Bishop was placed in charge of Llandaff. An attempt was made to win the people for the reforming movement by expounding to them its principles.[21]

In 1558, when Catholicism briefly became the official faith again under Mary, a report was written concerning the despoliation of Teilo's tomb and other treasures at Llandaff during the episcopacy of Richard Holgate. It seems that Llandaff's staff went against official orders to surrender their treasures to the King. Among the officials named for profiting from the plunder, the Treasurer, one Dr Smyth, was heavily implicated in taking jewels, plate and other valuables as was the Chancellor, John Boxholm.[22]

The report lists the precious items of Llandaff that were disposed, legally or otherwise, and makes a fascinating record of the portable artwork, metalwork, vestments, and reliquaries that the medieval Cathedral had acquired over the centuries. With extraordinary speed they went from being objects of religious veneration to items of purely monetary value, and were stripped wholesale from the building to enrich a handful of local worthies. Indeed the Crown Commissioners who oversaw the reduction of Teilo's tomb and the stripping of church wealth, were informed that the Canons of Llandaff had held much of the silver back for themselves, and compelled them to produce it. Later the treasurer of Llandaff was fined for his role in the affair but he stayed in post.

At the same time as the Cathedral's portable treasures were being seized, its lands were being sold off to local landowners. The Mathew family in particular benefited from the sale of the Manor of Llandaff itself and other lands throughout the Diocese ended up in the hands of major local families. The gentry had also acquired monastic lands in the 1530s when the great abbeys of South Wales were closed: Neath, Margam, Tintern and Abergavenny amongst them, along with friaries in Cardiff, Newport and elsewhere.

Not only were monks and nuns deprived of their monasteries but major shrines were closed down, with Teilo's tomb being the principal loss. Devotional shrines like the richly ornamented statue of Our Lady of Penrhys were demolished (the statue itself was taken to London to be ritually burnt in a symbolic destruction of Papist statues) and in churches the liturgy was altered to fit the new doctrines put in place by Cranmer and his reformers.

Bishop Kitchin lasted through all the changes of religion from Henry VIII's national church, Edward VI's extreme Protestantism, Mary's return to Catholicism and finally Elizabeth I's re-establishment of the Anglican Church. He died at Mathern in 1566 and Archbishop Parker appointed the Welsh-speaking Hugh Jones to replace him and reinvigorate the despoiled diocese. Jones started well but failed to carry forward his programme to ameliorate Kitchin's mismanagement of Llandaff. He was certainly constrained by long-standing members of Cathedral staff like Canon Henry Morgan, who was closely involved in plundering the Cathedral's treasures, as was the Archdeacon John Smyh.

Such rapid changes caused disquiet but there were no large-scale uprisings in Wales, as there were in the North (the Pilgrimage of Grace) and Cornwall. This was perhaps because the Tudor dynasty of Henry VIII had strong Welsh connections and the English monarchy was viewed more positively than in previous centuries. Henry had approved the Act of Union which brought Wales administratively in line with the English counties and established the Council of Wales and the Marches which replaced the often erratic authority of the Marcher Lords.

Instead the disquiet about the destruction of old forms of worship manifested itself in a scattered but firmly entrenched minority of recusants: non-churchgoing Catholics who held masses in secret. They were prevalent in Monmouthshire and became more visible and vocal towards the end of the sixteenth century. The Bishops of Llandaff, especially Bishop Blethin, used both religious and civil authority to root them out but the Monmouthshire Catholics were covertly protected by Lord Raglan and other traditionalists, who encouraged travelling priests and Jesuits to move throughout the countryside.

At the turn of the seventeenth century the Council of Wales fought a bitter local campaign against these die-hard faithful, who were particularly active in Abergavenny and the surrounding hills. Eventually by killing the Jesuits and some of their higher-profile protectors, the Council succeeded in blunting this religious revival but Monmouthshire retained a proportionally high number of Catholics into the eighteenth century.

This Elizabethan religious battle for the hearts and minds of the Llandaff diocese, combined with the poverty of the bishopric and a chronic lack of parish clergy, might explain why the Cathedral was left to decay in the late sixteenth century. When he was elected in 1584, Bishop Blethin made an effort to recover the lost records of the Llandaff Chapter and reform its Canons. His description of the Cathedral was as follows:

> "derelicta, solatioque pastorali destituta" – derelict and destitute of pastoral care. He described the fabric of the Cathedral as "untidy, full of dirt and almost beyond repair". The Canons had absolutely no respect for their church. Blethin states that he had to confront three evils: the ruin of the Cathedral fabric, Cathedral debts and the contempt of the Canons towards the Church. He placed the guilt of the galling poverty of the Cathedral on the heads of the Canons: "To whom have you not granted large manors, many lordships and farms? You have wasted everything, sweet toned books, precious vestments, golden vessels, unknown treasures. They are all reduced to nothing."[23]

Part of the problem was that the Cathedral's malaise also affected the city of Llandaff itself. Despite being granted an annual fair and other small benefits by Royal Charter, it remained in the shadow of Cardiff just a few miles down the road. The local gentleman Rice Merrick, writing in 1578, remarked on this problem and noted the sad state of Llandaff itself:

> I know not whether this city was at any time of any beauty or estimacion, but now it is in [ruin] which [came] to pass by the nearness and increase of Cardyf, being a Markett and a Haven Town, scarce one mile distant, and by the absence of the Bishops dwelling at Mathern.[24]

With meagre lands, a dwindling number of clergy and the often lawless state of Glamorgan where the landed families fought amongst each other with private militias, it is small wonder that the Cathedral was now in dire need of repair.

It was not until the short episcopacy of Gervase Babbington (1591-1594) that measures were taken to improve the state of the interior. No doubt shocked at the state of his Cathedral, Babbington himself funded the restoration of the stalls and seating, and arranged for a firm of Bristol plumbers to improve the state of the roof. His remedial repairs ensured that the building remained standing until the early eighteenth century despite its general neglect during and after the Civil War. Babbington's illustrious successor was Bishop William Morgan (1594-1601), the translator of the Bible into Welsh.

By the early seventeenth century the civil and economic situation seems to have improved, and despite the growing threat from Dissenters and Puritans the bishops were strongly supportive of James I and Charles I. Indeed, the mid-seventeenth century bishops were closely connected with Archbishop Laud and reintroduced certain High Church elements like surplices back into their services. But the Civil War was looming and as the power of the Parliamentarians grew, the supporters of Laud in the Church became increasingly embattled.

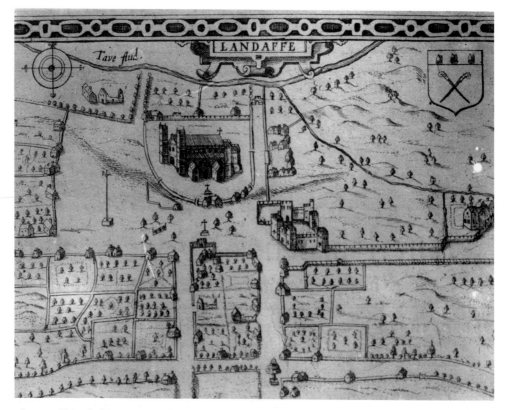

A map of Llandaff by seventeenth century cartographer John Speed

Bishop Morgan Owen, a close friend of Laud who was imprisoned in 1644 due to his religious views, died of shock when he heard of the Archbishop's death in 1645 and Llandaff remained without a Bishop until the Restoration.[25]

The Civil War inflicted more punishments on the Cathedral's structure, including its use for secular purposes like garrisoning troops and horses, and even as a feeding place for pigs. Having won the Battle of St Fagans, the Parliamentary forces were not seriously opposed in South Wales despite strong local support for the Royalists. Divine services did not begin again at Llandaff until after the Restoration of 1660.

One notable Royalist prisoner taken at St Fagans was Hugh Lloyd, who survived the Civil War to become Bishop of Llandaff in 1660. He took a strong interest in his diocese and particularly supported the establishment of free schools in Glamorgan, one of which was held in a schoolroom at the Cathedral itself. Lloyd was succeeded on his death in 1667 by his Archdeacon, Francis Davies, a Glamorganshire man who restored the Cathedral's library and the main bell.

Davies died in 1675 and was replaced by William Lloyd, who in 1679 was translated to become Bishop of Peterborough. Bishop Beaw replaced him and lasted until 1707, but the diocese was now seriously impoverished and the Bishops had to be pluralists, meaning they drew on other more lucrative appointments in England to sustain their position. Many were also Deans of St Paul's Cathedral. Even the Bishop's Palace at Mathern had been sold, although it was bought back for their use, but the Bishops tarried less and less at Llandaff.

By 1692 the Cathedral's main roof was unsafe; the pinnacles of the fifteenth century tower fell down in a storm in 1703 and finally the south west tower fell through the nave in 1722. As we will see, we are reliant to a great degree on Browne Willis's survey as a record of the unmodified medieval building. Other antiquarians such as Edward Lhuyd also passed through Llandaff and noted various monuments that no longer exist.

The Chapter Act Books reveal a picture of increasing desperation into the early eighteenth century, with non-essential staff like the organist and choristers being dismissed and various local people being co-opted into jobs to keep the building going. Despite the Cathedral's parlous state, there seems to have been some determination to retain it as the centre for the diocese even though it might have made more sense at this stage to move to Cardiff. Though still a small market town, Cardiff was the most populous place in early eighteenth century south Wales and moving the seat of the Bishop was proposed at one stage. The collapse of the south tower and resulting destruction of the nave resulted in Llandaff becoming partly ruinous; only the Lady Chapel and the eastern end of the building were still usable.

Dismissing proposals to remove the Cathedral to a new site in Cardiff, money was raised for restoration and in 1734 the Bath architect John Wood was commissioned to build an Italianate structure incorporating the choir and eastern nave. It also included the Lady Chapel and encased the Norman arch in plaster to achieve some kind of Classical interior. Though in line with eighteenth century tastes, the building was never finished and fortunately the medieval ruins were never cleared due to lack of funds. Although Wood was informed by eighteenth century scholarly ideas about the antiquity of Llandaff's past – he believed he was reconstructing an ancient Roman building – his efforts were later ridiculed. It should be remembered that, incongruous and incomplete as it was, the 'Italianate Temple' ensured the continuity of worship at Llandaff.

Nevertheless, the twilight of Llandaff in the late eighteenth and early nineteenth centuries also coincided with the beginning of the Industrial Revolution in the valleys of South Wales. This brought with it a massive growth in population and a sudden influx of wealth. As industrial towns like Merthyr Tydfil expanded, so did the ports along the Severn and consequently the Llandaff diocese started to attract a range of able clergy who began to reverse the decline. The resurrection of Llandaff Cathedral would commence in the reign of Queen Victoria.

Notes

1. Mark Redknap, 'Early Medieval Llandaff: The Evidence of the Early Christian Monuments' in John R. Kenyon & Diane Williams *Cardiff: Architecture and Archaeology in the Medieval Diocese of Llandaff* (BAA Conference Transaction Series, Maney Publishing 2006).
2. Mark Redknap, ibid.
3. James, N.A. & Lewis, J.M., 'Speed revisited: a reconstruction of the road map of Llandaff in 1610.' *Llandaff*: Llandaff Society, 1987.
4. from 'Introduction: The Welsh Cathedrals 1066-1300', *Fasti Ecclesiae Anglicanae 1066-1300: volume 9: The Welsh Cathedrals (Bangor, Llandaff, St Asaph, St Davids, 2003).*
5. Wendy Davies, *The Llandaff Charters* (1979).
6. John Reuben Davies, 'The Book of Llandaff: A Twelfth-Century Perspective', *Anglo-Norman Studies* XXI (Boydell & Brewer, 1998), pp.31-46.
7. Reverend R.W.D. Fenn, 'St Teilo and the Llandaff Tradition', Friends Festival Lecture 1968.
8. From the Parker version of the *Anglo-Saxon Chronicle*, entry for 917/918 AD: "In this year a great pirate host came over hither from the south from Brittany under two jarls Ohtor and Hroald, and sailed west until they reached the estuary of the Severn, and harried at will everywhere along the Welsh coast. They seized Cyfeiliog, bishop of Archenfield, and took him with them to the ships, but King Edward ransomed him afterwards for forty pounds. Then after this the whole host went inland with the intention of renewing their raids in the direction of Archenfield: they were opposed by the men from Hereford and Gloucester and from the nearest fortresses who fought against them and put them to flight. They slew the jarl Hroald and the other jarl Ohtor's brother and a great part of the host, and drove them into an enclosure and besieged them there until they gave them hostages and promised to depart from King Edward's dominion."
9. Jeremy Knight, 'From Villa to Monastery: Llandough in Context', *Medieval Archaeology*, 49 (2005, Maney), pp.93-107. Also see Knight in John R Kenyon and Diane Williams, *Cardiff: Architecture and Archaeology in the Medieval Diocese of Llandaff*, op. cit.
10. W.A. Strange, 'The Rise and Fall of a Saint's Community: Llandeilo Fawr 600-1200', The Journal of Welsh Religious History, new series 2 (2002).
11. Mark Redknap, 'Early Medieval Llandaff: The Evidence of the Early Christian Monuments', op.cit.
12. David Crouch, 'Cardiff Before 1300' in John R Kenyon and Diane Williams, *Cardiff: Architecture and Archaeology in the Medieval Diocese of Llandaff*, op.cit.
13. John Reuben Davies op.cit.

14. Malcolm Thurlby, *Romanesque Architecture and Sculpture in Wales* (Logaston Press, 2006).
15. Malcolm Thurlby, 'The Early Gothic Fabric of Llandaff Cathedral and its Place in the West Country School of Masons'. In Kenyon, John R. & Williams, Diane M. (eds.), *Cardiff: Architecture and Archaeology in the Medieval Diocese of Llandaff,* op.cit.
16. Ibid.
17. Ibid.
18. E.W. Williamson, 'The Lady Chapel', First Issue of the Friends' Report, 1933.
19. C. Given-Wilson, *The Chronicle of Adam of Usk 1377-1422* (Clarendon Press, 1997) p.173.
20. Madeleine Gray, 'The medieval bishops' effigies at Llandaff Cathedral'. *Archaeologia Cambrensis* vol 153 (2004), pp.37-50. See also Notes from 'Memorial inscriptions: Llandaff Cathedral', *Cardiff Records* volume 3 (1901), pp. 553-80, online at British History Online.
21. Lawrence Thomas, *The Reformation in the Old Diocese of Llandaff,* (1930) p.xvi.
22. 'Church goods of Llandaff cathedral and diocese (1558): Text', *Cardiff Records* volume 1 (1898), pp.372-86.
23. Lawrence Thomas, op.cit., p. 143.
24. Lawrence Thomas, op.cit.
25. Davies, Chrystal, 'They looked at Llandaff; Bishop Hugh Lloyd and the Battle of St. Fagans. Llandaff' (Llandaff Society, 1992).

Three Centuries:
Three Restorations

The repeated cycle of fall and rise – and fall again – of Llandaff Cathedral since 1700 can be most clearly documented using the descriptions and reports on the state of the fabric that punctuate the building's chequered career, written by visitors, travellers and, most importantly, by architects.

The four ancient cathedrals of Wales were the subject of a collection of surveys published in four volumes under the name of 'Browne Willis' which give a fascinating picture of the state of both the buildings and the staffing of these cathedrals in the early years of the eighteenth century, together with biographical details of Bishops and cathedral dignitaries from earlier times. The first to appear, in 1717, was that for St Davids with Llandaff following in 1719, St Asaph in 1720 and finally Bangor in 1721.

Following the publication of the St Davids volume, Browne Willis in his introduction to the Llandaff book, says:

> So I thought my self for the same Reason, besides others peculiar to Landaff, more strongly engag'd to publish some Account of that Cathedral, which is fall'n into a most deplorable Decay within these few Years: I might become instrumental in transmitting the Memorial of what they once were to Posterity. Wherefore it was, that out of a sad Contemplation lest so glorious a Structure as this Church, honour'd by being the ancientest Bishops See in the Kingdom, (as we have evident Authority to shew) rais'd, enrich'd, and beautify'd, by the Piety of so many noble Founders, should be utterly destroy'd, and become a woeful Spectacle of Ruin.

The Llandaff volume takes the form of a detailed thirty-four page description, with a floor plan and two elevation drawings by Joseph Lord, of the fabric of the building prepared for Willis by William Wooton (the Dr Wooton who appears in the entry for Browne Willis in *The Dictionary of National Biography* as having been his tutor for three years). There follows a lengthy section (69 pages) giving biographical details of Bishops, Deans, Archdeacons and the holders of the various stalls in Chapter.

This description of the medieval building as it stood in 1717 came at that point in its history which followed the two cataclysmic events that had precipitated Llandaff Cathedral's steady slide into decay and ruin. The Reformation had seen the Cathedral stripped of its wealth and its treasures, largely by those who should have cared for its welfare, whilst the Civil War had resulted in

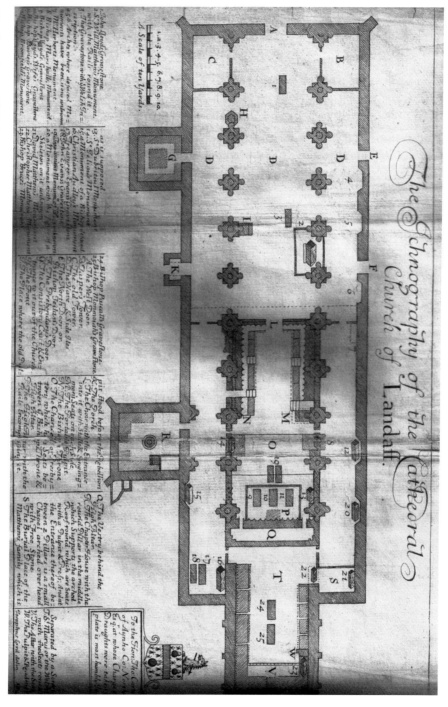

Plan from Browne Willis' survey, 1717

substantial damage to the structure of the building, the destruction of its library and its use for stabling and as an ale house. In February 1722-23, a mere five years after the Browne Willis survey was printed, the south west tower was to collapse through the roof of the nave and the building sank to the ruinous and unloved state that was to persist for well over a century.

The dimensions of the building listed in the survey agree closely with those of the fabric as it now stands – as one might expect – so it is in the detailed descriptions that there is most of interest. The writer commences his account at the west front and also includes, in passing, information about monuments, some few of which still survive.

> At the West End there are two Towers, one to the South, which seems to be as old as the Church, which is open within from the Top to the Bottom. This Tower, which now looks ruinous, had formerly coarse Battlements at the Top, most of which are down, with four small Pinacles at the Corners. [This is the tower whose collapse was to cause such damage in 1722-23.] The Tower on the North Side was built by Jasper (created Duke of Bedford, An.1485). This is a handsome Tower, and is still in pretty good Repair, all but the Battlements at Top, which were elegant enough, and entire, 'till the great Storm November 27, 1703, which threw down two of the Corner-Pinacles, and a good Part of the Battlements; the Wind, being Southerly, threw the Stones into the Church-Yard.

A description of the west front follows with the comment that the upper window, which now lights the interior of the roof space of the nave, was walled up. The figure that stood in the uppermost niche and which is now removed to the St David Chapel of the Cathedral was said to represent Henry I, and that immediately over the west door was taken to be St Dyfrig. The statue that is now in the St David Chapel has now been correctly identified as a figure of Christ in Majesty.

> The Church was then entered down seven or eight Steps. The Length of the Nave, from the West Door to the Screen that divided the Nave from the Choir was quoted as being about 110 feet, and the width of the building as 65 feet. The roofs of both the Nave and the Lady Chapel were covered in lead.

The roof within is described as

> consisting only of Couples, (as they are call'd in this Country) to which within are fram'd circular Beams of Timber, laid parallel to one another; which is the common Way of laying Roofs of Churches in South Wales: From thence to the upper End of the Choir, it was formerly ciel'd [sic] with Wainscot, which was painted; but the Roof being ruinous, the Ceiling was

taken down, in Order to repair the Timber some Years ago, which makes all that Part look very naked

On each Side of the Nave, over the Pillars, are twelve Windows, by two and two, with five Partitions between, [these are the clerestory windows, of which there are now fourteen on each side, in pairs] Close to the second Pillar on the South Side is the Font: Against the fourth Pillar on the same Side, was formerly a Pulpit, which was taken down in the great Rebellion. [The marks on fourth pillar where the pulpit and its tester were affixed can still be seen]

Against the fourth Pillar on the North Side, and so on to the fifth, stands the Monument of Sir William Matthew of Aradyr in Glamorganshire, about one Mile from Landaff: Its Length, including the Palisade round it, is sixteen Foot and a Half, its Breadth nine Foot and a Half. It is an Altar-Monument, on which lie the Images of a Man and a Woman, curiously wrought in Alabaster; the Man is bare-headed, in compleat Armour, with a Coat of Mail under his Corslet, and a Collar of SS. Over it: His Gauntlets are by his right Leg, and a Sword cross; at his Head is a Lion, and a Monk with Beads in his Hand: His Helmet is his Pillow: In his left Hand is his Dagger, and a Sword at his right: On his left Side lies his Wife, in the same recumbent Posture, habited after the Manner of the Time; the Lappets of her Head-Cloaths are lac'd, and the Lace gilt. The Inscription which is on the Edge of the Monument is this,

Orate pro Animabus Willielmi Matthew Militis, qui obiit decimo Die Martii, A.D M.CCCCC, vices VIII. ET ETIAM Jenette uxoris ejus que Deo reddidit Spiritum... Die Mensis... A.D. Mill.CCCCC. trices. Quorum animabus propitietur Deus Amen.

This monument has occupied several positions over the centuries, even being stored, in pieces, in the Chapter House for some years. It is now almost in its original place. The heraldry on this and the other Mathew tomb, of Sir Christopher Mathew and his wife, were restored and repainted in 1980 by Huw Mathew.

The two doorways in the north aisle are listed:

In this North Ile near the West End is a Door commonly call'd S. Teilaw's Door, thro' which, before the Reformation, Bodies were carry'd into the Church to be bury'd, it being look'd upon as meritorious to carry them that Way [this now leads from the north aisle into the St David Chapel]. To the East of S. Teilaw's Door, over against the sixth Pillar, is another small Door, which they call the Prebendary's Door. [Used no doubt by the prebends whose houses ranged on the northern and eastern sides of the Cathedral.]

The description of the north aisle notes "five irregular windows" in that part of the building which lay west of the chancel arch.

The reader's attention is then drawn to the south aisle and to the three structures that stood outside the line of the south wall but attached to it. Firstly, one bay east of the south-west tower, was a consistory court building, which was described as:

> a tolerable good Room, fifteen Foot square in the Clear within, with one Window six Foot broad and four Foot high, and two other lesser ones over that, one Foot three Inches broad, and three Foot high apiece. The Door that goes into it out of the South Ile is of Free-stone arch'd [this is the surviving South Door].

Against its western wall the consistory court appears to have had a small lean-too structure with an external door. This appears on the elevation drawing but not on the floor plan in the survey. Next, two bays further east and enclosing the small doorway that is now adjacent to the pulpitum arch, was a porch measuring "in Length seven Foot and a half, in Breadth six Foot nine Inches." The five windows between the Consistory Court and the Chapter House were described as 'handsom' [sic] and 'uniform'. These two small buildings appear on both the floor plan and the south elevation drawing in Browne Willis's survey but are now lost without trace.

The third structure that Browne Willis showed on the south side of the Cathedral is the Chapter House which still stands, albeit in a somewhat altered form. Its footprint is unchanged but the upper room now encloses a transition from a rectangular plan to the octagonal one that was introduced in the mid nineteenth century. In 1717 this upper room was approached by an external staircase against its eastern wall and was in use, together with an upper room in the eastern section of the south aisle, as a school. The Chapter accounts for 1706 record the annual payment of £8 to the schoolmaster and it was not until 1859 that a site for a school in Llandaff village was being sought. The roof of the Chapter House appears from the elevation drawing to have been a stepped gable. Strangely, the Chapter chose to hold its annual meeting in the Prebendal House.

Browne Willis does not show any internal means of access to the upper story of the Chapter House, but it is worthy of note that a spiral staircase with two slit windows now gives entry to the first floor level which houses the Cathedral Archive. The lower window of this staircase looks into the ground floor room whilst the higher one is blocked, as it would now merely open into the fill of the vaulting of the lower room. This is additional evidence that the Chapter House was constructed after the wall though which the stair rises. The stairway ends rather abruptly and untidily as if it had once extended to a higher level, leading to the conclusion that the small vaulted area in the south aisle outside door to the Chapter House, with its massive walls, blocked off chimney and vestigial window, represents the ground floor of a long lost tower. This vaulted area was divided from the south aisle and Browne Willis suggests that it had been a small chapel.

The interior of the Chapter House, says Browne Willis,

> which is East and West, twenty one Foot, South and North twenty three Foot) is pav'd with Free-stone, cut much of the Size of our common Paving Bricks: It is arch'd with Stone, and the Groyns of the Arches centre all in the Middle, where they are supported by one Pillar: Towards the South Wall, and a good Way to the East and West, there are Seats round it. At the North-East End there is a Press where they keep their Records, and by that there is a Pulpit.

He then turns his attention to the choir which occupied the same space as at present. It is, however divided by a screen from the nave and the side aisles and the stalls are in what might be termed 'collegiate' form, as in most ancient cathedrals. The title of the occupant of each stall was listed. The organ loft was over the stalls on the north side of the choir; there were in it some shattered remains of an organ within a wooden case, with some of the pipes lying loose and disordered in the case.

The Bishop's Throne, which he suggested was built by Bishop Marshall, stood at the eastern end of the south choir stalls.

> It is six Foot long and five Foot broad. Tho' the Beauty of it is pretty much lost by Length of Time, yet it appears to have been, when it was first made, a curious Piece of Work. The Back of the Throne that fronts the Choir is painted, and was cover'd with Lamp-black during the great Rebellion; but upon the Restoration of King Charles II. The Black was taken off, and the first Ornaments again appear'd... we see on the right Hand the Bishop praying to the blessed Virgin, who is ascending into Heaven with her Hands in a praying Posture, supported by seven Angels, one under her Feet, and three on each Side;

The throne disappeared during the eighteenth century but the painting survives and now hangs on the south aisle wall adjacent to the Chapter House door.

One of the most important parts of the Browne Willis survey of the Cathedral is the detailed description of the medieval reredos that stood to the west of the great Norman arch.

> The Altar-Piece, which is of Freestone, was made in Bishop Marshall's time. It looks well still, tho' the Colours are exceedingly faded. What we first see, is a Row of Niches, eleven in Number, painted with Roses and Hyacinths interchangeably. The Centers of the Roses and the little Knops of the Stems, with the Flowers of the Hyacinths, are gilt. The Roses are

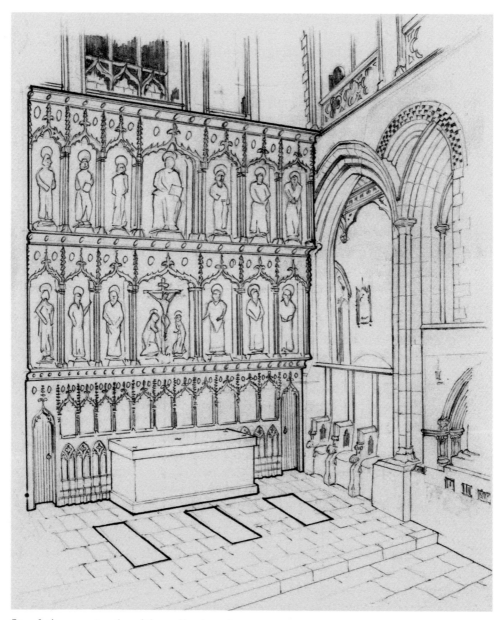

Speculative reconstruction of the medieval reredos

white, which confirms the Tradition of it being made by Bishop Marshall, since the white Rose was the Device of the House of York, which was never (as I believe) us'd singly in any public Decorations of Buildings, except in the Reigns of Edward IV, and Richard III, and then it was a proper Complement to his Patron Edward IV, under whom he was preferr'd.

Under these eleven Niches is a Row of eight Niches painted in Fresco, exactly like the former. At each end of these painted ones, are three real Niches, painted also in the same Manner. Within these are two little ones, with a Pilaster between; the Ground-work throughout, both in the Fresco and the real Niches, is interchangeably blue and red, and the Ornaments over every Nich are gilt. At each End is a Door which leads into the Vestry, painted like all the rest. Above the Altar-Piece are two Rows of large Niches, in which formerly have been Images. In both Rows the Middlemost Nich is larger than the rest, and on each Side are two lesser ones. The two largest Niches probably contained the Images of our Lord and the blessed Virgin; and the other twelve were for the twelve Apostles: Under the two large Niches are the ten commandments, written with gold Letters, within a Frame; over all is a handsome Free-stone Window.

During the nineteenth century restoration of the Cathedral by Prichard and Seddon the surviving lowest tier of this impressive structure was revealed again and moved to stand against the north wall of the Mathew Chapel, now known as the Dyfrig Chapel, where it can still be seen. Browne Willis's account of 1718 is the only known description of this reredos in its total and original form, but until now little attempt has been made to visualise what it could have looked like.

One of the series of circular stone bosses that fitted into the series of holes that appear two above each niche of the reredos has been identified amongst the miscellany of masonry fragments stored above the Chapter House. This is similar to the decorative bosses in equivalent positions on the reredos of the Lady Chapel. The decorative details of the remaining section of the reredos given by Browne Willis are confirmed by a coloured drawing made by T.H. Wyatt, (probably in May 1845) that is now lodged at the National Library of Wales, in Aberystwyth.

It would seem probable that the 'Images' to which Browne Willis refers would have been lost at the time of the Reformation and that the insertion of the Ten Commandments, and possibly the flower paintings, dates from the Commonwealth. The removal of the stone mensa, or altar slab, the outline of which is now visible as a whitewashed area in the centre of the reredos, proba-bly occurred at the same time, being replaced with a wooden table. The description that we are given corresponds in many respects to the great multi-tier reredoses, which still survive in some cathedrals such as Southwark and Bristol. The eleven niches that Browne Willis notes are still to be seen, as are the 'three real niches' at each side of the mensa. The 'eight niches painted in Fresco' would have filled the gap in the lowest level left by the removal of the mensa. The doorways to the vestry also survive.

But what of the upper levels that were destroyed in the eighteenth century? Let us start with a little measurement. The remaining tier is nine feet in height. Assume for the sake of argument that the two upper tiers were of a similar height and that they were separated by ornamental bands of, say, one foot in depth. Browne Willis's plan of the Cathedral indicated two steps from choir floor level to the Altar, so that the top of the three-tier reredos must have reached the level of the walkway of the clerestory. This could explain a puzzling omission in the Browne Willis description of the Cathedral – he makes no mention of the great Norman arch. If the reredos were a high as is now suggested, with its vestry behind, that arch would have been invisible. Thus it is entirely possible that when, early in John Prichard's restoration, the plaster with which the arch had been coated during the Wood 'restoration' of 1740 was stripped away, the Norman work appeared before the eye of the public for the first time in at least two centuries – no wonder that Prichard and the Dean were so surprised! If the central niches in the upper tiers were flanked by the figures of the twelve Apostles, as Browne Willis suggests, then there must have been three 'lesser' niches on either side of the larger, not two as he suggests.

It is unfortunate that the only place where the otherwise accurate plan presented by Browne Willis is in substantial error – by some twelve feet – is at the junction between presbytery and the Lady Chapel. Thus it is difficult to establish the exact position of the reredos. But Browne Willis does give us one further clue when he states that the vestry behind the reredos is five foot and three inches in breadth. The reredos that survives is one foot thick and there was, one presumes a rear wall, so that it would appear that the front face of the reredos would have been about eight feet west of the Norman arch. This would place it level with the rear face of the present mensa. Did George Pace deliberately and carefully place the altar at this point as a nod in the direction of the medieval plan? No correspondence appears to exist to support this supposition, but it may be significant that the dimensions of the post-war high altar both in height and length, and in the depth and overhang of the slab, agree almost exactly with those of the altar that stood before the medieval reredos.

And what of the 'images'? Here we can but speculate, as did Browne Willis. The upper central niche could well have been either a majestas in the style of that which is now affixed to a pier in the David Chapel or a calvary with the Cross flanked by the figures of St Mary and St John – or might the calvary have been in the lower central niche? The figures of the Apostles could well have been the occupants of the side niches of the two upper levels.

The overall effect of the gilding and the paintwork must have been spectacular. It is interesting to note that the tomb of Bishop Marshall stands just to the north and slightly forward of this great reredos as if in confirmation that it was of his time. Much of this interpretation of Browne Willis's description must be viewed as pure speculation, but the great medieval structure of which Llandaff possesses but a fraction deserves to be regarded as one of the Cathedral's great, lost, treasures.

Bishop John Marshall's tomb, on the north side of the high altar. Note the Minton tiling from the Victorian restoration, now lost.

The survey then turns its attention to the tomb of Bishop Marshall, which is described as being next to a doorway into the north aisle. Certainly the tomb as it now exists shows signs of being part of a higher structure, perhaps a chantry, within the fabric of a wall. Its two side panels are markedly different and the one on its north side seems to be made up from fragments.

> The first Thing we see on the North Side of the Choir, as we go down from the Altar, is Bishop Marshall's Monument. It stands in the Wall, between the ninth and tenth Pillars, and is of the Altar-kind. He is plac'd in a recumbent Posture, with his Crosier, and Mitre, and Pontifical Robes. In the Wall are his Arms impal'd with those of the See. The Arms of the See here are, Sable a Sword and two Keys in Saltire, Or, on a Chief, Vert, three Mitres of the Second. His own Arms are, Parted per Cheveron in Fess, Or and Vert, between a M Sable below, and a Faulcon, Or, above. At the Feet are the Cross, Nails, Ropes, and other Instruments of the Crucifixion, carv'd in Free-Stone upon the Wall. The Work of this Monument is very good, and favours of that Time when Arts began to revive. The Capital M of the black, or Gothic Kind, Which is in the Arms, which are also (as I remember) upon the Bishop's Throne, puts it out of Doubt to whom this Monument belongs; for there is no Inscription where-by we may be otherwise inform'd.

The carving of Marshall's arms is missing, but George Pace re-introduced them on a standard at the entrance to the St Dyfrig Chapel during the post war restoration.

After remarking on the two recumbent figures in the north wall of what is now the St Dyfrig Chapel, neither of which he identifies, Browne Willis records that towards the east end of the north aisle there was a screen which divided the final eleven foot from the rest of that aisle, forming a burial-place for the Mathew family. He goes on to note the monument to Sir David Mathew (known as 'the great') which now stands on the right hand side of the Dyfrig Chapel, but for several centuries prior to 1924 it stood against the east wall of this chapel in the space now occupied by the altar. This former positioning of the figure may explain the orientation of the 'squint' which lies on an alignment from the western end of the monument – as it would have been in times past – to the centre of the Lady Chapel altar. Sir David was, reputedly, Standard Bearer to King Edward IV at the battle of Towton, which was fought on Palm Sunday, 1461 and at which he is said to have saved the King's life.

He was the grandfather of both Sir Christopher Mathew and Sir William Mathew whose monuments also stand within this Cathedral. His effigy, which measures six feet two inches from head to toe, and is said to be life sized, is of alabaster, standing on a sandstone base that probably dates from the eighteenth century. The base that Browne Willis saw has long since been lost except for one square section that is in the Cathedral lapidarium. Sir David's armour is of the standard pattern of the day with the belt decorated with the Tudor rose, whilst he wears the Lancastrian Order of S.S. His helmet that is beneath his head bears traces of the figure of a Heathcock, the family crest. (Hence the naming of a public house in Llandaff!) Sir David was murdered at Neath about 1480. The size of his effigy is thought in medical circles to indicate that he suffered from acromegaly (Giantism).

> On the North Side, next to St. Mary's Chapel, between that and the North Ile, is a noble Altar-Monument about nine Foot in Length, on which are two Images finely wrought in Alabaster: The Man is in Armour, with a Collar of SS's about his Neck, and a Coat of Mail under his Corslet; by him lyes a Woman with lac'd Head-cloaths, and the Lace of the Lappets gilt.

This is the monument to Sir David Mathew's other grandson, Sir Christopher Mathew, and his wife. The remains of the paint on parts of this memorial give but a slight indication of the riot of colour that existed in medieval cathedrals and churches. The small figures on the side of this tomb which seem from his account to have been intact at the time of the Browne Willis survey are now badly mutilated.

The Lady Chapel was called the Welsh Chapel in 1717 and it was here that services were conducted in Welsh. It was divided from the side aisles by a pair of wooden screens. On the north side near the altar rails were a pulpit and a reading desk.

> Behind the Altar, and on the North and South sides, are Seats for the People. Over the Altar in this Chapel, towards the North and South, are two large double niches, in which are the Ten Commandments in Welsh: On each Side are two Rows of Niches, with three other Niches at each Corner.

Despite fitful attempts at salvage and partial restoration during the late sixteenth and seventeenth centuries, Llandaff was too poor, and in many ways too disorganised, to successfully repair its Cathedral. Browne Willis certainly knew how parlous this situation was:

> The whole Building is cover'd with Lead, which is pretty entire; only by reason of the sinking of the Timbers of the Roof, it appears uneven, and falling in in several Placcs. There is no painted Glass, nor any Escocheons in the Windows that I observ'd. This Church cannot, by any Means, be said to have been well kept. It is not many Years ago since the Roof was so decay'd, that the Rain which fell into the Choir, often interrupted Divine

Service. Now, indeed, that Convenience is well enough prevented; but the whole Fabrick looks out of Order. The Walls, however, seem to be pretty strong everywhere, except in the Old Tower; and the Stone-Frames of the Windows tolerably entire; so that it might still be made, without a very great Expence, considering the Largeness of the Structure, a very decent Cathedral. But the Revenue of the Church is so small, that, without foreign Assistance, much cannot be done under a very long Compass of Time. The Service of the Choir has been put down many Years, and the Revenues thence arising appropriated to the Reparation of the Edifice. Whether the Complaint is true, which indeed is pretty general, that the Monies so appropriated have not been duly expended, pursuant to the original Design of that Appropriation, is not my Business to enquire.

[Addendum: The putting-down the Service of the Choir was, as I find, done only by Permission, and not by any publick Instrument.] It is certain that of late Years, Necessity has compell'd the Persons concern'd, to lay out some Hundreds of Pounds to preserve the Roof from falling in and destroying the whole Church, and for other Necessaries.

In the same year that this survey was undertaken, other voices were raised with the serious proposal that the See should be moved to Cardiff, where, as Browne Willis recorded, "The inhabitants of that very elegant Town, have, within these few Years, beautify'd their Church [of St John the Baptist], and furnish'd it with an Organ, at their no small Expence." Fortunately for Llandaff, these voices did not prevail.

The Revd William Cole's manuscript described the rapid decline in the state of the fabric in the first quarter of 1723 in vivid detail.

February 6 1722/23 Wednesday, ten o'clock at night, the main couples of the roof and the south west tower fell down and bore with it the timbers of the loft that lay under it, and shattered and bruised a great deal of the tower wall (The other battlements of the north tower, at the east side, were blown down by a storm, November 20th, on a Sunday 1720 they fell on the north side, and beat down 20 feet of it in length to the ground. The storm also threw two pinnacles off the south tower, so that there is but one pinnacle now left. It broke the windows in divers places, and did about £100 damage.) On September 3rd, 1723 there fell down 50 feet of the roof at the west end, near the font, and on or about September the 6th the roof of the south aisle fell in, whereupon the choir service was removed into the Lady Chapel, and the west door shut up, and the entrance is now by the south door.[1]

The ruined medieval interior of the cathedral, drawn in the early nineteenth century

The Italianate Temple

Funds to attempt any form of repair were clearly in short supply and desperate measures were called for – the Bishop and Chapter purchased one ticket in the state lottery in July 1726. They did not 'come up' but nevertheless they were to repeat the exercise in 1731, again without success.

The situation was made the worse by the lack of the Office of Dean – the (absentee) Bishop acting as chairman of the Chapter – and prebendaries, many of whom were not resident in the Diocese, and who had little interest, other than financial, in the fortunes of their Cathedral. A new Bishop, John Harris, was appointed in 1729 and the tide began to turn with a report of a Survey of the building carried out in 1730 by John Wood, Senior, the Bath architect. In his lecture to The Friends of Llandaff Cathedral in 1955, entitled 'John Wood's Italianate Temple', Canon E.T. Davies gave a clear and detailed account of this next period in the Cathedral's history.

John Wood's report made alarming reading, showing clearly that very major problems existed and that total collapse was a real possibility. The outer wall of the north aisle was leaning eighteen inches out of the perpendicular; the battlements of the south wall needed to be taken down and reconstructed. The walls would have to be stripped of ivy and re-pointed, for they were already in danger of collapse "were they not held together by a strong iron bar that goes through ye walls from one side of the church to ye other". Some eighty feet of the south wall should be demolished and rebuilt as should the walls at the east end. Major work was needed on the Jasper Tower and the whole building needed repaving. Most alarming was his assertion that the roof was in a dangerous condition, with its rafters some eighteen inches out of position. Wood suggested that these and other works, which added up to a major reconstruction of the edifice, would cost well in excess of six thousand pounds, considerably beyond the current means of the Chapter. Nevertheless Bishop Harris and the Chapter accepted Wood's report and it is clear that restoration was to be their avowed aim.

Fund raising was put in hand, both by subscription and by brief, with a target of £6366. There is documentary evidence of the preparation of a list of families throughout the Diocese to whom an appeal for funds would be directed. Despite the increasing affluence of these families, the appeal was to fall on deaf ears and only £890 was forthcoming from this source.

A brief was a letter patent issued by the sovereign licensing a collection in the churches throughout the kingdom for a given object, in this case the restoration of Llandaff Cathedral. It was organised by a 'farmer' who charged a commission and expenses for his work. This fund raising scheme, which was launched in October 1731, also fell far short of what was needed with only £1986.1s.7d being collected by 1737.

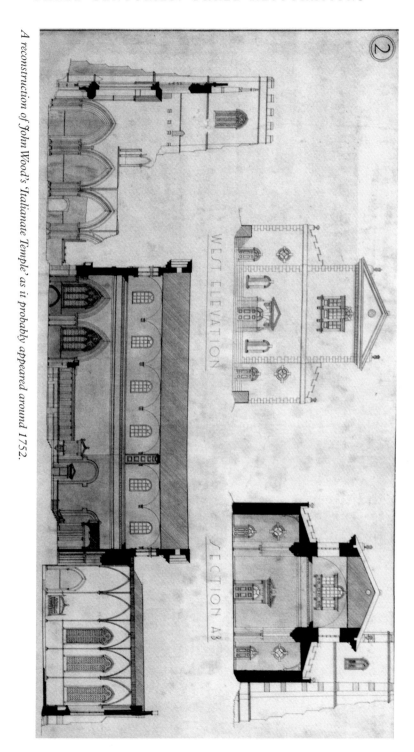

A reconstruction of John Wood's 'Italianate Temple' as it probably appeared around 1752.

Print of the Italianate Temple

Other less ambitious building schemes were now considered, with estimates from two different sources being received, both of which quoted costs which also proved to be beyond the Chapter's resources. Finally in June 1734 the Chapter met and entered into an agreement with John Wood for repairing the Cathedral at a cost of not more than £1700. The scheme now proposed involved taking off the whole roof and lowering it by about six feet, the walls above that level being very defective. Collapsed walls and those that were out of the perpendicular required attention, a new roof, re-glazing of the windows and recasting the lead for the roofs was to be included. This meant of course that the roof of the nave would now bear no relationship, in either height or pitch, to the west front gable. This anomaly shows very clearly in contemporary prints. There is still no mention of an 'Italianate Temple' but this eventual outcome was to become clear by 1736 when Bishop Harris gave a description of what had been achieved by that date.

> We have repaired the walls within 60 feet of the west door, and covered with new timber the choir, and carried a new roof from the east end of the church to the above-mentioned part of the body of the church and covered

it with milled lead; and as we have a quarry of alabaster near this place with other very good materials for stucco, we have employed a skilful plasterer to adorn the inside in such manner as decency requires and we are enabled by our stock to do. We propose to take down the two steeples which at present serve as a west front to the two aisles, for they are very ruinous, and to raise a tower over the front of the nave, and then finish with a rustic porch.[2]

The final stage in this 'restoration' started in 1739 when it was decided to remove the great window in the east wall of the Lady Chapel on the grounds that its tracery was "much decayed", and replace it with a smaller frame of oak. The surrounding gap was to be walled up. The deal board partition in the nave, put up as a closure to the new work, was to be tarred and secured against the weather. It only required this deal partition to be replaced by a stone wall in 1752 to conclude this extraordinary intrusion into a medieval structure. Fortunately the ambition to clear the western ruins failed to materialise thus allowing a future generation to achieve what the Chapter of 1731 had set out to do.

Professor E.A. Freeman, writing in 1850, was scathing in his opinion of what had been done and he was not alone in his views "The ostentatious rearing up of ugliness in the midst of beauty. Really the modern Choir of Llandaff is in no style at all. To call it Italian is a compliment almost as undeserved as to call it Grecian. It is simply hideous and unmeaning, without reference to any principles of art what ever."[3]

What trace of the 'Italianate Temple' remains? One of the stone urns that adorned its west front wall is now on display in the processional way and the ground plan of its west wall is marked by the eastern edge of the wood block flooring of the nave, a feature introduced during the post-war restoration by George Pace. The Italian Temple is as if it had never been.

Having reduced the Cathedral to about half its earlier size, its upkeep should have been more manageable, but the lack of a Dean at the head of the Chapter, together with a series of non-resident Bishops led to a failure to inject new vigour into the religious life of Llandaff Cathedral. The day to day running of the Cathedral and parish was in the hands of two Vicars-choral who also had posts in other parishes. Some of these junior clergy had unenviable reputations and all were poorly paid! The Ecclesiastical Commission which had been established by parliament in 1835 to introduce much needed administrative discipline and order to the Church of England, faced with the problems of a small and poorly funded diocese, was giving serious consideration to uniting the Diocese of Llandaff with that of Bristol, but by the following year Bishop Copleston was able to write to his Chancellor, Bruce Knight, to say that the idea had been abandoned and that Llandaff and its Cathedral were reprieved[4].

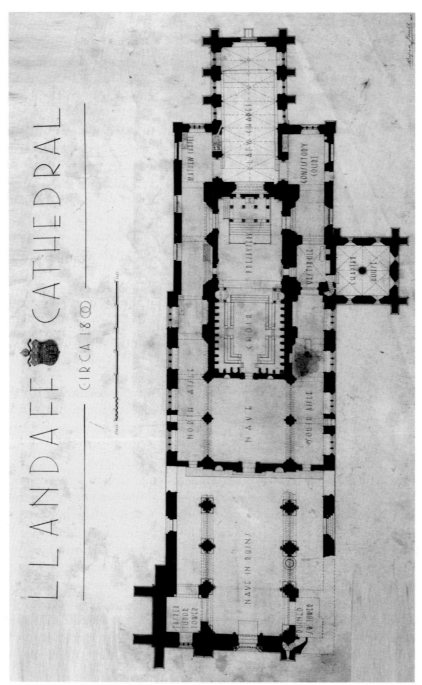

Speculative floor plan of the Italianate Temple, by John Wood

The Nineteenth Century Restoration

Edward Copleston had been enthroned as Bishop of Llandaff in 1828 and although he also held the Deanery of St Pauls, he was very much in control of his diocese through his trusted lieutenants Chancellor William Bruce Knight and John Montgomery Traherne with whom he carried on a constant correspondence. Amongst other innovations set in train by the Ecclesiastical Commission was the appointment of a full-time Archdeacon of Llandaff and it was Bruce Knight who was to fill this crucially important position in 1843. The Commissioners' scheme for the Cathedral itself came into effect soon after and Knight became the first Dean.[5]

In 1835 Precentor Henry Douglas had given the initial impulse to a major programme of restoration that was to fully rebuild Llandaff Cathedral, by placing his stipend for two successive years at the disposal of the Chapter, to be used for essential repairs to the nave roof and for the refitting of the Lady Chapel.

One of Knight's first acts as Dean was the commissioning of the architect T. H. Wyatt to report on the state of the fabric. Wyatt had already been associated with work at Llandaff and had been certifying contractors' bills in connection with repairs to the Lady Chapel since 1841. This report to Dean Knight, which is dated May 1845, is over the joint signatures of Wyatt and John Prichard.

Thomas Henry Wyatt (1807-1880), who had been articled to Philip Hardwick for his architectural training, was in partnership with David Brandon who was six years his junior and who seems to have played no part in the works at Llandaff. Instead, John Prichard (1817-1886) was very much the local lad who acted as Wyatt's assistant on the ground in the early stages of the restoration. A son of the Reverend Richard Prichard, who had been appointed as senior Vicar Choral at Llandaff in 1821, he had trained in London as a pupil of A.C. Pugin's chief assistant, Thomas Larkins Walker.

Prichard had carried through an extensive restoration of the Lady Chapel which involved lowering the floor to its original level, cleaning the stonework of many years' accumulation of grime, ochre and white wash (this on the outside), restoring the tracery and mullions of the side windows, lowering the ground surrounding the outside of the chapel to form a proper drain around the walls, provided new furnishings throughout and, designing, in 1844, a new east window in the Lady Chapel reputedly modelled on the tracery of the windows of the Chapter House of York Minster. This replacing the crude and small wooden casement that had been inserted in 1739. The new east window was filled with painted heraldic glass by Thomas Willement.

Wyatt and Prichard's report opens with a scathing comment about the last attempts at restoration that leaves little doubt about their views:

John Prichard, architect

It cannot be necessary to dwell on the incongruity, and unsightliness of the present structure which intervenes between the ruined portion at the west end and the Lady or Welsh Chapel. How melancholy a specimen of the bad taste of the last century could have been erected in connection with this beautiful ruin it is difficult to conceive.[6]

They then report that the restoration of the Lady Chapel is complete. Next they turn their attention to the future and in doing so give us an additional view of the Italianate Temple.

On the strength of this report, Dean Knight, having already appealed to the clergy of the diocese, prepared a general and persuasive appeal to the laity. Sadly, before it was published, Dean Knight died and it was left to William Daniel Conybeare, his successor, to launch this renewed appeal in November 1845 together with details of the £2360 that had already been subscribed by the clergy. Dean Conybeare came from a family of clergy, his grandfather having been Bishop of Bristol, and combined his knowledge of theology with considerable expertise in the field of geology, being a friend of William Buckland the palaeontologist.

Preserved in the Cathedral's archive are the minutes of the Cathedral Restoration Committee for the nine years 1855-1864, a period that was so

Llandaff from the west, c.1852

crucial in the history of the building, together with printed reports and lists of subscribers to the restoration fund for most of the years between 1845 and 1866. From these papers it becomes possible to form a picture of the continual struggle to encourage the flow of funds and to maintain the impetus of the work. There are repeated attempts to convert subscribers' promises into hard cash. The funds reported as being available at the year end rarely exceed £500 and in four of the years for which an account still exists the balance in hand was less than £100.

By the beginning of 1847 the appeal of 1845 had raised £1,409 and in his printed report Dean Conybeare recorded that, after paying for the work already done, a balance of £1,415 remained in hand. And that

> The Eastern extremity of the South Aisle intervening between the Chapter House and the already restored Eastern Chapel, is now rapidly resuming its original character.... And this portion will afford an excellent sample of the general design; it will be crowned by the beautiful open work parapet intended to replace the wretched battlements [this section of parapet, east of the Chapter House, still survives] and two fine windows in the early decorated style will again replace the modern deformities which had usurped their station. The expense of this portion is estimated under £300.

The next step was the restoration of the Choir and Chancel.

> A beautiful screen or reredos behind the Communion Table, before covered by plaister, has been laid bare, and above this a perspective has been opened into the Eastern Chapel beneath the deeply receding chevron mouldings of a fine Norman Arch, which was previously entirely blocked up and concealed – the arches also which here opened into the side aisles have been disencumbered from the modern walls by which they have been filled.[7]

It is said that when a workman first uncovered traces of the Norman arch, Prichard, who was called from his breakfast, took over the delicate task of removing the plaster, working throughout the day, and that when the Dean saw what was coming into view said to his architect "John, I've always liked you but now I love you!"[8]

Bishop Copleston died in October 1849 and was buried within the sanctuary of the Lady Chapel, being the last person to be laid to rest within the walls of the Cathedral. He was succeeded by Alfred Ollivant who later described his solemn entry into his Cathedral thus:

> The demand of the Bishop to be admitted to his throne was responded to by the Vicar Choral, the only ecclesiastic at that time in residence, having all the Cathedral, parochial, and pastoral duties of Llandaff, then including Canton and Ely resting upon him. There were at that time no Residentiary Canon, nor houses of any kind for Canons, Residentiary or Minor, nor even for the Dean. There had been no choir since 1691.... On the opening of the door, in reply to the Bishop's summons, the musical arrangements of 1691 were found to be still in force; the National Schoolmaster, heading the procession, gave out a Psalm, which was sung by about a dozen of his scholars, a bass viol being the only instrument then in the possession of the Cathedral.

The new Bishop was the first holder of that office in modern times to be resident within walking distance of the Cathedral and, having no extra-diocesan responsibilities, he was able to take an immediate and active interest in the continued restoration programme for his Cathedral.

By Christmas Eve 1851 Dean Conybeare was able to say in his annual report

> the first work which devolved to my care was the restoration of the Presbytery. This has now been completed at an expenditure of about £2,800." The balance in hand was "rather more than £1,100"
>
> The next work...consists in raising a new roof, and constructing a new Clerestory, over four arches. The expense of this estimated...as falling within £2,500.

With promises of some £550 already given he appealed for £900 more "that we may proceed boldly to the completion of this most desirable work."

By Christmas 1852 £1,400 was forthcoming but when the work of constructing a new clerestory and roof to the old Choir had been paid for a mere £140 remained in hand. One now feels that, weighed down by worries about his son Crawford Conybeare who was ill in Madeira, and whom he had visited on more than one occasion, as well as by his own advancing years, Dean Conybeare began to retreat from the immediate objective of complete restoration No doubt dismay at the constant struggle to raise funds also contributed to his view, expressed in his Christmas 1852 report:

> Whether my successor may judge it desirable or expedient to undertake the reconstruction of the Western roofless Ruin must be left to his discretion, and the circumstances of the times.

In 1852 John Pollard Seddon, who, as a young London architect was building an hotel in Southerndown, heard of the restoration work being undertaken at Llandaff and paid it a visit armed with an introduction to Prichard. There was clearly a meeting of minds, because Seddon records that, on his return to his London office, he received an offer of partnership from John Prichard which he immediately accepted, moving to Llandaff forthwith. This new collaboration brought a fresh dimension to the remainder of the restoration, introducing valuable links through Seddon's brother Thomas with the Pre-Raphaelite circle and with the extensive furniture manufacturing enterprise of John Seddon's father.[9]

Thomas Wyatt was to depart from the scene in 1853 amid public controversy regarding the terms of his contract – or lack of it – with the Dean and Chapter, leaving John Prichard in charge of the restoration together with his new partner. In that year, Dean Conybeare was again in Madeira where, in April, Crawford died and was buried in Funchal's English Cemetery. The Dean was away from Llandaff for six months.

Further building difficulties loomed. In October 1854 the Dean reported that during the previous year alarming discoveries had been made whilst the nave floor was being levelled. The nave piers were found to have been built on the loose gravel of the underlying ground without any prepared foundations and the situation was made worse by the numerous burial vaults that had been excavated in close proximity to them. Nevertheless the work continued to complete the restoration of that part of the building that had been the Italianate Temple in a manner which was generally in the form which we see today with a high pitched roof, albeit clad in lead. It was reopened for worship on 16 April 1857 when once more the Service was choral and the preacher was the Bishop of Oxford, Samuel Wilberforce. But there was no organ, no bishop's throne, no stalls, and the Chapter House had still to be restored. Even the choir, that of Gloucester Cathedral, was 'borrowed for the occasion'. Nevertheless what might be regarded as phase two of Llandaff Cathedral's resurrection was substantially complete, but within six months Dean Conybeare was dead. He was buried near to the Chapter House below a memorial cross designed by his son Henry. The new Dean was Thomas Williams who, as Archdeacon of Llandaff, had been an active member of the restoration committee since its inception. He was 56 years of age and his Bishop was 59. The reopening service of 1857 had created a new surge of enthusiasm and all was now in place for the third and most ambitious phase of the restoration.

In the summer of 1857 Prichard and Seddon set out their plans for the restoration of the ruined west section of the Cathedral:

> We are of the opinion that the first step will be to repair the arcades on the North and South sides and to connect them with the piers now imbedded in the modern west wall (of the Wood Temple) & to strengthen them by a range of three buttresses on either side similar to those that have been lately erected further eastward, but having equilateral arches spanning the aisles as was evidently intended from this point westward from the different disposition of the piers in the ruined portion of the Nave from that which is now under cover. Having thus made the lower part thoroughly substantial we would proceed to continue the Clerestory on either side until it abuts against the western towers – and the roof should then be carried from the modern to the ancient western wall.
>
> Although it would be desirable to include the above works under one contract yet it would be practicable to divide it into three – namely: 1. the restoration of the arcades with the buttresses; 2. The Clerestory and 3. the Roof [the "three contract option" was, in the event, how it was organised].
>
> To accomplish either or all of these works it will be necessary to disengage the real building from the modern west end wall & as it is the object to do this with as little interference as possible with the present interior arrangements, we propose to cut channels & to pierce the ends of the aisles filling in the same with brick studded partition as also the upper part in the roof reinserting for the time being the modern west window. We propose also to restore and repair only those portions of the western façade which absolutely require it. They quote the estimated costs for this programme of works to be £3,756.4s.6d.
>
> Subsequent steps would be the rebuilding of the South Tower to the height of the clerestory, the rebuilding of the walls of the aisles and roofing them, the completion of the tower and the paving, these being undertaken as funds permitted.[10]

By November 1857 plans and tenders for that phase of the undertaking were in preparation, as were estimates for the stalls, the bishop's throne and flooring work. This ambitious stage of the programme had been made possible by a substantial inflow of funds during 1857 and the early part of 1858 that had included the sum of £1,000 from the Marquess of Bute and contributions of £100 or more from over thirty individuals, including the Prince of Wales.

The contractor who gained most of the structural work throughout the restoration was Thomas Williams – no relative of the Dean of the same name – who was based in Canton and who also constructed several other buildings in Cardiff for Prichard & Seddon. His firm was to build the landmark tower and spire which were the final statement of the restoration. The majority of the carving throughout the years of restoration was undertaken by the Llandaff family firm of Clarke's.

In January 1858 a major debate started regarding the material to be used to cover the nave roof. That part of the Cathedral which had been brought back into use in April 1857, including the steeply pitched roof that had been constructed over the Lady Chapel, had been clad with lead, but now Prichard and Seddon put forward their view that Westmorland slate should be used for all the steep roofs leaving only the aisle roofs covered in lead. They pointed out that the pitched roof of Ely Cathedral gained its picturesque appearance "mainly from the frequent patches made by those most expensive of artisan, the plumbers, who constantly hover over every large building covered in lead." They also drew attention to the costs that these repairs invariably incurred as could be clearly demonstrated by reference to the Chapter's own accounts. There would be a substantial cost benefit! The Ecclesiological Society's committee met to discuss the proposal and the views of George Gilbert Scott and Benjamin Ferry (the diocesan architect of Bath and Wells) were sought. Opinion was not unanimous but came out in favour of slate with a metal cresting along the length of the nave.

The Dean's report in June 1859 tells us that "the ruin is a ruin no longer, and it is hoped that the subscriptions already promised may suffice to secure the execution of the essential portions of the work in view". In the same month Prichard and Seddon were asked for detailed estimates for the stalls, and for doors and window glazing for the western part of the building. In September the contracts for the doors and windows were let and estimates were presented for the introduction of gas into the Lady Chapel for lighting and heating.

Prichard's drawing in which he depicted the way he expected the completed Cathedral to appear, included, above the chancel arch, a Flèche, or small spire, to house a light bell, and in March 1860 the construction of its foundation was authorised. In the event the Flèche was never completed but its foundation platform was a feature of the roofline of the pre-war Cathedral.

By June 1860 the nave roof had been slated and the doors and windows were being fitted. September saw a contract being let to Messrs Gray & Davison for the construction and fitting of the organ, advice having been taken from Sir Frederick Gore Ouseley regarding its specification. The cost was not to exceed £900 and the organ fund was to benefit from a second edition of Bishop Ollivant's *Account of the Condition of the Fabric from 1575 to the present time*. There were considerable contractual difficulties with Gray & Davison which finally had to be taken to arbitration, so it proved somewhat ironic that the instrument was eventually considered inadequate for a building of the size of the Cathedral and was replaced in 1900. The Gray & Davison organ was sold to St Mary's Church, Usk, where it continues, in its original Seddon case, to give good service.

By the following June the wall which had, for 120 years, divided the Cathedral into two was finally removed and the whole length of the building could at last be seen. In revealing the totality of the building from west door to high altar, Prichard had made what was probably the most radical change to the ritual layout of the Cathedral in the whole of its existence. In the medieval cathedral and in the Wood 'temple' which succeeded it, the nave had been divided from the choir and sanctuary by a screen or pulpitum that enclosed the clergy and the mysteries of the altar. Prichard was faced with a requirement for a Cathedral which could equally well serve a growing parochial function, but, in dispensing with the screen, the building had become, in many people's eyes, just a very large parish church. It would be for another restoring architect to resolve the conflict between having a conventional 'cathedral' plan with its pulpitum screen and 'collegiate' choir layout, and a church that could place the altar in full view at the centre of public worship. Demarcation without isolation would prove to be the solution.

On Tuesday, 17th September 1861 the organ was in place and a full choral service was held to the mark this milestone. But the stalls and the bishop's throne were incomplete and the laying of floors was still in progress. Reference to the contract for the bishop's throne first occurs in August 1858 when a Mr Ratty withdraws his claim to the contract for its construction and the responsibility is left with Prichard and Seddon. They had contracted Edward Clarke to execute the carving, but Prichard was also building a large mansion at Ettington Park in Warwickshire, for Mr E.P. Shirley. Coincidentally, John Prichard's brother Richard was the incumbent of the parish in which Ettington Park stood. John Prichard employed Henry Armstead to design decorative panels for the house and Edward Clarke, and his family, moved to Warwickshire for a couple of years for Edward to carve Armstead's designs. This accounted for the lack of progress with the throne and prompted an entry in the Restoration Committee minutes on 15th March 1862 which said that "Messrs Prichard & Seddon were directed to contract with Mr Williams for fixing & completing the screen at the end of the stalls… and also for completing the Throne for the sum of £100. It is understood

The completed spire with the timber scaffolding still in place, 1869.

that Mr Clarke is to execute the carving as soon as the work in Warwickshire has been completed or that some equally competent person shall be employed." It is also clear from the minute book that economies were being made particularly in the quality of the materials employed. Funds were, as usual, very tight.

The fine lectern by Skidmore of Bristol was given by Col. Edward Stock-Hill of Rookwood and Dean Thomas Williams provided a font designed by John Seddon. The Rossetti Triptych was still unfinished and the Chapter resolved not to pay the one third of the cost of it that they had promised until it was put up in the Cathedral!

September 1862 saw the dissolution of the Prichard-Seddon partnership and from that date it is Prichard's name alone that appears in the minutes. Their work at Llandaff was all but done and the only major project that needed attention was the rebuilding of the south-west tower. The two architects could now concentrate to a greater extent on their work of building and restoring churches, schools and parsonages across the diocese. Prichard worked largely within the Archdeaconry of Llandaff whilst Seddon took the Monmouth Archdeaconry. Each had produced over the years buildings of great merit. Prichard designed such churches as St Catherine, Baglan, St John Evangelist, Canton, other buildings such as Nazareth House in Cardiff, St Fagans Rectory, Llandaff School whilst also restoring many of the small and ancient country churches in Glamorgan. Seddon's hand appears at St Woolos Cathedral in Newport, Newchurch in Gwent, Llangwm Uchaf, and many others, but perhaps the most interesting of Seddon's new churches is that at Hoarwithy, in Herefordshire, which is built in an Italianate idiom.

In 1863 Prichard presented designs and estimates for a new south-east entrance to the Cathedral and work to complete the restoration of the Chapter House. In 1864 gas lighting was installed along the string course below the clerestory, a measure "rendered absolutely necessary by the adoption of a third service on Sunday evenings. No mention is made in the minute book of the hazards involved in actually lighting this installation! The Rossetti Triptych was, at long last, complete. It is clear that the physical restoration of Llandaff Cathedral had been accompanied by an equally important spiritual revival, not only in Llandaff itself, but across the diocese. It should be noted that during the episcopate of Alfred Ollivant (1849-82) about one hundred and seventy churches were either built or restored in the Diocese of Llandaff.

Minor Canon Edward Fishbourne recorded in his memoirs that "the choir stalls were extended to their present length in 1869". The stalls that were initially installed by Prichard, probably at the same time as the Gray & Davison organ, occupied just the first bay west of the chancel arch and provided seating for only six members of the Chapter. The pulpit, with its panels by Thomas Woolner, stood against the first pier west from the chancel arch and the Sir William Mathew table tomb stood in bay three. The second phase of furnishing the choir, completed in 1869, entailed moving the pulpit one more bay further west and also re-siting the Mathew tomb in the fourth bay, where it had been at the time of the Browne Willis survey of 1717. Now the second bay west from the chancel arch could be filled with canopied stalls for all the members of the Chapter and two ranks of desks for an enlarged choir of men and boys.

The final act of this restoration took place in 1869 when Bishop Ollivant, who for his enthronement had entered a Cathedral which was in ruins, lowered the last stone of the spire into position, completing thirty years of rebuilding. At the great service of thanksgiving on 13th July Bishop Wilberforce returned to

Drawing of the Moses panel from the pulpit, now in store

preach once more, and Llandaff Cathedral was again the active mother church of a rapidly industrialising diocese.

If there can be any criticisms at all of this heroic restoration they must firstly centre on the decision to place the high altar on an excessively elevated platform, thereby destroying the proportions of the Norman arch that the restoration had restored to view. Secondly, the design of the upper story of the Chapter House, elegant though it be in appearance, introduced structural problems that were to affect the upper room for over a century. Prichard had arranged for the rain-water from the new octagonal roof to drain via a gutter which ran continuously around the top of the walls. Failure of any part of this gutter, which had no 'fall', let the rain water drain into the structure of the wall. Also the stonework chamfers at each corner of the building had vertical construction joints which again let rainwater into the walls beneath. These are minor criticisms when the magnitude of what was achieved is considered.

John Prichard died on 13th October 1886 and was buried with his father, near to the south-east door of the Cathedral that he brought back to life. A small brass

The new Victorian pulpit from the Prichard restoration

plate below the spire which was his crowning contribution to the restoration records his life, and on the south side of the exterior of his steeple, at belfry level, is a carving of his head placed there by his successor as a restorer, George Pace.

Prichard was succeeded as the Cathedral's consulting architect by his former partner John Pollard Seddon, who served until his death on 1st February 1906. During Seddon's period of office the decision was taken to replace the Gray & Davison organ, which had a 'tracker' action, with a new and larger instrument, by Hope Jones, with an electric action that allowed the organ loft to be sited in the facing bay on the south side of the choir. The oak case of the instrument was given by George Insole in memory of his father and his brother. Its design and integration into the existing choir furnishings would have been Seddon's.

Early in the new century Seddon submitted an alarming report to the Chapter in which he suggested that a major problem had arisen which threatened the stability of the towers and he proposed an elaborate programme of work that involved cross bracing being built between the two towers to allow

A contemporary print of the Victorian nave

each of the supporting piers in the nave to be rebuilt sequentially. This produced
consternation in Chapter and a call for a second opinion. John L. Pearson, who
was currently part way through the building of the new cathedral at Truro, was
called in. He suggested that the problem could readily be solved by a competent
builder. Such work as was considered necessary was swiftly completed.
Frederick R. Kempson (1838-1923) who had won the competition in 1889 for
a design for a new daughter church in Llandaff Yard, was appointed to succeed
Seddon as the Cathedral's consultant architect in May 1906. He was in partnership with Charles B. Fowler.

In 1908 the Venerable Frederic Edmondes, Archdeacon of Llandaff, offered
to pay for the re-furbishment of the walls and ceiling of the Lady Chapel. The
Dean and Chapter consulted Kempson and commissioned Geoffrey Webb to
carry out an ambitious scheme. At the same time the reredos, which was believed
at that time to be no more than a recent insertion and which impinged upon the
height of the window that Prichard had rebuilt, was removed. It was more than
a decade before a drawing of 1803, discovered in the British Museum, indicated
that the reredos was no modern copy! Fortunately the stonework that had been

Kempson's Lady Chapel

taken out had been preserved in Messrs Clarke's yard and would eventually find its way back to its proper place.

Kempson's only other known contribution to the Cathedral was the design of an elegant internal porch at the Teilo door. The drawings for this porch, including the joiner's construction plans produced by Clarke's, are in the Cathedral Archive, but the porch itself did not survive the bombing in 1941.

Following the death of Kempson in 1923, the Dean, F.W. Worsley, and Chapter appointed <u>Sir Charles Nicholson</u> to be their consultant architect in May 1924. The eldest of three brothers, all of whom excelled in various branches of the arts, he had served his articles under J.D. Sedding. Sir Charles was, eventually, to be consulting architect to six cathedrals including Lincoln and Wells. He was noted for his technical and practical knowledge coupled with a profound sense of atmosphere which was to serve him well in his time as Llandaff's Architect that was to extend over a period of twenty-five years. His first project at Llandaff was the refurbishment and extension, in 1926, of the Prebendal House to which he added the upper room, with the song room beneath it and a short east wing that

Charles Nicholson's Lady Chapel

provided an elegant new entrance and internal stairwell.

In the following year plans were mooted to re-furnish the Lady Chapel, including the restoration of the recycled reredos. Nicholson's plan for the reredos also suggested for the provision of statuary in the twelve niches and for arcading (probably to be painted) on the wall below the east window, to carry the line of the window opening down to the floor. These details were not incorporated in the programme of work in 1927, but have since been carried out, with Frank Roper's 'Flowers of Mary' filling the niches in 1965 and the addition of *trompe l'oeil* arcading below the reredos by Donald Buttress with Larkworthy in 1987. Nicholson designed new furniture for the Lady Chapel to replace the pulpit and pews that were to be given to a new church in Bargoed. Chairs replaced the heavy pews. Old bench ends were incorporated in new clergy seats and the heating and lighting were improved.

In 1931 it was the turn of the Chapter House to be refurnished and panelled, in memory of Archdeacon David Davies. September 1931 saw the installation of David J. Jones as Dean of Llandaff and a partnership between Dean and Architect was formed that was to be meeting of minds. These two knowledgeable men carried on a correspondence in which they explored, as between friends, ideas and possibilities for the Cathedral which they both loved.

In 1933 Dean Jones founded The Friends of Llandaff Cathedral a body that over the years has provided superb support for a succession of Deans, together with continual and substantial funding that has contributed enormously to the work and maintenance of the Cathedral. Through the contents of its annual reports it has also provided an invaluable source of record about the fabric and activities of the Cathedral.

Some of the ideas that passed between Dean and Architect were totally speculative in character and in 1936 Nicholson produced a drawing, now in the Cathedral archive, that first put on paper an idea that both men thought could never be carried out. From the day it was installed, the Rossetti triptych had been criticised for its positioning and lack of proper lighting. Nicholson also felt that the high platform on which the altar table stood effectively destroyed the proportion of the Norman arch whilst both Dean and Architect were conscious of the problem presented to elderly and infirm worshippers in negotiating the steps to take their communion at the high altar. Nicholson proposed to move the Rossetti painting to the east end of the south aisle (where the St Teilo Chapel now stands), reduce the altar platform to one step and to insert a light metal screen in the Norman arch whose bases would once more be exposed to view. "Between ourselves," Nicholson wrote to his friend the Dean, "we know that, much though we would wish to, we cannot do it". Time would tell!

More pressing matters were to occupy the minds of both Dean and Architect. Death watch beetle had been found in the timbers of both the nave roof and the north aisle, and the clerestory windows were in urgent need of replacement following storm damage in successive winters. A major reconstruction of the organ had been necessary during 1937 and 1938. Funds were tight and it was The Friends who were able to fund a rolling programme of window replacement. The nave roof was continually being deferred.

The nave during the nineteen thirties, probably the enthronement of Bishop Timothy Rees, 1931

Second World War

A cathedral is a difficult, if not an impossible, building to 'black out' so that the first effect of the declaration of war in September 1939 was the combining of parish and cathedral evensong services during the winter months. Not so obvious were a careful review of the fire-fighting arrangements in the Cathedral and the establishment of a 'fire-watching' rota. By mid-1940, with the fall of France, the incidence of bomb damage became an even greater possibility and by September The Friends were busy raising funds to pay for the removal and storage of major works of art. By the end of that year no less than twelve of the stained glass windows were taken out and stored, the Rossetti triptych was boxed and placed behind a bank of sandbags in the south aisle and the figure of the

Virgin and Child in the Lady Chapel was also protected by a wall of sandbags.

On the evening of January 2nd 1941 these precautions proved fully justified when a mine exploded in the south churchyard after snagging its parachute cords on the spire as it fell. The damage to the building was enormous and Dean Jones, who was in the building with Bob White the verger, was lucky to escape with his life. Despite injuries, the Dean set about organising such salvage and repair work as was practicable and rallying support and aid. A large proportion of the southern side of the nave roof collapsed leaving the northern half precariously balanced. The south aisle roof collapsed and all the tracery of the windows in the south wall was blown in. Every scrap of glass which remained in the building was lost and much of the furniture and interior decoration was damaged beyond repair. Much of the west wall of the Chapter House as well as its conical roof had to be demolished. The top third of the spire, where the parachute had snagged it, was shifted sideways and also had to be taken down. Some brave souls ventured into the ruins and salvaged all the Colours of the Welch Regiment and many other items of value.

The Cathedral was completely unusable. The bomb had fallen on a Thursday evening and there is no record of any formal services being held on the following Sunday, but on January 12th services were resumed in the dining room of the Deanery with 65 communicants. By January 26th it had been possible to patch up the Prebendal House sufficiently for it to become the Cathedral – and it was duly licensed as such by the Bishop. The altar was at the southern end (where the kitchen now stands) and the shutters between the two halves of the building were lowered into their boxes.

The Dean had quickly taken command of the situation and immediately summoned Sir Charles Nicholson by telegram. The Architect was quickly on the spot to examine the damage and to produce a short but comprehensive assessment. Within days, and despite his injuries, the Dean also wrote the following initial thoughts and impressions in an exercise book:

> No words of mine are needed to bring this home to each of us who are Trustees of the Cathedral and what it stands for. It is a severe break with the past – but a temporary one; and we shall, some of us, rebuild the Cathedral, and set it going on its functions again. But as one on the spot I ought to describe as briefly as possible what happened; and offer suggestions for carrying on in some degree the functions of a Cathedral: and the question of rebuilding will be one of interest to all of us equally.

THE DAMAGE DONE.
i. To the structure.
A land mine presumably fell in the churchyard at 15 yards from the south

nave aisle wall. It blew off most of the South Aisle roof of the nave, the south side of the Nave roof, severely damaged the Chancel roof, destroyed the roof of the Museum, displacing 15 feet of the top of the spire, shook severely the Jasper Tower bringing down some of the smaller pinnacles and leaving one of the large corner pinnacles out of plumb.

All the glass in the windows was blown out and destroyed. The walls, especially the S. Walls, were severely shaken especially the Chapter House ones, and half of that structure will probably have to be taken down.

ii. To the interior furnishings.

Chairs & seats were smashed, including the Choir Stalls, some of which can be salvaged.

The organ was injured, its console on the south side very severely most having been destroyed: case much damaged.

Two of the pulpit's Woolner panels were broken as well as the hand rail and the body slightly damaged.

iii. To the other Dean & Chapter buildings.

a. The Prebendal House large Library room had its doors and windows blown in, 2/3 of the upper Library ceiling came down, the slating of its roof was damaged: and the new ceiling of triplex boarding lost one section only. But the roof seems to have been lifted off the walls slightly.

b. The White House is very extensively wrecked and cannot be lived in. The tenants have moved away. It might have to be reconstructed.

c. The White Cottage is very severely damaged. Roof and interior. But it might be worth rebuilding it.

d. The Cathedral Cottage is very severely damaged and it is doubtful if it is worth while rebuilding it.

e. The Well Cottage is badly damaged and can be fairly easily repaired.

f. The Cathedral School has a large number of its windows blown out and its roof damaged.

The Headmaster says it is not as bad as he thought: he hopes to begin school again on Jan 17.

WHAT HAS BEEN DONE.

Mr Teather was immediately notified of the calamity & he employed Messrs Knox & Wells, Mr Boswell and Mr Guy Clarke to remove the debris, to salvage what was possible of the building of the Cathedral and its contents & to roughly repair the dwelling houses where that was practicable.

A wire was sent to Sir Charles Nicholson to come and examine the Cathedral and advise. He was here Friday and Saturday Jan 10th & 11th & will be sending his report to the Representative Body at its next meeting on Friday next.

Mr. Teather asked Mr Gill, a local organ builder, to salve the organ and

The bombed cathedral, from the south side, showing the crater

Messrs Norman and Beard were notified so that Mr Norman came in person & their representative Mr Gough and they [Hill & Norman & Beard] working together have removed a large quantity of pipes to a place of safety. [Herbert Norman produced a written report on 16th January.]

Mr. Teather has asked Messrs Taylor's of Loughborough to examine the clock and bells.

I gather Messrs Haden are to come and examine the heating apparatus when the debris has been cleared. We have emptied the water out of it.

The bombed cathedral, interior looking south at the entry to the choir

A Lancashire firm of steeple jacks was asked to ascend and examine the spire. They did it on Jan. 10.

As much as possible of the furnishings have been carried out and stored either in the Deanery Basement or at the Prebendal House. The contents of the Muniment Room are dumped at one of the rooms in the Deanery Basement and the organ will probably be stored in the interior on the north side possibly under the Jasper Tower. This is not finally decided.

Mr Teather will be claiming with the District Valuer for damage done to the buildings of the Cathedral and the Chapter's other houses.

I shall be making a list of damaged interior furnishings, in cooperation with Mr Teather.

PROSPECTS FOR THE CATHEDRAL.

Mr Norman thinks that about 80% of the organ can be salved. Sir Charles says the whole of the Nave Roof must be brought down at once to save the clerestory and the walls.

The organ case and the choir stalls are to be stored inside the Cathedral.

Sir Charles seemed to think that the Chancel and the Lady Chapel together can be adapted for a place of worship to seat 250 persons in about three months.

As to the Dean and Chapter Administration.
a. The Services

Holy Communion was administered in the Deanery Dining Room on Sunday Jan 12 with 65 persons present.

For the immediate future, I suggest that

The usual services of Holy Communion and the Choir Offices with the Parochial occasional offices shall be held in the Prebendal House.

Then after about three months we can hold our usual regular services in the East End of the Cathedral....

By the end of January 1941 Sir Charles had prepared four alternative schemes any of which he hoped could be completed within six months. All of these schemes envisaged using the Lady Chapel as choir and sanctuary, with the high altar area, presbytery – and perhaps the choir – serving as a nave. He had reckoned without the Office of Works which controlled the issue of licences for all building work. Some restoration work to render a church usable was permitted but alterations were definitely not allowed. Unfortunately each of Nicholson's schemes required the removal of both the Victorian high altar reredos and the high stepped platform on which the altar stood. This, claimed the Office of Works, was definitely alteration and was most certainly not permitted. Letters flew and meetings were held but all were met with a stony refusal. Eventually the Minister of Works in person was drawn into the debate by the MP for the constituency, Judge Temple-Morris. Finally on October 6th the Minister, Lord Reith, swiftly recognised the stupidity of the situation and ordered that the work could and should proceed.

By 7th February 1941, Sir Charles had produced a ten page report that detailed what needed to be done in the short term to preserve the fabric from further deterioration, and outlining a programme for reinstatement and eventual restoration when the time came. His prompt action undoubtedly did much to save the Cathedral from even worse damage from the elements in the intervening years. A further report from Sir Charles dated 2nd May 1941, dealt with possible damage to the vaulting of the Lady Chapel and detailed instructions for the stabilisation and protection of damaged walls, the demolition of the upper stage of the Chapter House and the securing of loose pinnacles on both of the towers.

On April 1st 1941 a service of re-interment for those bones which had been scattered by the bomb in the churchyard took place. A year later, on Saturday April 30th 1942 a service of reconciliation marked the return of clergy and congregation to Nicholson's 'Emergency Cathedral' which was separated from the remainder of the ruined and roofless cathedral by a huge wooden and asbestos screen that completely filled the chancel arch. In bad weather this screen creaked and groaned in the wind and rattled noisily with rain or hail. The heating plant was unusable and such portable heating as could be found did little to combat the cold. The windows of the emergency cathedral were closed with asbestos sheeting – except for a narrow strip of reinforced glass at the very bottom. A Moustel organ (a sort of harmonium) sat on the north side of the Lady Chapel, which was furnished with salvaged pews and chairs. A row of salvaged Canons' stalls – less their canopies – was ranged across the foot of the asbestos screen and the remainder of the area between the chancel arch and the Norman arch was filled with very closely packed chairs. A rudimentary pulpit was placed in the southern side of the Norman arch and the Lady Chapel was reached from this makeshift nave down a flight of three steps.

Thoughts of Restoration

On the 18th May 1942, Sir Charles wrote for the Dean a three page summary of his preliminary thoughts about the form in which the Cathedral should be restored. This was to be the beginning of a correspondence between Dean and Architect in which ideas were exchanged and developed, many of which were to have a profound bearing on the sort of Cathedral that would finally emerge from the ruins. His summary read:

> The two perspective drawings [unfortunately, these do not survive] show alternative suggestions for the eventual restoration of the interior. In most aspects these are alike but they differ as regards the internal treatment of the high roof. Externally neither design involves any departure from the pre-war appearance of the Cathedral except the omission of the stump of the unfinished spirelet over the chancel arch.
>
> The destroyed Nave roof was not a very sound piece of construction

The roofless nave looking westward from the presbytery

and in my view was not well suited to a building of Cathedral dignity. My first suggestion was to replace it with an arched cradle roof of West Country character. But the original thirteenth century roof undoubtedly had a flat ceiling like that of the Nave of St. Albans Abbey and this flat ceiling existed in Browne Willis' day. The larger of the two drawings shows the Nave ceiled [sic] in this fashion. To my mind it would be proper to adopt this alternative rather than that of an arched cradle roof or an open timber one. I believe the interior would look more spacious and more dignified with a flat ceiling than with a roof of any other practicable design (vaulting being of course out of the question). Next the adoption of a flat ceiling would have many practical advantages, being excellent from the acoustical point of view, extremely strong in construction, and a good deal less costly than any other form of covering. There are other advantages in having all the roof timbers easily accessible above the flat ceiling, and in the very considerable protection such a ceiling gives from the cold.

The one great difficulty with a flat ceiling is the height of the modern chancel arch, which would have to be underbuilt if a flat ceiling was

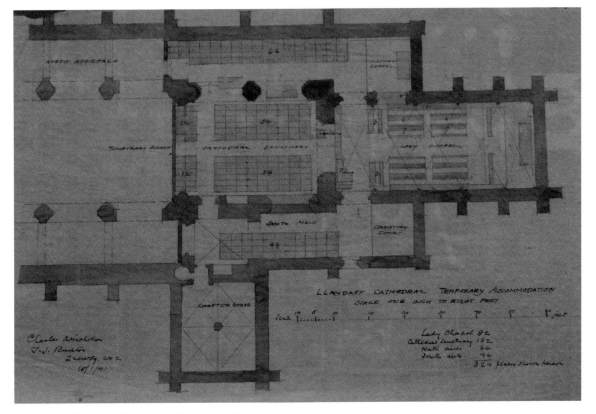

Nicholson's plan for the Emergency Cathedral

adopted. The cost of this could, I think, very well be saved by the simpler construction of the roof.

This arch is believed to have been built on the site of a Norman arch which had been destroyed in the thirteenth century when the Nave was rebuilt. It is quite clear that no such arch existed in Browne Willis' day – indeed the nineteenth Century restoration of this part of the Church was in no sense a faithful reproduction of what had existed at any former time. It would, however, I think be impractical to do away with the arch altogether as this would necessitate considerable alterations to the Presbytery which would needlessly interfere with very good 19th Century work and which would be costly as well as unnecessary.

The principal alteration in the design, other than the alteration of the Nave roof, consists of the proposed re-arrangement of floor levels and the opening out of the Norman Arch together with the removal of the former reredos to a suitable position in the South Aisle where the paintings could be properly seen without artificial light. The reredos here would be the principal feature of a chapel and would also serve as a screen to the choir vestry.

The interior of the 'Emergency Cathedral'. Note the asbestos window.

As regards the Norman Arch I feel that now it is exposed it deserves to be treated as an important architectural feature and that it should never be partly blocked up with a reredos.

No doubt this arch was entirely covered up from the time of the fourteenth Century, when the reredos now in the Mathew Chapel [now the St. Dyfrig Chapel] was built across the Presbytery in front of the Arch.

This reredos was a high one with three tiers of niches of which only the lowest tier has been preserved. In Browne Willis' time all three tiers were complete and reached up to the sill of the East window.

This being the case Prichard was certainly right in not retaining the lowest tier of the reredos in its original position, it would have partly blocked the Arch which should obviously either be left open or else entirely

An aerial view of the bombed and roofless cathedral with its asbestos windows and shortened spire.

concealed as was done in the 14th Century at Llandaff and a little later at Winchester, St. Albans and Christchurch. Unfortunately Prichard blocked the Arch with his reredos and buried the piers with his steps but the opportunity of modifying these arrangements should I think be welcomed and the reredos can be preserved intact in a very favourable position.

The modern sedilia I should retain with very slight modification to suit the new floor levels and the solid backs of these could be pierced to let more light into the Sanctuary.

As regards the old furniture although much of it is damaged most of it can be worked up again, in doing this I should advise eliminating the excessively high platforms under the choir seats and I should question the

Charles Nicholson's first sketch of buildings on the north side of his postwar cathedral

advisability of replacing the stall canopies as they formerly existed. The details of the arrangement of fittings deserve careful consideration but these matters are of less importance than questions affecting the main fabric.

I venture, however, to think that a good deal of knowledge regarding details of church arrangements has been acquired since the Cathedral was restored in the middle of the 19th Century and that it would not be wise to reproduce the furnishings exactly as they were before the Cathedral was damaged.

This flow of ideas continued and expanded over the years to include provision of a War Memorial Chapel for the Welch Regiment and additional vestry, toilet and office accommodation. Initially it was the intention to site these on the south side of the Cathedral, where they could be integrated with the necessary reconstruction of the south wall, but this plan was soon superceded by ideas for a more extensive scheme on the north side of the Cathedral. The matter that generated the most correspondence and the greatest range of options was the future position of the Rossetti triptych and the stone screen in which it had been mounted, with the only common theme being that it should not again block the

Nicholson's proposed restoration of the bomb-damaged nave

Norman arch. The flat ceiling was readily accepted both on historical and aesthetic grounds and because of the many practical advantages that it offered, not least the lack of outward thrust on the nave walls.

Conversations that Sir Charles held with Hill, Norman & Beard, explored the possibility of siting the main body of the organ, which needed major reconstruction whatever was decided, one bay west of its pre-war position. This position would be less cramped and would have addressed problems of balance and sound projection about which recent organists have frequently complained.

Nicholson's concept for the new extensions on the north side of the Cathedral envisaged a vaulted Regimental Chapel that would, effectively, form an additional aisle. It would be orientated east-west with a small courtyard development containing vestries, toilets and offices at its eastern end. The Teilo door would lead from the north aisle of the Cathedral into a narthex at the west end of the Chapel and, in a letter that he wrote in January 1948, Nicholson envisaged what he described as "a connecting cloister from the Church to the Prebendal House". The existing windows of the north aisle would be moved to form the outer north wall of the Chapel.

A set of drawings, plan, sections and elevations, are in the Cathedral archive, and include a perspective drawing of the restored nave that he proposed. The flat ceiling, open Norman arch exposed to its full height, repositioned organ, absence of pews and the low profile Canons' stalls are all clearly shown. The drawing also shows that it was the intention to return to the 'collegiate' form of layout for the chapter stalls which had been abandoned in Prichard's restoration. This would be the only form of division between nave and choir which would indicate Cathedral status.

In October 1945 thoughts could turn, at last, to the commencement of rebuilding, with the attendant difficulties of licenses, shortages of materials and skilled labour, with much of the available resources being employed on the reconstruction of housing and industry. Negotiations with the War Damage Commission were protracted and involved, with difficulties in drawing the line between what could be considered war damage and what was due to the dilapidations resulting from the normal passage of time! Costs of building were estimated to have at least doubled since before hostilities started and fund raising was not proving easy. Even by 1948 there was very little to see in the way of building other than repairs to the east end of the south aisle.

Dean David Jones had valiantly led the efforts to maintain and restore his Cathedral in the face of the ill-health which had dogged him ever since the bombing, and on 16th July 1948 he resigned and was appointed Dean Emeritus. His successor at the Deanery was Chancellor Glyn Simon, then Warden of St Michael's College, and a member of the Restoration Committee.

On 14th February 1949 Sir Charles wrote to Dean Simon enclosing "The Specification for Reconstruction of the high roofs of Nave and Choir being Section 4 of the General specification for War Damage repair at Llandaff Cathedral". Just three weeks later, on 4th March the sudden death of Sir Charles Nicholson was announced, to be followed a further ten days later by that of Dean Emeritus David Jones.

★ ★ ★

The Dean and Chapter wrote to T.J. Rushton, Sir Charles Nicholson's partner, on 6th April 1949 inviting him to continue to deal with the war damage aspects of the work at Llandaff which consisted of the main roof, the south presbytery aisle, the towers and the whole of the north aisle. The Dean and Chapter then proceeded on 11th April to invite George Pace of York, a young and virtually unknown architect, to complete the restoration in all aspects other than war damage. Both men swiftly accepted their invitations. These two architects were not known to each other and the boundaries of their remits had the makings of a fertile field for disputes, but they would seem to have worked together over a period of about five years in reasonable harmony.

One of the areas where demarcation problems could have arisen between the two architects was the nave roof. Rushton was responsible for the war damaged main structure but that did not embrace the construction of the flat ceiling. That was in Mr. Pace's camp. In the event, the weight of the panelling of the ceiling designed by Pace made necessary the design of a stronger main structure – by Mr. Rushton. The restoration of the Chapter House was another area in which they had to work together.

George Pace's first task after taking up his post was the construction of a setting in the ruined and roofless nave for the enthronement of Bishop John Morgan as Archbishop of Wales. He had four months to prepare. A tarpaulin covering over a scaffolding framework would form the roof from which was suspended, over the altar, a massive maroon cross that stood out boldly against the white of the screen which filled the chancel arch. The Archbishop's throne was placed in the centre of an arc of chairs ranged behind the altar and everyone else had a chair or just stood. It rained and water from the roof poured in torrents over the Bishop of Newcastle as he preached. But Llandaff suddenly came to life again and the ruined nave was transformed once more into a stately church, albeit for one day.

In his approach to the restoration Pace took on board many of the design decisions that had been made by Sir Charles and Dean Jones. The flat ceiling and the lowering of the Prichard chancel arch, the opening up of the Norman arch and the consequent need to re-site the Rossetti, the substitution of chairs for pews and the possibility of a link between Cathedral and Prebendal House were all retained: But in doing so Pace was to place his own distinctive design imprint on all aspects of the work. Prichard and Seddon had been able to introduce work by outstanding artists of their day into the building. The 'Seed of David' triptych by Rossetti, sculpture by Woolner and Armstead and glass by a range of Pre-Raphaelite artists. Dean Simon was determined, as was George Pace, that the twentieth century would make a similar artistic contribution to this ancient cathedral and they set about making approaches to Jacob Epstein, John Piper and Patrick Reyntiens, Stanley Spencer, Frank Roper and Alan Durst. All except

The nave prepared for the enthronement of Bishop John Morgan in 1949

Stanley Spencer were to leave their mark on Llandaff, as did Geoffrey Webb who added three more windows in the Lady Chapel to those from the 1920s that had been saved from destruction.

In describing the progress of the rebuilding of the Cathedral it is almost impossible to treat the contribution of either of the two architects in isolation as, upon occasions, progress of one was dependent on progress by the other. The restoration was undertaken in two major phases, the first being construction of the

George Pace inspects a pinnacle on the spire

Welch Regiment Chapel together with the link to and extension of the Prebendal House and the restoration of the building to the west of the chancel arch. On the completion of this phase the screen that had closed off the ruined nave was removed for a great service of re-hallowing on 10th April 1957. The nave was then brought into use, the screen was replaced and the eastern part of the building, which had served for fifteen years as an 'Emergency Cathedral', became the subject of what can be considered as the second phase of the restoration.

Reconstructing the roofs of the nave and Chapter House

In the first phase, the south wall, west of the Chapter House, had taken the brunt of the bomb blast and needed major rebuilding. New window tracery had to be cut to match the profiles of the glass that had been removed and stored in 1940, and the opportunity was taken by Pace to add four label stops that depicted turning points in the Cathedral's history to the external drip mouldings of the two windows nearest to the Chapter House. The elaborately pierced parapet built by Prichard was replaced with a solid wall which would eventually be matched by a similar parapet wall above the clerestory. The cross arches and flying buttresses in the aisles had been repaired or reconstructed and aisle roofs repaired. The north aisle roof was of conventional timber construction, covered in copper sheet, whilst the south aisle roof was made of closely butted transverse reinforced concrete beams that carried a lead roof. Internally the south aisle ceiling was constructed of plastered metal mesh supported on a timber frame-work. Pace was to use this technique again in the Welch Regimental Chapel.

Once the walls had been repaired the chancel arch was taken down as far as its capitals and rebuilt so that its apex was now below the level of the proposed new ceiling. This procedure was not without its hazards, as at one stage in the

Formwork for the arches in the Welch Regiment Chapel

operation the structure that was supporting the partially demolished arch moved and the building had to be evacuated until the arch had been stabilised. The roof was then built from a series of closely spaced triangular frames that were fabricated in a workshop in the north churchyard, starting from the chancel arch and working westward. These frames rested on the repaired clerestory walls without exerting any outward force – one of the potential problems that had reinforced the argument in favour of the flat ceiling design. The purlins, boarding and Westmorland slate quickly followed, as did the ceiling panelling. The timber from which the roof was constructed, sapele, opele and yang are varieties of hardwood resistant to beetle attack!

By 1953 the windows of the nave were installed and the building was at last weather-proof. But as 1954 dawned, Dean Glyn Simon was elected to be Bishop of Swansea and Brecon. As Chancellor, and then as Dean, he had made a learned and energetic contribution to the planning and implementation of the restoration. His successor as Dean was Eryl Thomas who, like Glyn Simon

The spire laid out in the nave, prior to reconstruction

before him, had been Warden of St Michael's College. It was soon clear that he was to be a forceful and effective leader of the restoration, not just of the fabric but also of the worshipping community, continuing the work initiated by his predecessor.

The Dean makes the long climb up the scaffolded tower

The upper third of the spire had been dismantled and stored in 1941 with all the blocks of stone carefully numbered to show their position so it should have been a straightforward matter to restore the spire in 1955. All the blocks were laid out on the nave floor and sorted into their rings. After the first few

Capping the reconstructed spire, 1955: Canon Delme Jenkins and Dean Eryl Thomas

courses had been rebuilt it became apparent that all was not well and these courses were taken down and examined. Either the rings were being erected anti clockwise rather than clockwise, or the start point of each ring was wrong. The problem was resolved, building proceeded smoothly and on 28th July 1955 Dean Thomas caught the imagination of press and bystanders alike by emulating Bishop Ollivant's act in 1869 of lowering the last piece of the spire into position. Bishop Ollivant did this whilst standing safely on the ground – Dean Thomas climbed the ladders in his decanal gaiters through the two hundred feet of scaffolding to place the weathercock back in its place with his own hands!

In designing the new Welch Regiment Memorial Chapel, Pace discarded Nicholson's plan for a Gothic addition in favour of a distinctively modern interior, within an outer shell whose river-washed stone exterior (garnered from demolished cottages in Llandaff) blended with the old building. This new build departed from tradition by being oriented north-south with an annexe on its western side. He linked it, through a processional way, with the Prebendal House which he had extended with new two story block housing vestry and toilet facilities, neatly connecting with Sir Charles Nicholson's extension of 1926. A large

The modern Welch Regiment Chapel

services duct connecting the heating and power between the Prebendal House and the Cathedral nave was provided. A network of heating pipes was laid beneath the floor slabs of the Chapel, a system continued in the nave. The dedication of the Chapel took place on 22nd December 1956, with full military ceremony, in advance of the completion of the nave.

With the heating system installed, the nave floor was laid with dark hardwood blocks under the seating areas and with slabs in all the walk ways. The profile of the front edge of the blocks on both sides of the nave reproduced the line of the front wall of the eighteenth century Italianate Temple. Alas, all the splendid decorative Minton tiling of the Prichard restoration was swept away.

Pace was very aware of the need to produce a 'cathedral' atmosphere, which was lacking in Prichard's restoration, without resorting to the introduction of the traditional division formed by a screen surmounted by an organ, interposed between nave and choir. His first scheme involved positioning a section of the organ on a platform, standing on four columns, over a fixed nave altar. The underside of the platform would be painted, and Stanley Spencer's name sprang to mind as the proposed artist. This solution was overtaken by a new design for

The pulpitum in the course of construction

a pulpitum arch in reinforced concrete that was to provide the setting for Jacob Epstein's 'Christ in Majesty'. This massive aluminium figure was to create widespread controversy and international interest when the restored nave with all the new work was rehallowed by Archbishop John Morgan on 10th April 1957. George Pace's pulpitum with Epstein's towering figure that looks out to the world beyond the Cathedral through its clear west window was the twentieth century's greatest contribution to Llandaff Cathedral's renewal, continuing to generate debate and controversy even after more than fifty years. This modern interpretation of the concept of a pulpitum allowed for the convenient deploy-ment of a nave altar as and when required without precluding other uses of this

View of the restored nave from the Urban arch

central space, whilst still allowing a clear view of the high altar from the nave.

The 'positive' division of the organ that was enclosed in the concrete drum of the pulpitum was not as great a success as had been hoped, at least in part due to the instability of tuning caused by heat from the sunlight streaming through the clerestory windows. The majority of the boxwood figures of Saints and Doctors of the Church that had adorned the Victorian chapter and choir stalls had been salvaged and, having been covered in gold leaf, were ranged on small platforms around the pulpitum. Three angels playing musical instruments, now placed on the eastern face of the concrete drum, had been saved from the pre-war organ case – three more of them eventually finding a new home high in

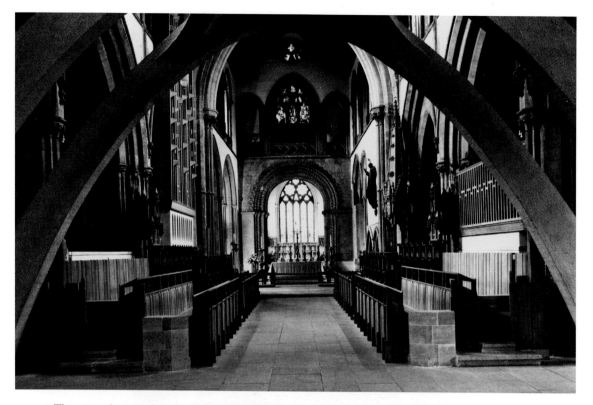

The restoration complete: the choir and presbytery

the roof over the high altar.

The new stalls for the Chapter and choir were not ready when the rehallow-ing of the nave took place, so that temporary arrangements had to be made using such salvaged furniture as could be found. This make-shift choir was laid out in 'collegiate' form using the two sets of stalls from the Lady Chapel placed across the western end of the choir to provide seating for the Dean and senior members of the Chapter. Strangely, this format was not perpetuated in the permanent stalls that George Pace designed.

A new font with carving that depicts the Fall and Redemption of Man, together with scenes from the legends of the cathedral's Celtic patron saints was cut from Hoptonwood stone by Alan Durst ARA, who was a descendant of Charles Sumner, Bishop of Llandaff 1826-27.

The second phase of the restoration was undertaken on the eastern end of the Cathedral that had only had temporary repairs in 1941. With the chancel arch once more blocked by a screen, work could begin. The high roof and the aisles were all reconstructed, the aisles being covered in copper. The concept of a flat ceiling was not carried through east of the chancel arch, so that the form of roof that Prichard had designed for the whole length of the Cathedral can still be seen. The interior of the Lady Chapel was lime-washed with the roof bosses providing the only splash of gold and colour. John Seddon had designed an altar table, with inlaid lettering, for the high altar and this was now brought back into use in the Lady Chapel, together with its accompanying credence table. Eighteenth century screen work and gates from that earlier restoration were refurbished for the entrance to this chapel.

Pace solved the perennial problem of where to place the Rossetti triptych, by using it in a new side chapel as the reredos mounted in a simple frame that displayed a Dutch influence. This chapel, below the Jasper Tower, dedicated to St Illtyd, was furnished as its War Memorial by the 53rd (Welsh) Infantry Division. This army unit had links with s'Hertogenbosch, in the Netherlands, which they had liberated in October 1944. Their Divisional sign of a red bardic crown is inlaid at the centre of the chapel floor. The Chapel was dedicated on 26th April 1958. The cathedral in s'Hertogenbosch has a cross made from timbers that once formed part of the nave roof of Llandaff Cathedral.

The Rossetti triptych now resited there was nothing to prevent the Norman arch being displayed in its original entirety. The high altar, of Purbeck Marble, was placed on a shallow foot-pace seven feet forward from the Norman arch, interposed with a gradine wall, also of Purbeck Marble, to carry the crucifix and six standard candle sticks which date from the seventeenth century. Sufficient space was allowed between the gradine wall and the altar for the celebrant at the eucharist to stand behind the altar facing the congregation, a practice that was to become the norm as the altars in the Lady Chapel and the St Dyfrig Chapel were moved forward from their respective reredoses.

The Prichard and Seddon sedilia was foreshortened and lowered with one seat converted into a credence table. Only two of the four Evangelist figures that were in the canopies above the seats have survived and now flank the memorial to George Pace in the south presbytery aisle. New houselling benches and servers' stalls are to George Pace designs. The window in the east wall above the high altar was installed in 1959 having been made by Patrick Reyntiens to a design by John Piper. The nave pulpit, again a Pace design, was dedicated in 1960. Clarke's of Llandaff had once again been deeply involved in the work of restoration and had been joined in the enterprise by Messrs Hinkins & Frewin of Newport for much of the new work.

On 6th August 1960, nineteen years after the Cathedral's destruction, a service of thanksgiving for the completion of the work of restoration took place in the presence of Her Majesty the Queen and the Duke of Edinburgh, complete with an anthem composed for the occasion by Sir Arthur Bliss, Master of the Queen's Musick.

Three centuries and three restorations. The first incomplete and largely unsuccessful, the other two brought to triumphal completion. There are many parallels between the two successful restorations. In 1840 Dean Knight set out with Wyatt to rebuild a Cathedral overwhelmed by natural disaster but the Dean was soon dead and the Architect departed in controversy. The task fell firstly to a new partnership of Dean Conybeare, and subsequently Dean Williams, working with Prichard and Seddon to reverse the decay of centuries. They lived in a time when the church's influence and drive was recovering and there were huge demands for new church buildings to meet the needs of rapidly growing communities.

After 2nd January 1941 Dean Jones and Sir Charles Nicholson had the responsibility of reversing a disaster of war that they could not have foreseen. They valiantly prepared the ground for renewal but both had died before they enjoyed an opportunity that would have allowed them to convert their visions into a revitalised Cathedral. The new partnership of Dean Simon, and later Dean Thomas, with George Pace, achieved that aim in the face of shortages of materials and skilled labour, and the competition for funding that was also being sought for the building of churches in newly developing housing estates. All three of these restorations took place during times when the Church was challenged by changes in theological thought and liturgical practice for which the architects of the day had to provide relevant ecclesiastical settings.

Postscript

George Gaze Pace died on 23rd August 1975, aged 59. His restorative work at Llandaff was all but complete and such small details as remained were seamlessly dealt with by Ronald Sims, his associate and latterly partner in his architectural practice. But the completion of a programme of restoration is not the end of the matter, as this chapter on Llandaff's architectural past has suggested. Since 1975 the building has been in the care of succeeding architects who have left their individual marks on the place.

Robert Heaton of the Anthony Clark Partnership in Wrexham, was appointed in June 1977 and was responsible for the refurbishment of the St Dyfrig Chapel that included an entrance screen in memory of Archbishop Glyn Simon who, as Dean, had guided the crucial early stages of the post-bombing restoration. This memorial introduced to the Cathedral, for the first time, work by the West Wales artist and calligrapher, Ieuan Rees.

1985 saw the reroofing of the St David Chapel to a design that provided a better 'fall' to combat persistent water ingress, and the start of an extension to the Prebendal House to give additional vestry and office space. This was part one of a projected scheme to build a quadrangular enclosure in the space

The north side of the Cathedral with the re-roofed St David Chapel

between the existing Prebendal House and the course of the former Mill Stream.

Robert Heaton retired in June 1986 and was succeeded by Donald Buttress, much of whose work at Llandaff entailed the kind of routine maintenance that is necessary on every building. The copper covering of the low roofs that had developed defects – and which produced a great deal of noise during rain or hail storms – was replaced with lead. The profile of the slate roof of the Chapter House was altered in its lower courses so that rain water was thrown clear of the walls. The problem introduced by Prichard's guttering on the wall head of this building was, at last, solved and the upper room of the Chapter House was dry.

In 1987 the Lady Chapel was given major attention both externally, with a comprehensive programme of repointing and reroofing work, and internally where a generous bequest made possible the recovery and reinstatement of Geoffrey Webb's decorative scheme of 1909. Peter Larkworthy and his staff, who had painstakingly uncovered what remained of Webb's original paint beneath the 1950s limewash and brought the Chapel roof to life again with newly cut stencils, were then employed by Buttress in the St Illtyd Chapel for which he had designed a splendid and glittering setting for a newly cleaned and restored Rossetti 'Seed of David', as a true folding triptych, guarded by a metal parclose screen.

In his design of a new scheme for the revitalising of the St Teilo Chapel at the east end of the south aisle, Donald Buttress incorporated a dorsal curtain supported by decorated riddle posts that are capped with pre-Raphaelite birds salvaged after the bombing in 1941. In a niche in the south wall of this chapel, Dr. Buttress constructed a reliquary for the reputed skull of St Teilo using a stall canopy, also salvaged from the war damaged Cathedral. Buttress, whose study of the architecture of Llandaff Cathedral began whilst he was carrying out his National Service at St Athan RAF Station and had lead to a thesis for his Master of Arts degree, announced his retirement as Consultant Architect in 1997.

Notes

1. British Library xxix fol.14b
2. Canon E.T. Davies, *John Wood's Italianate Temple*, Friends' Annual Report no. 23, p.25.
3. E.A. Freeman, *Remarks on the Architecture of Llandaff Cathedral* (Pickering, London, 1850).
4. *The Letters of Edward Copleston, Bishop of Llandaff, 1828-1849.*
5. Ibid.
6. Restoration Committee minute book.
7. Dean Daniel Conybeare, Restoration Committee Annual Report 1847.
8. Rev. Edward A. Fishbourne, *Notes on the Cathedral Establishment at Llandaff from October 1871 to December 1882.*
9. Michael Darby, *John Pollard Seddon* (V&A, London, 1984).
10. Report inserted in Restoration Committee minute book.

The Art of Llandaff Cathedral

Introduction

Throughout the history of Christianity, churches and cathedrals have patronised artists, offering them a place to develop their creativity and inspire us with their work. Art transforms the interior from a mere building into a sacred space.

Most cathedrals are known for some special piece of architecture or art. In Llandaff Cathedral a variety of artists, both lesser known and famous, all contributed to the building's history and life. The Cathedral has one of the greatest paintings of the Pre-Raphaelite Brotherhood, 'The Seed of David' by Dante Gabriel Rossetti; a set of mesmerizing panels of the 'Six Days of Creation' by Edward Burne-Jones; and the superb aluminium 'Christ In Majesty' by the renowned sculptor, Jacob Epstein.

There are also bronzes by the uniquely talented Cardiff artist William Goscombe John and the ever-present hand of the energetic Frank Roper, who was Vice-Principal of Cardiff Art College. From the Victorian restoration onwards, a succession of Deans and Architects worked with artists over the years to make Llandaff what it is today. The letters preserved in the Cathedral archives show their deep love of art and their concern for the visual quality of the building.

The most natural starting point for viewing Llandaff is from the hill above the Cathedral which gives the building an unusual physical closeness. As you walk down a long slope you pass the ruins of the medieval bell tower and mature trees to arrive at the paved area facing the famous west front. The west door is surmounted by the carving of an unknown bishop with his mitre and staff blessing all who enter.

Like the entire west front, the bishop is carved from the distinctive creamy-yellow Dundry stone from near Bristol. Many different types of stones were used in the building of Llandaff, including some materials not to be found elsewhere in Cardiff. The early Norman parts of the Cathedral use Sutton stone (from Ogmore and Southerndown) or Radyr stone with river pebbles. Later the greyish lias limestone from southern Glamorgan was introduced. The nineteenth century reconstruction used Bath stone, oolite from Chipping Camden in Gloucestershire, stone from Wiltshire, Radyr and the Forest of Dean as well as some Caen stone from Normandy. The upper part of the nineteenth century spire is of a yellowish stone from Rutland. In the David Chapel, Doulting stone from Shepton Mallet in Somerset was used with river pebbles from the Taff and recycled stone from demolished cottages in Llandaff. Portland stone was used

The unknown bishop on above the west front

for the foundation stone of this chapel and for the panels of inscribed battle honours in its east wall.

From the steps inside the west door, the interior opens out beyond and below the viewer. In many cathedrals one is instinctively moved to look upwards towards heaven but from the west door at Llandaff one looks down, through and up at once. The building's layout enables much of the Cathedral to be instantly visible and the columns rise like great tree trunk with leafy foliate carvings.

Periods of Art at Llandaff

A small amount of art at Llandaff, mainly monumental statuary, dates back to the medieval period. Changes to religious belief during the Reformation and the establishment of the Anglican Church reduced artistic activity. Many medieval artworks disappeared from Llandaff after the destruction of St Teilo's tomb, and the Civil War caused both damage and neglect. As we have seen, the dispersal of its treasures and lands made Llandaff very poor compared to English cathedrals. For a number of centuries little was built, but eventually changing architectural fashions called for the reconstruction of the Gothic cathedral.

The nave, looking towards the altar

During the nineteenth century Cardiff was transformed into one of the great industrial ports of the world, fuelled by the coal and iron of the Welsh Valleys. The Llandaff diocese now covered several major urban centres and this increased population offered enrichment for the diocese and new opportunities for the arts and for the Cathedral. As its central position was restored in the nineteenth century, Bishop Ollivant, who was an enthusiastic promoter of the arts, organised exhibitions locally in order to raise revenues to support the work at the Cathedral.

Whilst the architects John Prichard and John Pollard Seddon were restoring Llandaff's fabric in the 1850s, they conceived of the Cathedral's furnishings and decoration as part of this project. Seddon's brother Thomas was a minor member of the Pre-Raphaelites and connected to the circle that included William Burges (restorer of Cardiff Castle under Lord Bute) and Dante Gabriel Rosetti. Drawing on ideas of the Gothic propounded by Pugin, and decorative concepts expounded by John Ruskin, they sought to develop an appropriate ecclesiastical style for the Anglican Church's rediscovery of ritual.

Three major sculptors were involved in this Victorian renovation: Thomas Woolner (of whose quartet of panels for Prichard's pulpit, only one survives), Henry Hugh Armstead, who sculpted some fine figures for Prichard's spire, and

Some of the figures carved by Milo ap Griffith, now gilded and arranged around the Pulpitum.

Milo Ap Griffith, who produced many figures that now adorn the Majesta's pulpitum.

In late 1856 Ollivant and Seddon organised the first exhibition of fine art in Cardiff Town Hall. They aimed to create a new awareness of the arts, support the Cathedral and to establish an "Art Museum and Literary Institution on a scale to the rising importance of the town." The *Public Library Journal* of June 1903 recalled that the 1856 event was "an exhibition of works of Art, Manufacturers, Natural Curiosities, Antiquities etc." which lasted six weeks. It was opened by Bishop Ollivant, Lord Aberdare gave a lecture, and concerts were held. The article suggests it was held to benefit Canton Church and schools and contribute to the cost of Rossetti's painting. The exhibition included many works of art from Cardiff Castle by well known artists including Opie, Edward Lear, and even a Fra Angelico lent by John Ruskin.

Exhibits were also lent by local collectors and friends of the organisers and included paintings by Ford Madox Brown, Arthur Hughes, Gabriel Dante

The late nineteenth century Choir and Presbytery

Rossetti and Thomas Seddon, and the sculptors Alexander Munro, Thomas Woolner, John Evan Thomas, his brother William, and examples of the sculpture from Llandaff Cathedral lent by Prichard and Seddon. Public interest was such that a new subscription to the exhibitions in 1857 enabled Bishop Ollivant to begin work on the choir stalls, south west tower and bishop's throne. A number of further exhibitions were organised for various fundraising activities, with the Cathedral administrators at their heart.

Although an art museum did not materialise until the 1880s, these exhibitions and the foundation of the School of Art, along with the influx of artists from London working on William Burges's restoration of Cardiff Castle and Castell Coch for the Marquess of Bute continued. Bute owned the mineral rights for much of the south Wales coalfields and became possibly the single greatest art patron of the age. Llandaff's Victorian art must be seen in the context of Bute's city and the artists he encouraged to work in Cardiff.

This rich supply of nineteenth century art gave Llandaff a distinct character, defined by its Pre-Raphaelite heritage. The interior of the building remained largely unchanged until the 1930s when the Lady Chapel was renovated and the sculpture of the Madonna and child installed. Dean David Jones and Cathedral architect, Sir Charles Nicholson, began to examine new ways of reordering the Cathedral and considered moving 'The Seed of David', at that time in a stone reredos behind the high altar, to a different position.

The destruction of the 1941 bombing of the Cathedral and the subsequent restoration offered many possibilities for reordering. The key figures, Architect George Pace who replaced Nicholson following his death, and the farsighted Deans Glyn Simon and Eryl Thomas, tapped into Britain's postwar artistic talent and invited significant figures such as Stanley Spencer, John Piper and most famously, Sir Jacob Epstein to add to the Cathedral's sacred art. Later, the talented Cardiff artist Frank Roper became Pace's collaborator for many years in enhancing the details of the interior.

In the following section, we will look in turn at the major sculptures, paintings and monuments in the Cathedral. Only from the nineteenth century onwards do we have records of the artists themselves. Many who have made Christian art have been touched by the message of the Gospel, and made aware of a world that often does not share its view. In this sense the Christian building is also a sanctuary, a place to feel safe and sense the love of God.

The visual traditions of churches are intended to be an aid to worship rather than objects of worship in themselves. They reinforce the idea that we worship God but also appreciate the talents given by God to His people. The themes of sacred art are numerous and most paintings with Christian iconography have a multitude of meanings. This chapter is too short to delve into the deep and rich tapestry of art history related to the church but it attempts to unravel the history of some of the major pieces commissioned at Llandaff.

Llandaff's Art and Religious Symbolism

The sacred art of Llandaff follows European tradition in the use of symbols, obvious and concealed. The dove is a symbol of peace, of the Holy Spirit and in the law of Moses of purification, especially after birth. It appears in a number of artworks including Rossetti's 'The Seed of David' and the font. The cockerel which appears on one of the Passiontide lecterns designed by Frank Roper is not only a symbol of the Passion and reminder of Peter's denial of Christ but also of vigilance and watchfulness. The peacock that appears in a number of places in Llandaff has eyes to symbolise the 'all seeing' church. It also represents immortality, especially in nativity paintings, through the belief and tradition that its flesh does not decay. The pelican, carved by Edward Clarke to a design by Rossetti, makes up part of the memorial to Pace in the south presbytery, created

The eagle lectern, by Skidmore of Bristol

from the remains of the Victorian Sedilia. In medieval bestiarics, female pelicans were allegories of Christ's passion because they were reputed to feed their offspring with own their blood.

The eagle is found spreading its wings on a lectern to hold the Bible. Associated with John the Evangelist, as the eagle soars high near the noonday sun and is a symbol of the resurrection and of Christ Himself. Here the eagle rests on lions and medallions with the evangelists, crosses and angels. The lectern, originally in shining bronze which has now blackened, is a superb piece of Victorian workmanship.

*The medieval majestas from the west front,
now situated in the David Chapel*

Sculpture

In the late 1980s Dean Alun Davies launched a successful appeal to enable the cleaning of the west front. As this work went forward, the statue in the topmost niche, directly above the central lancet window, was examined more closely. It had previously been referred to by J.H. James as being the figure of 'A Majesty', "thought to represent King Henry II, who was reigning at the time the west front was built".

Close inspection confirmed the view that this outstanding example of sculpture of its time was actually a medieval Majestas, a Christ in Majesty. It stood, precariously unattached to the building, on a narrow ledge and had suffered so much from erosion that it could only be saved by pinning it together where it

The medieval dormition carving in the south aisle.

stood and then lowering it to the ground for further conservation work. Once this work had been completed it was brought into the cathedral and fixed to the first pier in the David Chapel as one enters from the Nave. It depicts a figure in a seated position, and may be the oldest piece of statuary in the Cathedral.

The medieval Flemish or North German wood carving of the 'Falling Asleep of the Blessed Virgin Mary', dating from about 1430, was given to the Cathedral in 1950 and was for many years affixed to the organ loft. It is now enclosed in a niche at the east end of the south aisle behind a wrought iron frame supporting a sheet of sandblasted and engraved laminated glass. The engraving was carried out by Sally Scott and depicts flowers traditionally associated with the Blessed Virgin together with the Welsh version of 'Hail Mary' saying "Mair – fendigaid – henffych – well" (Hail Blessed Mary). The whole setting was designed by the Cathedral Architect Donald Buttress.

The wooden carving depicts 'The Dormition': the falling asleep or death of the Virgin in a bed watched over by eleven apostles. Following the traditional configuration, St Peter is at the head and St John at the foot of the bed, with the other apostles between. Here St Peter reads to Mary while St John holds a book. The figure kneeling on the right is, unusually, wearing spectacles. The bottom left hand figure is the only one with no beard while on the right hand side a disciple covers his face in grief.

On a plinth by the door to the processional way in the David Chapel rests a statue, carved in oak, of a seated bishop. The figure is about four feet in height and has been dated to about 1500 by the Victoria and Albert Museum. George Pace, who was the Cathedral Architect at the time of its acquisition, felt that the crozier held by the bishop in his left hand is of a later date, replacing the original, which had been lost. The face is finely carved and looks (suggested Dean Simon) "as if it were a portrait of some fifteenth century prelate".

No statues apart from monuments were erected in the Cathedral during the nineteenth century until the restoration. With the establishment of Clarke's stonemasons at Llandaff and Lord Bute's carvers involved in the building of Cardiff Castle, a pool of talented local craftsmen became available for sculptural projects within the Cathedral's fabric. Major artists of the day also contributed sculptures to the refurbishment, including Edward Coley Burne-Jones (1833-1898) whose 'The Six Days of Creation' is situated in the Dyfrig Chapel.

Burne-Jones was born in Birmingham and, like William Morris, was of Welsh ancestry. Two of his sisters became mothers of famous sons, one the Prime Minister Stanley Baldwin and the other writer Rudyard Kipling. Burne-Jones originally studied at Birmingham College of Art before undertaking a theology course at Exeter College, Oxford. There he met and befriended Morris and Dante Gabriel Rossetti and became part of an intimate society called 'The Pre-Raphaelite Brotherhood' which looked back to the artistic principles of the Middle Ages. He became a founding member of Morris, Marshall, Faulkner and Company with Morris, Ford Madox Brown and Philip Webb in 1861, designing tapestries and stained glass for them. The company changed to Morris & Co in 1875.

Although 'The Six Days of Creation' is a series of elaborate tiles they are in fact carved from clay and as such are listed here under sculpture as they have been called 'ceramic icons'. Their subject matter is taken from the book of Genesis: "In the beginning God created the heavens and the earth." Genesis

Dyfrig Chapel reredos: 'The Six Days of Creation' by Edward Burne-Jones

Ch.i v.1. The earth which produces growth and habitat for mankind is often a symbol of the church which shelters us.

Each new day shows an additional angel holding a globe in her hands with appropriate symbols taken from Genesis. Each angel, except the one in the first tile, has a flame attached to her head, signifying the presence of the Holy Spirit. The sixth tile features an almost hidden seventh angel: Burne-Jones's mother died tragically six days after his birth and this may account for the extra angel in the last panel, and be his own intimate signature for the piece, unknown to anyone else. The angels were probably modelled on Elizabeth Siddal, Rossetti's wife, whose mother was of Welsh descent.

Burne-Jones made some watercolours on the theme in 1863 and mentions that Jane Morris was also one of the models. The art historian Christopher Wood suggests he did this after his second trip to Italy, with John Ruskin in 1862. While in Venice they visited the 'Creation Mosaics' in San Marco. These beautiful mosaics are particularly linear in design, something Burne-Jones reflected in his own work. Wood also suggests that they may originate in cartoons made for the Middleton Cheyney window in 1870.

The tiles are glazed in soft blues, yellows and greens made by the Della Robbia Pottery in Birkenhead (named after the great Italian artist Luca Della Robbia, 1400-1482, acclaimed for his bronze and marble but also for terra cotta reliefs and his majolica glazes still known as 'Della Robbia'), made to Burne-Jones's designs by Harold Rathbone, the managing director. After appearing in an auction, the panels were bought and donated to the Cathedral in the 1960s by Don Richards and his two brothers in memory of their mother Margaret Richards of Dowlais. They were eventually framed by Frank Roper in aluminum with Tudor roses.

A major Victorian sculptural collaboration was formed at Llandaff between

Henry Hugh Armstead (designer) and Edward Clarke (sculptor). Armstead, who was born in London and initially concentrated on work in precious metals, was a friend of the Pre-Raphaelite artist Holman Hunt. He is nationally recognised for his design, between 1863 and 1872, of many of the sculptural reliefs on the plinth of the Albert Memorial and for the figure groups representing 'Agriculture', 'Manufacturing', 'Commerce' and 'Engineering' on the same memorial. He was also responsible for a number of figures on the Foreign and Colonial Office in Whitehall. His earliest work at Llandaff was the pair of bas-relief panels on the rear wall of the memorial to Henry Thomas of Llwyn-Madoc in Breconshire, which is in a double arcaded niche in the north aisle, adjacent to the entrance to the David Chapel. As befits a memorial to a member of a family long associated with the law, these two panels depict, to the left, the 'Judgement of Solomon', and, to the right, 'Moses with the tablets of the law'. They were carved in Caen stone by Edward Clarke of Llandaff to Armstead's designs. The remainder of the memorial and its setting were designed by John Prichard, and, until it was relocated by Pace at the time of the post Second World War restoration, the stained glass window which is now directly opposite across the nave – another 'Thomas' memorial – occupied the window space immediately above this memorial.

The south western tower, also known as the Prichard Tower, replaced a medieval tower that stood on the same site and collapsed in the eighteenth century. Here can be found another collaboration between Armstead and Clarke. Armstead designed the deep bas-reliefs of the four Evangelists on the rear south side of the Prichard Tower facing east. The figures are one of the great carvings of the cathedral but often missed as you have to stand at some distance from the building to fully appreciate them. Each of the gospel writers are represented by their symbols: a man for Matthew, a lion for Mark, a bull for Luke, and an eagle for John.

The niches of the tower contain sculptures that include symbols of the worldwide spread of Christianity. The patron saints of the Cathedral, St Peter and St Paul, appear in the south-west fronts, as does Alfred Ollivant who oversaw the restoration of the building in the 1850s. At the belfry level are a selection of images intended to represent the worldwide nature of the Church. They include an Ethiopian Warrior (possibly referencing the first convert to Christianity in the Acts of the Apostles) and a Roman Soldier (Jesus being born into the Roman Empire). There is a Hindu and an Anglo Saxon warrior in the south and a North-American Indian and Chinese Mandarin in the East, with a Jewish teacher and Greek Philosopher on the north side. The tower's statues might also reflect the growth of Cardiff into an international city at the height of the British Empire in the Victorian era.

In 2001 extensive conservation work was undertaken on these figures, two of

The four evangelists, on the Pritchard Tower

them being replaced with new carvings made to the original drawings. The figure of Bishop William Morgan, who translated the Bible into Welsh, also graces this tower.

The heads of British kings and queens along with the uncrowned heads of Cromwell and Edward VIII run along the south aisle wall. This ambitious set of carvings by William Clarke were meant to finish with the head of Queen Victoria. However a measuring error ensured that the series had to continue as Victoria's head was not at the end of the aisle. W.R.P. (Bill) Clarke told the story in his lecture to 'The Friends' in 1978

> The truth is this – and I quote from William's notes which perhaps are in the form of a confession: 'I made a mistake; the heads were supposed to finish with Queen Victoria, but I was three short.' If he had not included Cromwell – much to the annoyance of Col. Hill of Rookwood, the donor – there would have been four. Incidentally, William was a great admirer of Cromwell. William eventually donated 'Cromwell' to settle the argument.

The twenty-two heads, most of which were carved in situ from rectangular blocks of stone, pose some intriguing questions. The series starts immediately west of the Chapter with the head of Richard III, which seems an odd point in

The heads of Cromwell and the uncrowned Edward VIII on the Pritchard Tower

the British monarchy at which to begin when the next head represents Henry VII and the commencement of the House of Tudor with its Welsh connections. The third head, that of Henry VIII, has suffered some war damage. The series continues with Edward VI, Mary and Elizabeth I.

After James I (whose crown is damaged) and Charles I, comes the head of Cromwell wearing a rather jaunty cap. The monarchy resumes with Charles II, James II, William III (damaged) – but no Mary – and Queen Anne. The four Hanoverian Georges follow – George III having also suffered some damage – then William IV and a rather stern-featured Victoria. The last three heads on the south side were – obviously – later additions and were again carved in situ using the remaining blank blocks; Edward VII (carved by Harry Stokes), George V (carved by Wyndham Clarke) and, uncrowned, Edward VIII (also Wyndham Clarke).

There developed a local legend which said that when the south wall parapet could house no more sovereigns' heads, disaster would befall the monarchy and the Cathedral. With the abdication of Edward VIII and the bombing of the Cathedral in 1941 it seemed to some that this prediction would be fulfilled, but the Cathedral has a north side and it is there that the heads of George VI, again carved by Wyndham, and Elizabeth II, carved by Jan Brozavic, a Hungarian refugee, and John Excell, found their place. The monarchy survived and the Cathedral, although grievously damaged, rose again from the rubble.

One of the greatest sculptors produced by Wales was William Goscombe John (1860-1952). The breadth and depth of his work has still not been widely recognised, yet scattered across Britain are significant pieces made by this uniquely talented artist. Cardiff Civic Centre is home to three of his sculptural masterpieces – bronze figures of the shipping magnate John Cory, John Crichton Stuart and Godfrey Morgan, First Viscount of Tredegar, together with a marble sculpture of St David in the City Hall.

William John (he added 'Goscombe' – his mother's family name – early in his career) was born in February 1860 in Gray Street in Canton, the son of Thomas John, a foreman woodcarver and inlayer in the Tyndall Street works that produced so much of the fine craftsmanship for the Third Marquess of Bute at Cardiff Castle.

William learnt to draw at an early age and was trained in woodcarving by his father, and both sang at the Cathedral long before the foundation of the Cathedral School in 1880. John would have seen Prichard's soaring spire being built with its sculptures by H.H. Armstead. At the age of fourteen William started his training as a woodcarver under his father's tuition, remaining there for some seven years. He had already been attending drawing classes at Cardiff School of Art for some four years. In 1881 he moved to London to work as a pupil assistant in the studio of Thomas Nicholls, whilst continuing his studies at the Lambeth School of Art. Nicholls had been responsible for carving the figures representing 'The Planets' on the Clock Tower of Cardiff Castle. It was during this period that John became interested in the Pre-Raphaelite movement, and the revival of the technical skills of medieval arts influenced this early part of his life.

Goscombe John joined the Royal Academy in 1884 where he won the Landseer Scholarship in 1887, and he also won a gold medal in Paris. On becoming a Royal Academician and travelled extensively. Throughout his life he maintained close ties with both Llandaff through his friendship with the Clarke family, being a mourner at the funeral of William Clarke in 1923, and with Cardiff. He was a member of the Council of the National Museum of Wales from its inception and was a great benefactor of that institution.

John's contributions don't lie inside the cathedral alone. On the upper reaches of the Green above the steps to the Cathedral he made the Great War Memorial 1914-18 with a crowned female figure in the centre holding a shield with a cross sprouting from an oak. She is like a mother and queen, flanked by two male figures. Cast in bronze on a base of Grey Shap, it is memorial to both the local young people who died in the Great War, and to the fallen who were former pupils of the Cathedral School. The three bronze figures that John made and which stand on pedestals of granite, were named 'Llandaff' (the central figure), 'The Workman' (representing the village) and 'The Student' (representing the Cathedral School). Contemporary descriptions from the *Llandaff Parish Magazine* and the *Western Mail*, respectively, say that:

The central figure is symbolic of Llandaff. On her head is a mural crown, so called because the band of the crown is in the form of an embattled wall. On her left hand is a shield ready to protect her sons – the children of the City. On the face of the shield is traced a Cross growing out of an oak. Christianity, as it were, superseding the ancient Druidism. Her right hand is lifted to bless as she accepts the service of Gallant young hearts.

Calm, majestic, strong, loving, protecting, she stands as a mother beloved and as a queen to be worshipped. The side figures tell their story clearly, simply, eloquently – the youth from his game, the strong young man from his work, betaking themselves to the rifle, ready for the training as we remember them, over ten years ago.

The memorial was unveiled on 11th October 1924 by the Lord Lieutenant, the Earl of Plymouth, and dedicated by Bishop Pritchard Hughes whose only son was amongst the fallen whose names were inscribed thereon.

Within the Cathedral, in the north aisle is a good marble effigy of Dean Charles John Vaughan by John. Vaughan accepted the position of Dean at Llandaff by Bishop Ollivant's invitation on the basis that he could spend half of the year in London continuing his mastership of The Temple in London. He was renowned for his brilliant mind, and became Headmaster of Harrow at the age of twenty-eight. Vaughan took a great deal of interest in the rapidly expanding Cardiff. It was said "the fact of his mere residence in the city was potent in its influence in promotion of church interests" and that "his genuine love of people overcame the temptation to hurt for the sake of intellectual triumph, and that love was returned." His effigy was highly regarded when it was exhibited in the Royal Academy in 1900. There is a good marble effigy of Dean Vaughan, by Goscombe John in the upper room of the Prebendal House, with another copy in the Cathedral School.

In 1909 Goscombe John also exhibited at the Royal Academy the bronze mural figure of Bishop Richard Lewis (Bishop of Llandaff 1883-1905) which hangs on the south presbytery wall. The figure seems to be blessing people as they walk towards the high altar. It is quite Baroque in its appearance, with two small angels either side of his mitre at his feet. The pastoral staff is a copy of Bishop Lewis's actual Crosier which had been designed by H.H. Armstead. Lewis was an enthusiastic figure who brought in new ideas to the diocese and increased the number of clergy through St Michael's College as the population of Cardiff and its surrounds grew.

To the right of the entrance to the David Chapel in the north aisle is one of two Goscombe John medallions at the Cathedral. This first is in memory of the Venerable James Rice Buckley, Canon of Llandaff 1907-1924, Archdeacon of Llandaff from 1913-24 and Vicar of Llandaff for 45 years. Four figures sit around the portrait of Buckley: the first is a nun with the word 'Fides' – faith,

Goscombe John's statue of Canon Rice Buckley, on the Cathedral Green

trust, loyalty; the second is a woman with a child with 'Caritas' – dearest, love; the third is a woman wearing a breastplate inscribed with the word 'Fortitudo' – strength, courage, valour; and the fourth is a woman with a crown and sword entitled 'Justiti' – justice. A more public bronze statue of Rice Buckley, also by John, is to be found on the Cathedral Green, facing the Cathedral. This too found a place at a Royal Academy Exhibition, this time in 1927.

Looking towards the high altar on the presbytery wall east of the Bishop's throne is the second John bronze medallion, a late bas-relief of Bishop Joshua Prichard Hughes (Bishop 1905-1931), which was exhibited at the Royal Academy in 1940. The Bishop is posed in the style of a Renaissance portrait,

Walker's Madonna and Child, 1935

with a Bible in his hands and the lower part of his body protruding. It was worked from a photograph received from the Dean.

The Royal Academician Arthur George Walker (1862-1939) was invited to sculpt a Virgin and Child to fill a niche in the Cathedral's fifteenth century Lady Chapel reredos running along the eastern wall. Walker was a friend of Goscombe John, and also knew the Clarke family, and had seen the Cathedral from the outside before they both went on a trip to Italy. He had already worked on projects for other cathedrals and had sculpted the late Queen Mother when she was Duchess of York, a statue of Florence Nightingale in Waterloo Place and an equestrian statue of John Wesley in Bristol.

It having been decided to restore the ancient reredos in the Lady Chapel and insert a figure in the central niche, Sir Charles Nicholson, the Cathedral Architect, in writing to the Dean in 1934 said

> ...with regard to the Lady Chapel reredos, the best sculptor I know for the purpose would be Arthur Walker and I feel sure he would be glad to do it for £300, which I think is an ample figure... he has the faculty of visualising his finished work inside the rough block of stone and of chipping away the superfluous envelope until the figure appears... they seem to be real sculptor's work and not stone reproductions of clay models. There is a lot of this quality in much of Walker's work even where models have to be used and that is what seems to me to give it its peculiar merit... personally I have every confidence in him and would advise giving him a free hand as far as possible as too many suggestions would probably hinder him from producing his best work.

Walker wrote to the Cathedral discussing the type of stone. The donor had specified that the figure was to be left plain and never painted. For Walker, "Portland Stone... is not very much darker than Bath stone which is a very pale cream." He declared a preference for Portland's fine grain and even hardness: "very good qualities in stone for figure carving." Walker requests a piece of the stone "even an inch large" to help him, and says in a letter of October 1934 "I like Portland as it is a strong hard and very durable stone indeed it has been called English Marble."

The Llandaff sculpture, made for the space, is typical of its period and not unlike many Bible illustrations of the day. Mary, in flowing clothes, is looking down and the child is moving freely within her arms. There is a sister piece in Wells Cathedral which is more fluid, but so similar that it is as if one was posed a few seconds after the other. However, just as Epstein's Majestas was to cause controversy later, the Virgin and Child caused much indignation at the time as it was seen as too 'Catholic' and the argument even reached the pages of *The Times* in June 1935.

A figure not unused to controversy was Allan Gairdner Wyon (1882-1962). He was the son of Allan Wyon, the Chief Engraver of Seals to Queen Victoria, a post that had been held by successive members of the Wyon family since Peter Wyon came to England in 1727 as 'Silver chaser and Medallist' to the Court of King George II. The young Wyon, who studied sculpture in the Royal Academy Schools between 1905 and 1909, was a Landseer Scholar there and won a series of medals and prizes for his work. As a carver in stone he was part of the team commissioned in 1928 by Charles Holden to make a series of figures for the new London Transport Headquarters above St James's Park Station in London. These figures provoked a storm of controversy – not surprisingly for a team that also included such names as Henry Moore, Jacob Epstein, Eric Gill and Sam Rabin. Wyon later took holy orders and became the Vicar of Newlyn, in Cornwall, in 1936.

Wyon is well-known for a series of memorial brasses at Truro and Edinburgh Cathedrals, and it was for such a brass for Bishop Timothy Rees that he was commissioned following Rees' death in 1939. Possibly the new Bishop of Llandaff, John Morgan, who had been a Minor Canon at Truro Cathedral in the 1920s, knew of Wyon's brass work there and suggested his name. The Rees memorial was completed in 1942 and was originally placed in the centre of the Lady Chapel, though to save it from undue wear it was later moved into the Lady Chapel Sanctuary. In its initial location the figure faced east, as is traditional, but in its new setting it defies convention and looks westward, no doubt so that the figure can be appreciated by visitors.

One of the most substantial pieces of sculpture commissioned after the Second World War was the font by Alan Lydiat Durst (1883-1970), which stands towards the western end of the south aisle. The original Victorian font of 1863 by John Seddon, with its depiction of the Flood and its base representing a miraculous catch of fishes, had been badly damaged in the bombing and needed replacing. Durst had trained as a carver in both stone and wood in London, and taught wood carving at the Royal College of Art from 1925-1940. He was invited in the 1950s to create a new font for the Cathedral, funded by Charles Lionel Taylor in remembrance of his wife Olive.

At first glance one immediately notices the wooden cover with its Celtic style knot work carving, and an image of a dove with a halo and cross behind its head on what looks like a half sphere helmet, perhaps a reminder of the end of war and the beginning of a new peace (Durst had served in the Royal Marines). The dove in Christian iconography is a symbol of the Holy Spirit, a reminder that it was revealed above Jesus when he was baptised by John the Baptist in the River Jordan. Luke Ch.iii v.21-22 says "And as he was praying, heaven was opened and the Holy Spirit descended on him in bodily form like a dove." The dove is often seen in churches above fonts because Noah sent a dove out from the ark

The font by Alan Lydiat Durst

to see if the waters had receded, it came back with an olive branch. This may be appropriate for a vessel holding the waters of baptism, and certainly for the remembrance of Olive Varcoe Taylor.

The font is carved out of Hoptonwood stone and depicts images from the Old and New Testaments around the theme of the Fall in the garden of Eden and redemption through Christ's birth, alluded to by the appearance of the Angel

Gabriel to the Virgin Mary. There are also scenes from the life of St Teilo – riding on a celestial horse, preaching and blessing a pig and litter. St Dyfrig is represented founding a church, and with his remains arriving at the Cathedral. There are a number of Biblical quotations too including a Latin inscription "He that believeth and is baptised, shall be saved" (Mark Ch.xvi v.16) and a Welsh inscription which says "It is not good to contend with God" There is also a Chi Rho.

The upper half of the font shows the Tree of Knowledge with the angel holding the flaming sword. Eve kneels with a scroll or ribbon while the Serpent coiled around the fruit tree aims at her heel "the Serpent deceived me...". Below is the Tree of Life with the Angel Gabriel with the serpent and its bruised head "it shall bruise thy head...". Isaiah is there prophesising within his visions "Behold a Virgin shall conceive..." (Isaiah Ch.vii v.14) and St John with his symbol of the eagle also in a vision "the leaves of the Tree were for the healing of the nations" (Revelations Ch.xxii v.2). While Mary is represented with Christ in his crib above which is a five pointed star.

Durst wrote to the Dean on 28th June 1951 from his studio: "I do not think that early Christians and Medieval art ever mixed the fundamental teachings of the Bible with legends and events in the lives of the saints on an equal footing. Whenever the two themes occur together, the latter is always subordinate in someway to the former." He later writes on 9th June 1952 "You will notice that I have included two angels, both with flames to their heads representing the Holy Spirit – the one with a flaming sword at the Tree of Knowledge and... the Tree of Life... it came to me when I was thinking about the font in Chartres Cathedral last month." It has been suggested that the font has a Saxon touch about it, and certainly the elongated figures resemble the proportions of the magnificent carvings at Chartres. The font was exhibited at the Royal Academy before being brought to Llandaff and according to letters was a contributing cause of Durst being elected an ARA.

As one enters the Cathedral one's eye is instantly caught by Jacob Epstein's extraordinary Christ in Majesty, sometimes known as 'The Majestas'. It occupies a central position, displayed on the cylindrical organ case designed by George Pace to take the place of a rood-screen. Held aloft by its concrete arch, the Christ figure makes an open-armed gesture of welcome and looks into the distance, seemingly rising towards the heavens. Whether seen from the west door or from immediately beneath in the nave, the statue presents a dramatic affirmation of Christ's ascension and makes a fitting symbol for Llandaff Cathedral's resurrection from the ashes of war. The cross-inscribed halo behind Christ's head also echoes the Greek Orthodox icon of the Pantocrator, and the beardless face references some of the earliest Roman images of the Saviour.

The sculpture is an integral part of the concrete arch and organ case which

Jacob Epstein's controversial Majestas

George Pace introduced into his postwar restoration. He wanted to give the Cathedral the equivalent of a rood screen without losing the open view towards the High Altar. His ideas moved from a baldachino supported on four pillars to a more radical vision of a concrete arch spanning the nave. Just as the medieval rood screens featured a figure of Christ on the Cross – the Rood – so Pace wanted a similar figure to surmount his arch. Writing in 1957 Bishop Glyn Simon described the moment in 1952 when, as Dean of Llandaff, he and George Pace had the conversation that was to lead to the most controversial aspect of the Cathedral's post-war restoration.

One evening, looking down on the Cathedral from the path leading up to the Green above, Simon said – "I am sure that we must have a Rood there, but who is to carve it?"

> "There is no-one alive" Pace replied "who can do the kind of Rood I have in mind." We discussed two or three names, and silence ensued.
> Then Pace said, "Well, there is one man who would be exactly the man and that is Epstein; but I suppose you wouldn't have him?"
> Now, as it happened, I had made a special point of seeing all Epstein's great religious works and had been profoundly impressed by them. So I answered at once – "Of course I would, but surely he would never come down to a place like this."
> "We will write at once" was the reply "and see what happens."

The letter to Epstein was written the following morning and produced an enthusiastic response. Epstein, together with Stanley Spencer who had been approached about a separate project, visited Llandaff on January 12th 1953. After further discussions between sculptor, Architect and Dean, Pace formally commissioned Epstein on October 28th 1953 supplying him with both drawings and a model of the proposed pulpitum arch on which the work was to be mounted.

In his invitation Pace had said that

> "The most important work will be the creation of a great parabolic arch at the entrance to the ritual Quire which is to carry a small echo organ and to support on its West face a great figure of Christ Reigning from the Cross. Both the Dean and I greatly desire that this figure shall be of outstanding quality and a major work of contemporary sculpture. I am writing to you in the hope that you might be interested in and be prepared to undertake this figure".

Jacob Epstein (1880-1959) was a New York-born son of a Russian-Polish Jew who had studied in Paris and later became a British subject. His sculptural work consisted largely of portrait heads or Biblical figures cast in bronze, and more than a few caused controversy. It is interesting to compare Christ in Majesty with his other famous late commission, the large bronze piece of St Michael's victory over the Devil on the outside of the new Coventry Cathedral on which he worked with Sir Basil Spence. Whereas St Michael is a dramatic composition showing the saint's triumph over Satan, posed with wings outstretched and spear in hand, the Christ figure at Llandaff is quite serene.

At Llandaff, Epstein's work was by far the most controversial part of the post-War restoration. Although the Majestas was not created as a memorial, its unpolished aluminium structure with the machine-like precision of the vertical seam on Christ's robe recalls the industrial processes that drove the War. This contrasts with the realistically-modelled hands, feet and face, whose serene expression shows the surrendering of the mind to God's purpose and will.

The original plan was to make a plaster figure to be gilded and burnished at a cost of between £500 and £600 – casting in aluminium would cost £1500. But both Pace and Epstein felt that an aluminium cast was the preferred option and the Dean and Chapter agreed to this course of action in January 1955, part of the cost being met by deferring the placing of any commission for a work by Stanley Spencer (whose death soon after prevented him making a painting for Llandaff). In the end, Epstein himself contributed a considerable amount of his fee to ensure his work was transformed from plaster into aluminium. It was cast by the Morris-Singer works in Lambeth.

It was not until the eve of the rehallowing of the Cathedral nave by Archbishop John Morgan on 10th April 1957 that Epstein sat, watching nervously, as the figure was lifted into position. Alongside him at the rear of the nave sat the newly appointed curate of Llandaff, the Revd. Bob Evans, who vividly recalled that moment in his book *The Way to Liverpool*:

> Epstein stopped talking. We just gazed.
>
> For the first time I saw Christ as Epstein saw Christ. Truly it was majestic.
>
> The arms hung down with the hands open towards those who dared to look. They seemed to beckon and strain to lift each one of us. These were the hands come down from the Cross to call mankind to enter the Kingdom, which Christ had made ours. Here was the strength of Christ made visible to man. Words were not needed....
>
> Then, at last, he turned to me. "Well?" I told him what I could see. He made little comment, but seemed to listen. Later with the foolishness of youth... I went in feet first "Was it difficult for you, a practising Jew, to create a Christ for a Christian congregation?" I can recall almost his exact words.
>
> "All my life I have searched for truth and beauty and, in the end, I discovered that it is in the idea of the Christ that they are to be found."

*Angel minstrels, saved from the 1900 organ case, on the east
side of the Majestas*

The west windows of the Cathedral, were filled with dense stained glasss before the bombing in 1941, but are now made up of clear leaded lights so that the piercing eyes of this great figure of Christ look out to the greater world beyond the walls.

Many people were unhappy with Epstein's sculpture and setting, and numerous letters were written to the Cathedral. One letter, from Viscount Knutsford, of Munden, Watford dated April 9th 1957, summed up the tone of those days. He wrote:

Most of us have grown up with a mental picture of Our Lord in human form, which we have probably taken from some church window or old picture book... instead of a piece of worship you now have an 'exhibit' which will claim the attention of trippers and the curious. What a really terrible tragedy.

Others argued that the statue was an inappropriate addition to the previous plan of the pre-war Cathedral. There were also complaints even about using graven images. Arguments about the Majestas and its position still continue in some quarters.

But the Majestas remains a crowning achievement for its sculptor and for the farsighted Cathedral that commissioned it, especially in view of the economic situation in the postwar years. Epstein said "Were the Majestas the last work I were ever to make I would rest content. I do not believe I will ever make another 'act of Faith' similar to it."

The Majestas is the main sculpture upon the parabolic arch designed by George Pace in conjunction with architects Ove Arup & Partners. However it is accompanied at the rear of the organ case by gilded Pre-Raphaelite figures from the Old Testament, saints and angels holding musical instruments. These figures appear like a heavenly host encircling Christ as he rises, as if into heaven – perhaps referencing Luke Ch.xxiv v.51 "while he was blessing them, he left them and was taken up into heaven."

Some of these figures were made by the Pembrokeshire-born Royal Academician James Milo Ap Griffith (1843-1897), who also made the famous 1885 statue of John Batchelor standing in The Hayes in central Cardiff. These box-wood figures were originally made for forty six niches of the Victorian choir stalls in 1878 and the majority survived the 1941 bombing.

After Epstein's aluminium figure was created, the original plaster cast took on something of a life of its own. George Pace wrote a series of letters saying that the cast should be destroyed, claiming that he and Epstein had verbally agreed this before the latter's death. The debate continued, with the Tate Gallery supporting the right of Epstein's widow to do what she wanted with the cast. Sally Ryan, an American sculptor, admirer and patron of Epstein wrote to Eryl Thomas, Dean of Llandaff in March 1966:

> Lady Epstein, as Executor of her husband's estate, has a very onerous task in deciding the fate of the original plaster of her husband's work. [...] There is now the possibility of placing this cast of Llandaff Christ in the nave of Riverside Church [in New York]. Lady Epstein is particularly anxious that this project should not go forward without your knowledge.

Discussions as to whether the plaster cast should be sent to the United States

Epstein relocated: the gilded Majestas at Riverside Church,
New York

were exchanged, given the fact that Epstein was born in New York. Robert J. McCracken wrote from Riverside Church on May 27th 1966:

> I had rather hoped that you would be gratified by the placing of the cast in a church on the other side of the Atlantic. A bond could thereby be established between Llandaff and Riverside. You may be sure that we shall always make clear that Llandaff commissioned the work and that the original is in the Cathedral.

Dean Alun Davies suggested that Sally Fortune Ryan gave the plaster cast to Riverside Church rather than see such a great work of art destroyed and this settled the matter. It can be seen at Riverside to this day, gilded and mounted.

The existence of this second 'Christ in Majesty' had an impact later. In the 1980s the Representative Body of the Church in Wales suggested making a copy of the original maquette, converting it into a bronze and selling it!

Whereas Epstein's great figure dominates the Cathedral, Llandaff's most prolific twentieth century artist is represented in many places. Frank Roper (1914-2000) was a highly talented sculptor who worked on projects in many British churches and cathedrals besides Llandaff. Here he was asked by George Pace to contribute to the Cathedrals restoration and the two collaborated extensively. Coming from a family of Yorkshire stone-carvers, Roper was a student at the Royal College of Art (1936-39) and like many postwar British sculptors he worked with Henry Moore. He spent many years as Head of Sculpture at Cardiff College of Art and eventually became the Vice Principal.

Roper had a facility with many materials including bronze, aluminium, silver, wood, ceramics and glass, and lettering. He developed a modelling technique that used polystyrene in the place of wax giving a unique surface texture to many of his works. He also had a distinctive way of treating figures, making his figurative pieces instantly identifiable.

Passion lecterns designed by Frank Roper

In 1963, using this method, he cast in aluminium a frame for 'The Six Days of Creation' by Edward Burne Jones (p. 127), and three Passion gospel stands for use in Passiontide. These stands carry portrayals of the crowing cockerel, the crown of thorns and the instruments of the Passion. In the same year Roper cast, in bronze, for the restored bishop's throne, the two versions of the Diocesan Arms with angelic supporters, and a mitre that was affixed above the Assistant Bishop's stall on the north side of the choir.

On 12th March 1964 the new choir and chapter stalls were dedicated. Both the Dean's stall and that of the Archdeacon of Llandaff were canopied using various pieces of Prichard's carved castles from the pre-war stalls embellished with cast aluminium pinnacles made by Roper. Over the years these have proved rather fragile and some damage to them has occurred.

As early as 1933 the then Dean and Sir Charles Nicholson, the Cathedral Architect, were discussing the possibility of commissioning twelve decorative panels for the reredos including an Annunciation, the Magi, Flight into Egypt and the risen Lord. After the war, the famous religious artist Stanley Spencer was asked by Dean Eryl Thomas to decorate the niches in the reredos but his death brought an end to the idea. His letters to the Dean survive in the Cathedral archive. It also seems that Spencer was asked to paint a 'Doom' under the proposed baldacchino over a nave altar, which later metamorphosed into George Pace's concrete arch.

The twelve niches around the sculpture were eventually filled by Frank Roper and are arguably his finest work in the Cathedral. George Pace conceived of using a selection of flowers traditionally associated with Mary in medieval plant lore, appropriate to a Lady Chapel. Pace originally suggested that they be titled in English: "Having English wild flowers associated with the Virgin during the Middle Ages cast in lead or aluminum and gilded. I would suggest Mr Frank Roper as the sculptor for this I would imagine the cost would be about £60 to £70 per panel." At some point a decision was made to title the flowers with their Welsh names, which all included a reference to Mary.

Roper depicted the flowers and their Welsh names woven onto blackthorn twigs in each niche. In fact they resemble the crown of thorns put on Christ before his crucifixion, and as such remind us of the destiny of the child Jesus, seen sitting comfortably on the Virgin's knee in the Walker sculpture below the stained glass window showing his Old Testament ancestors.

The niches were painted in green and red by the painting department at Cardiff Art College, and more than a hint of the influence of Matisse can be seen, possibly even referencing one particular work, 'The Snail'. Matisse was one of the most influential contemporary art figures at this time who was working on his Chapel at Vence in Southern France. Upon this background Frank Roper made his individual sculptures which are superb pieces of art, highly imaginative and

Frank Roper's twelve decorative panels in the reredos

technically brilliant, using gilded bronze with the ancient Welsh names of flowers as the basis for the plants' shapes with their petals and leaves. They were paid for by the family of Mr and Mrs Walter Gould who were Friends of Llandaff and benefactors of the Cathedral. Their various names include

Gold Mair - (Mary's Gold) - Marigold
Miaren Mair - (Mary's Briar) - Briar Rose
Clustog Fair - (Mary's Pillow)- Sea Thrift
Gwniadur Mair - (Mary's Thimble) - Foxglove
Gwlydd Melyn Mair - (Mary's Yellow Stem) - Yellow Pimpernel
Mantell Fair - (Mary's Mantle) - Ground Ivy
Esgid Mair - (Mary's Slipper) - Monkshood
Llysiau'r Forwyn - (The Virgin's Herbs) - Meadow Sweet
Ysgol Fair - (Mary's Ladder) - St John's Wort or Centaury,
Briallu Mair - (Mary's Primrose) - Cowslip
Chwys Mair - (Mary's Sweat) - Buttercup,
Tapr Mair - (Mary's Taper) - Snowdrop.

The traditional site of St Teilo's tomb is on the south side of the presbytery just inside the rails of the high altar. Mounted on the wall below the thirteenth century lias limestone effigy is a frieze of six small bronzes depicting the Saint's life, and legends of him. This was funded by donations from a flower festival and the Friends of Llandaff, and completed by Roper in 1966.

Pace responded to it initially: "I can't say that I am altogether happy about this cast metal 'fringe', but I am willing to be converted. I think we shall have to be very careful that we don't get too much metal work in the Cathedral and that,

St Teilo's tomb, with Roper's metal figures

without intending it, we may get an effect of fussiness or over much work on art nouveau lines." However Roper's sculptures are spare and ascetic, and are carefully situated to avoid taking over the space. With their spiky linear quality and open frames, they catch the eye and embellish the area they occupy. The Teilo Frieze is understated and fits naturally into the line of the tomb. It illustrates:

i. St Teilo as Bishop sitting on a throne or sedilia, rejecting a throne of precious metals in favour of a modest seat of cedarwood that was once used by the Lord.

ii. Three figures – St Teilo, St David and St Padarn - receiving gifts on a visit to the Holy City of Jerusalem: a miraculous bell, a portable altar and a pastoral staff.

iii. The three saints sitting on a boat with a sail and an oarsman with their hands in prayer on their way to Jerusalem.

Frank Roper's panels depicting the life of St Teilo

     iv. St Teilo planting an apple orchard in Brittany where he lived for some years
     v. Teilo turning his back on temptation represented by a group of four female figures gathered near him.
     vi. Teilo riding a large stag, while wearing his mitre and staff, securing the boundaries of the Parish of Landeleau in Brittany.

The openness of the design clinging to parallel bars somewhat resembles the decorative gatework that Roper designed for a chapel at St Davids Cathedral.

Frank Roper's final piece for the Cathedral was a bronze made in 1990. St Francis stands in an oval mandorla within which the sculpture is framed. It was made to be seen against a plain backdrop so its forms would stand out. The saint is represented with his hands held high above his head preaching to the birds and animals and a line from his 'Canticle of the Sun' – "Praised be my Lord for all beings". Nature is represented in the sun and stars, a crescent moon, birds, squirrels, an owl, a deer and a wolf. The feeling of the whole piece is joyful and was given in memory of Ken Clayton by his family.

Paintings

The wall of a new church or one whitewashed for decoration is like a new canvas for an artist. Paintings can help with meditation and prayer. Many churches were endowed with wall paintings – which unlike sculpture or stained glass windows were painted on site at the time of the structure of the building itself.

High up on the south wall of the Lady Chapel is an old medieval painting showing the Cross of Lorraine or the Patriarchal Cross, a form of cross popular on Mount Athos and in wide usage during the Middle Ages. The painting stands out among the stencilled designs produced by Geoffrey Webb for Kempson's refurbishment of the Lady Chapel in 1908.

'The Assumption into Heaven of the Blessed Virgin' painted on vertical planks is set in a sedilia designed by George Pace. It was commissioned by Bishop John Marshall (at Llandaff between 1478-96) in 1480, whose chest tomb stands in the entrance of the St Dyfrig Chapel. The painting is a superb and unique work which was part of Marshall's episcopal throne. In it the Virgin is being 'taken up' in body and soul to heaven by angels. The Bishop can be seen in the lower right of the panel robed in cope and mitre and speaking in Latin: *O Virgo scandens sis Marshall celica pandens* (O Virgin that goest up in state / Open to Marshall heaven's gate).

The shield held by angels on the bottom left is the arms of the diocese with those of Marshall. Stars and clouds form a pattern across the whole painting and the background looks like the sea. The Virgin stands in a white dress with a red mantle and ermine trimmings, decorated by Tudor roses with a tassel on the bottom like the ones on the Elizabeth Mathew tomb nearby. Mary's hands are joined in prayer inside a mandorla, a symbol of divinity and supreme power. The Virgin is held up by six angels with a variation of white, green and red wings, while the seventh and eighth angels play musical instruments – probably a harp and lute – and an angel swinging a censer each emerge from a cloud or possibly a bed of flowers. In some ways it resembles the birth of Venus, a classical subject and no doubt a subject known to the painter. It is possible the painting was executed by the same artist who painted the Doom Painting in Wenhaston, Suffolk (c.1480). This painting is now considered by some to be the greatest in its genre of apocalyptic medieval paintings of its period in England.

The 'Assumption' was removed from the bishop's throne and covered with lamp black to obscure the image during the Reformation. This ensured its survival during the iconoclasm of Edward VI's reign and the Puritans during the Civil War. It was later set at the top of the Palladian portico of John Wood's 'Italianate Temple' high altar in 1736. A note on the clothes of one of the central angels says 'Part of Bishop Marshall's Throne done in the year 1480 and set here in the Year 1736 September...by Thomas Omar & Robert Davies Joyners'.

'The Assumption into Heaven of the Blessed Virgin, from Bishop Marshall's Throne

The painting found its way to the Bishop's Palace and Palace Chapel (now the Cathedral School) and a letter of 1916 suggested it should be placed back in the Cathedral. It has always been an object of curiosity and even Bishop Ollivant discusses it in a letter, saying there were differing opinions about whether it belonged to the Cathedral or Palace originally:

> I have been under the impression that at the time it was painted, which seems to have been in the latter part of the 15th century, the bishops of Llandaff lived at the palace at Mathern.

The painting was taken to the parish church of Llandefalle in Breconshire for safe keeping during the Second World War and subsequently taken to the National

*Oil painting of the Madonna and Child in the south aisle, attributed to the
School of Murillo*

Museum of Wales. In a letter to Rollo Charles, of the Museum Art Department,
in 1959 George Pace successfully petitioned for its return to the Cathedral.

The Virgin is also the subject of a fine seventeenth century painting (above),
in which she is seated on clouds with Christ standing on her knees. Six angelic
heads surround them and below is the outline of a building's foundations, which
may represent the miraculous foundation of the church of Santa Maria
Maggiore, whose plan was indicated by a fall of snow. The painting was given to
the Dean and Chapter by Mrs Hanbury of Pontypool Park in April 1924. It had

documentation from the Ministry of Fine Arts in Rome in 1866 and was believed to be painted by the Spanish artist Bartolome Esteban Murillo (1617-1682). Known for his religious work, Murillo was born in Seville and the 'Madonna and Child' was previously attributed to him.

The Rijksmuseum in Amsterdam has another 'Madonna and Child' painting by Murillo which has similar-looking models for the Virgin and child. Moreover, there is a letter in the Cathedral archive from an Elsie Hanbury of Gordonstoun, Elgin in Scotland enclosing papers as to the authenticity of the Murillo left to her care from her mother-in-law Mrs Hanbury-Leigh, and there exists a document dated 1867 authenticating it as a Murillo. In 19th August 1936 a letter sent to the Dean about Mr Drown who cleaned the picture states:

> He has cleaned a good many Murillos. His opinion is that this work is genuine. It certainly is not a copy.... Drown says that the sweeping brush lines now visible, though formerly obscured by woolly over painting and the skillful way in which the lips of the main figures and the heads of the cherubs are sketched rather than painted in detail and the general nature of the work leave no doubt in his mind that the painter was Murillo.

Subsequent examinations in 1949 by both Mr J. Steegman, the then Keeper of Art at the National Museum of Wales, and Mr Neil MacLaren of the National Gallery led to the conclusion that this painting – which had spent the war years stored in the cellars of what was then Llys Esgob – was not by Murillo. Further expert research carried out in the late 1990s confirmed this earlier opinion, whilst not making a firm attribution.

The Cathedral's 'jewel in the crown' in terms of painting is 'The Seed of David' by Dante Gabriel Rossetti (1828-1882) (opposite). It was painted between 1858 and 1864 and was originally set in a stone reredos designed by John Seddon, behind the high altar below the Norman arch. It depicts the Nativity and Jesus's ancestor King David from the line of Jesse.

In early 1856 it was suggested by Seddon that Rossetti should paint an altar piece, as long as the Bishop and Dean approved and the appropriate funds were raised. Seddon was, at that time, carrying out work at St Margaret's, Aberdare for Henry Austin Bruce MP (Later Lord Aberdare) and when the proposed scheme was outlined by Seddon to Bruce he proved to be very enthusiastic, becoming the driving force behind both the fund raising and the negotiations that were necessary. Jan Marsh, Rossetti's biographer, writes "As the first step in negotiations, Seddon's brother Tom escorted Henry A. Bruce, MP for Merthyr Tydfil and chair of the subscription committee, to meet Rossetti on 4th March."

We know that Rossetti wrote to his brother William asking him to read him some of the Gospel so that he could study the background for the piece. His draft watercolours are now held by the Tate Gallery in London. From a letter we learn

that he had already sent a watercolour to Ruskin on the subject the previous year. In Belgium in 1849 he had admired an Adoration by Memling and only two years previously in 1845 the National Gallery in London has acquired an 'Adoration of the Kings', after Joos Van Cleve – which showed the Magi kissing the hand of Christ. It was Rossetti himself who proposed a triptych. Rossetti's own description of the triptych is in the Cathedral archive, and he wrote as follows:

> This triple picture shows Christ sprung from high and low, as united in the person of David, who was both shepherd and King: and worshipped by high and low (by King and shepherd) at his birth.
>
> The centrepiece is not a literal rendering of the event of the Nativity, but rather a condensed symbol of it. An angel has just entered the stable where Christ is newly born, and leads by the hand a King and a shepherd, who bow themselves before the manger on which the Virgin Mother kneels holding the infant Saviour. The shepherd kisses the hand, and the King the foot, of Christ, to denote the superiority of lowliness to greatness in His sight; while the one lays a crook the other a crown at His feet. An angel kneels behind the Virgin, with both arms about her supporting her; and other angels look in through openings round the stable, or play on musical instruments in the loft above.
>
> The two side panels represent David, one as shepherd, the other as King. In the first he is a youth, and advances fearlessly but cautiously, sling in hand, to take aim at Goliath; while the Israelite troops watch the issue of the combat from behind an entrenchment. In the second he is a man of mature years, still armed from battle, and composing on his harp a psalm of thanksgiving for victory.

The over-riding theme of the triptych is complex. Certainly we have a scene of the Nativity with two side panels of King David. The first panel shows David as a young shepherd and a hunter, holding a sling – no doubt the famous moment when he aims it at Goliath, with Israel's army in the background looking on. The third panel shows David as a mature King dressed for battle yet sitting with a lyre, probably composing a psalm of thanksgiving for victory. Around him are roses and a peacock, a symbol of immortality. This panel is possibly one of the greatest works by Rossetti.

The centre panel shows us Mary sitting in a wooden structure, with three supports (possibly suggesting the three crosses at Calvary) and has a familiar feel to the temporary like structures of Piero Della Francesca's and Sandro Botticelli's nativity paintings in the National Gallery, with which no doubt Rossetti would have been familiar. Another of Francesca's paintings of the baptism shows a white dove in a sunburst hovering above the scene. There are many angels including two the size of the other figures – one on its knees and the other unusually clasping Mary from behind as if to steady her or hold her.

A king and a shepherd with a staff in his hand bow before Mary, who is kneeling holding Jesus, whose hand it is suggested is being kissed – but the perspective of the scene is difficult to read from the viewer's angle. The story is taken from both Matthew and Luke, who follow different traditions of the magi and shepherds. Both the shepherd's crook and king's crown are laid at Christ's feet. Jesus's foot is kissed by the King, something traditionally part of Near and Middle Eastern culture even today.

On the shield of the King is a faint representation of two figures carrying grapes on a yoke – a familiar symbol often found in stained glass windows including Canterbury Cathedral – possibly from Numbers Ch.xii v.23: "And they came unto the brook of Eshcol and cut down from thence a branch with one cluster of grapes, and they bare it between two upon a staff".

It was common for the Pre-Raphaelites to use each other and their wives as models. In this painting Rossetti used William Morris for King David. According to Ford Madox Brown's diary 24th August 1856 he wrote "Yesterday Rossetti brought his ardent admirer Morris of Oxford, who bought my little 'Hayfield' for £40." It was around this time that Rossetti made a study of Morris's head for the triptych – whether he considered this because Morris had Welsh heritage through his paternal grandfather (and apparently the first to drop the Ap from the family name) one cannot be sure. But it is true that wherever the Bible is illustrated cultures take on the familiar imagery and physical types of their own people. Rosetti may have utilised Morris's 'Welsh' characteristics for this reason in his painting for Llandaff.

While Morris's wife Jane Burden was used for Mary, it is believed the poet Swinburne was used as the adoring King who kisses Christ's feet and the painter Edward Burne-Jones as the shepherd. The angel kneeling before Mary is Rossetti's wife Elizabeth Siddal, and David the Shepherd in the left hand panel is based on Timothy Hughes, a friend and husband of Fanny Cornforth, the subject of many of Rossetti's paintings.

Rossetti wrote to his aunt in 1864 when the piece was complete that his idea was to unite poor and rich "to show Christ sprung from high and low in the person of David, who was both shepherd and King, and worshipped by high and low – a king and a shepherd – at his nativity". Jan Marsh wrote:

> According to Rossetti's brother William, the 'real subject' of the picture was "the equality in the eyes of God, of all sorts and conditions of men from the monarch to the peasant; their equality both in the act of faith which they perform and in the means of divine grace by which it is sanctioned and accepted".

Rossetti visited Llandaff in 1866 and tried to lighten the painting which blocked out the light from the east end. He was well aware that the triptych's situation in the brightest part of the Cathedral, with light streaming through from behind the high altar, made it seem dark by comparison. He even suggested offsetting the effect by painting the whole of the Sanctuary black! (The Chapter refused this idea).

The setting for this triptych painting was criticised from the outset on the grounds of poor lighting and lack of accessibility for those wishing to see the detail of the panel. No alternative was put forward until, in the mid-1930s, Sir Charles Nicholson proposed opening up the space beneath the Norman arch and relocating the triptych at the eastern end of the south aisle. A drawing of the suggested placement is in the Cathedral archive. This scheme was not carried out, although the paintings were removed in 1935 for cleaning and restoration, work that was to prove more extensive than had been envisaged as sections of the paint were separating from the canvas because of the type of heavy chalk priming that Rossetti had used.

In September 1940, as part of the efforts made by the Friends of Llandaff Cathedral to protect stained glass and other works of art from potential war damage, the triptych was removed from its frame and stored in a large wooden crate behind a bank of sandbags near the entrance to the Chapter House. Thus, when the Cathedral was severely damaged on January 2nd 1941, the paintings survived unharmed.

With the post war restoration came the opportunity to realise Nicholson's vision of opening the vista through the Cathedral unimpeded by the Victorian high altar reredos. George Pace followed this line of reasoning and reused the Rossetti triptych as the reredos of the St Illtyd Chapel below the Jasper Tower. The frame then provided was the subject of some criticism as areas of unpainted canvas, previously hidden behind the cusps of the stone Seddon reredos, were exposed to view, whilst the pale blue of the frame was thought to be an unhappy choice.

In 1988 the paintings were again cleaned and restored in conjunction with the provision of a parclose screen to enclose the Illtyd Chapel and the installation of a new and more fitting frame against a wall sumptuously decorated by Peter Larkworthy. The whole work was designed by Donald Buttress, the Cathedral Architect.

Memorials

Unsurprisingly the Cathedral contains monuments and memorials which preserve the memory of those who contributed in some way to the history of the Cathedral, although only twelve major tombs survive from before 1800.

Llandaff's earliest tomb is that of Bishop William De Breuse (or Bruce or de Braose) carved in lias limestone which is positioned in the north east side of the

Lady Chapel. He was the creator of the chapel and was Bishop of Llandaff between 1266 and 1286/7.

The tomb is beautifully executed. The bishop's robe flows in a loose classical style with the folds of the gown forming a pattern. He wears a mitre with a dogtooth decoration and at his sides are decorative carved stones with a fleur-de-lys, oak leaves and spiraling foliage. Around his neck is what looks like a torc, shaped like a crescent, and may be a reference to the crusades. He has a crosier which is quite decorative and not unlike the ancient ones held in St Davids Cathedral. There is an inscription around his head and an amice with a fringe, showing his dress was of unique quality. Alongside are a set of angel heads running along two columns.

In the south aisle lies an effigy of Henry of Abergavenny, previously the Prior at that Abbey before he became the Bishop of Llandaff between 1193 and 1218 and who was present at the coronation of King John.

The effigy of Henry of Abergavenny

DYFRIG
CHAPEL

The tomb of a bishop, possibly St Dyfrig

Not far away is the tomb of St Teilo, said to be a bishop in South and West Wales c. 545-569 and Llandaff's second Celtic patron saint. His thirteenth century tomb is carved in Dundry stone with Victorian diaper work completed mostly in 1856 by the sixteen year old Edward Henry Clarke. Notice the sun in the centre of the canopy (see page 149). St Teilo, according to tradition, has his head on a cushion and wears a mitre and pontifical robes. There is no lion at his feet but a bird-reptile figure.

In the Dyfrig chapel is found the tomb of an unnamed bishop. The effigy is sometimes described as St Dyfrig but is probably that of Bishop Edward Bromfield. The figure, executed in Dundry stone, lies in full bishop's dress and was probably carved in the west of England at the end of the fourteenth century. He looks past the instruments of Christ's Passion to a figure of Jesus rising from his tomb above his head. This might be a sign of the bishop's anticipated resurrection on the Day of Judgement. On the front of the tomb is a robed figure of Christ pronouncing a benediction. It is a beautifully carved tomb.

A figure of a bishop in the north aisle wall near to the Sir William Mathew memorial is currently thought to be that of William of Radnor, Bishop from 1257 until 1265.

In the north choir aisle is a cadaver monument made of Painswick stone. This 'memento mori' depicts the inevitability of future death is one of only three known in Wales, the others being in St Mary's Tenby and St Dogmael's Abbey, Cardigan. It resembles others in England, especially the tomb of Bishop Beckingham (d 1465) in Wells Cathedral, which suggests a West Country origin of around that date. It is probably a notable figure of the Cathedral. The skeletal form of this sculpture lies on a shroud which has fallen away from much of the body. Its head flung backwards, sunken cheeks and eyes and skin drawn tightly across the body and it is badly damaged probably from some unknown vandalism. It is the legs that are missing and series of dowels suggest that they were once fixed here, or repaired, although lost to us today. Above and around the effigy is an ogee-arched recess.

Nearby on the right side of the Dyfrig Chapel lies the chest of Bishop John Marshall (1478 and 1498) who was a Fellow of Eton College and of Merton College, Oxford and Canon of Windsor. It was during his time at the cathedral that the Jasper Tower was built, with other parts of the medieval cathedral. The chest is a most interesting monument as the clothes fall in a pattern not unlike an ancient Syrian sculpture, in fact so similar that one wonders if the sculptor had in fact travelled or learnt from someone who had visited the Holy Land and Near East. The chasuble on the fifteenth century effigy of Bishop John Marshall (1478 to 1496) is pointed in front and bands of embroidery are sewn around the edge in the traditional Y-shaped 'orphrey' of ancient design made with braid or embroidery. There are angels at his head and a mitre full of jewels and studded with flowers and unusually his eyes are open. His staff is decorated with a rose and his feet rest on a lion. On the pedestal is an 'Image of Pity', the emblems of Our Lord's Passion and a wounded Christ.

There are three notable monuments to the Mathew family in the Cathedral. In the wall between the Lady Chapel and the Dyfrig Chapel is a monument to Sir Christopher Mathew and his wife Elizabeth carved in Chellaston gypsum, a form of alabaster. Alabaster is a soft, easily carved stone, that gives excellent detail of chain mail, a sword and sheathed dagger, with a Tudor Rose on the belt of Elizabeth and her striking headdress with its exquisite decoration. Christopher Mathew's helmet shows a heathcock, part of his family crest, and his collar has the intricate links of the Lancastrian Collar of Esses (or SS) that is still used today. Elizabeth's dress is typical of the period, with a necklace, and the sculptor rests her head on a cushion supported by two angels. The hands of both figures are in prayer and Elizabeth's rest on a heart. Above the canopy still bears traces of the rich colours that once adorned our cathedrals. The armorial bearings were repainted by Huw Mathew in 1980. Around the pedestal it says

The effigy of Sir Christopher Mathew

"Pray for the souls of Christopher Mathew, Esquire, and of Elizabeth his wife. Elizabeth indeed died on 30th January, A.D. 1523, and the aforesaid Christopher died A.D. 1500, to whose souls may God be gracious."

A monument to Sir William Mathew and his wife Jenette stands on the north side of the nave and is also carved in alabaster. It was once broken in pieces but was reassembled during the nineteenth century restoration. Sir William was a grandson of David Mathew, and was knighted on the Battlefield of Bosworth in 1485. Here his head rests on a helmet with the now damaged figure of some creature, where only the claws are left. His hands are in prayer, a sword lies at his side and his feet rest on a lion. Jenette's head is covered in a beaded and embroidered headdress, belt and embroidered sash, and lies on a tassled pillow. Many figures surround the tomb, of angels, monks, knights and ladies, along with heraldic crests. A damaged inscription roughly states "Pray for the soul of William Mathew, Knight, who died 10th day of March, A.D. 1528: also Jenette his wife, who gave back her spirit to God on ....A.D. 1530, to whose souls may God be gracious."

An uninscribed but truly beautiful effigy probably of Sir David Mathew lies on the right hand side of the Dyfrig Chapel. The monument is 6ft 2 inches and said to be life size. He was of great repute as a standard bearer and is said to have saved King Edward IV at the Battle of Towton, fought on Palm Sunday 1461. Sir David was called the 'Keeper of the tomb of St Teilo' for protecting the Cathedral from the danger of pirates lurking in the Bristol Channel. Made of alabaster on a sandstone base, he also wears a Tudor rose and the Lancastrian Order S.S. like his grandson Christopher, and also bears traces of the heathcock. He was killed in Neath in 1480 in an armed conflict with the Turberville family.

The monument to Bishop Ollivant on the northern side of the sanctuary was also by the nineteenth century sculptor Armstead. It is a fine piece of work showing him in full canonical dress, but not in the mitre or chasible. Note the red and green serpentine shafts (also used near the Teilo tomb) from the Lizard district of Cornwall, named as such because they look like a serpent skin. Ollivant was succeeded by Richard Lewis and Armstead also designed his episcopal crosier which can be seen in the large portrait bronze of the Bishop by Sir William Goscombe John, east of the choir stalls.

John Evan Thomas FSA created the elaborate memorial to John Nicholl (1797-1853) in the Dyfrig Chapel which was installed in 1856. From a Glamorgan family Nicholl left Oxford University with the highest academic honours and was called to the Bar and elected a member of Parliament and a "zealous devotion to public duties". He became Judge Advocate General and Privy Councillor. The monument to him is huge and dominates that part of the Chapel with figures of Wisdom and Religion standing on either side. It is a number of important pieces in the Principality by Thomas, a sculptor who also worked at Buckingham Palace and the Palace of Westminster. His Welsh work includes the sculpture of the Duke of Wellington in Brecon and the iconic figure of the Second Marquess of Bute which has recently been moved from St Mary Street to Callaghan Square. His first piece for the Cathedral was on the south wall of the Lady Chapel – the mural memorial of Bishop Edward Copleston.

The pair of bas-relief panels in the north aisle, a memorial to Henry Thomas of Llwyn-Madoc in Breconshire were designed by Armstead and carved by Clarke. They have recently been relightened and make a superb pair when viewed from a distance. Armstead also designed the figurative work on the bishop's throne, again executed by Clarke.

The calligrapher Ieuan Rees was responsible for executing Donald Butress's design for the stone near the bishop's throne to the scholar William Morgan, who translated the Bible into Welsh in 1588 and became Bishop of Llandaff in 1596. Rees also carved the memorial stone outside the Cathedral in the Garden of

Remembrance, on the south side of the Cathedral. It marks the spot at which the land mine detonated on January 2nd 1941, and the stone was erected to mark the 50th anniversary of that event. A plaque to Bishop Glyn W.H. Simon also by Rees is located in the Dyfrig Chapel.

Furnishings

Behind the high altar the crucifix and candlesticks create a dramatic screen beneath the Urban Arch acting like a lace cloth and framing the figure of Christ on the cross with such perfection that even at the entrance to the Cathedral through the west door the eye is drawn towards it. The crucifix on the altar is medieval German work and the altar candlesticks and standards are Italian – an extra mounting was made for the medieval cross to fit with the others. It was originally intended for Malty parish church after the Second World War, but as they wanted a George Pace cross instead, the Architect obtained it for Llandaff.

Pace wrote "The High Altar Crucifix speaks so effectively that one does not

The High Altar: Crucifix and candles

want to load the place with others." And on 26th January 1960 he wrote:

> I was in London last week and visited Wolsey's. The seven candlesticks have
> been cleaned and treated and look very well. I had a talk with Mr Wolsey
> about the cross which is to be fitted on the central candlestick and to bear
> the medieval figure.

The seven candlesticks, six bought, a seventh made to hold the cross at a cost
of £50 carved, silvered and lacquered, were cleaned at Wolsey's "to bear the
Medieval figure".

One of the most distinctive pieces of Victorian decorative work is the
grandiose bishop's throne. In November 1857 Prichard and Seddon had
produced designs and estimates but, after numerous problems with contracts
and contractors, it was not until 1864 that the work was completed. The
designs for much of the figurative work were by Armstead and were carried out
by Edward Clarke. On the eastern face of the timber spire of the throne is a
bas-relief panel showing St Paul preaching to the Athenians, whilst on the

The Victorian bishop's throne and stalls, before the installation of the new organ

western face is a representation of Christ's command "Feed my sheep". The bishop's prayer desk is flanked by 'The Adoration of the Magi' and 'The Annunciation'.

The David Chapel is a rich repository of twentieth century furnishings and memorials. The building and everything in it were given by the Welch Regiment and allied regiments in Canada and Australia. Dedicated to St David and to the memory of those who fell in many wars, it was consecrated on 22 September 1956. It has a tranquil atmosphere. As the entrance an inscription tells the story of the chapel.

> This chapel is built of stones recovered from four cottages built in Llandaff during the reign of Queen Elizabeth I. They were taken by the workmen from the bed of the River Taff. The cottages were demolished in January

The cool white interior of the David Chapel, with Pace's frontal on the altar

1941 by enemy bombers during World War II. As soon as possible after hostilities had ceased Mr Leonard Mitchell, a Cardiff Accountant and treasurer of the Friends of Llandaff Cathedral who then owned the land on which the stones lay, made a most generous gift of these lovely stones to the Dean of Llandaff. Today they form the rounded walls of the Welch Regimental Chapel, completed in the reign of Queen Elizabeth II.

The river pebbles line the exterior walls of the chapel. Inside, David Chapel is suffused with a lightness and simplicity that is in marked contrast with the main body of the Cathedral. The clear glass and highly elevated windows with whitewashed walls create an almost arctic atmosphere and if you stand in the south east and look upon and back to the west with its series of pointed arches, similar to many Vale of Glamorgan churches. The folding curves of the ceiling increase the feeling of being inside a large tent, in a remote terrain. There is very little colour in the chapel but the soft wooden pews with memorials and Prince of Wales feathers and other symbols are also restful to the eye.

The few stained glass windows are miniature panes of sixteenth century French glass. They depict various Biblical figures in medieval clothes, and are vigorously designed with rich colours. The eight coloured panes are fixed high up in the windows and do not interfere with the monochrome purity of the space. They were donated by relatives of members of the Regiment and represent the best of a collection that was sent to the Cathedral.

Set against the east wall is a listing of the Battle Honours of the Regiment, carved in situ by Geoffrey Kaye of York. The letters interleave, join and mutate; rules of spacing and alignment are subservient to the total design whilst still retaining clear legibility. This is the most outstanding lettering in the Cathedral and must be one of the best examples of twentieth century letter carving in the whole of Britain.

On the floor are a series of brass tablets commemorating officers of the regiment, as do the pew ends. On 23 July 1968 George Pace wrote to the Dean saying "In the Welch Regimental Chapel from time to time bronze floor plates are needed." The Regiment supplied the wording and the plates were intended to decorate the floor almost like metallic foot prints, heading towards the altar.

On 11 June 1969 the Welch Regiment was amalgamated with the South Wales Borderers to form the Royal Regiment of Wales. In January 1970 it was suggested by Col. Lionel Evans that an inscription recording this be incised in the chapel stonework. Pace felt that there were only two people in Britain who were capable of the standard needed to accompany Geoffrey Kaye's incised Battle Honours, and they were busy on other projects. At the time Pace was working with Frank Roper to complete a cast metal text monument to the Venerable Bede at Durham Cathedral, and he decided to produce something similar at Llandaff.

Geoffrey Kaye at work in the David Chapel, 1958

On 26th November 1969 Pace wrote "Welch Regimental Chapel: Inscription. The great series of lettering from Durham Cathedral is finished and in position and had received general acclaim. This means that the experiment that I carried out to achieve this lettering have proved to be reasonably successful and can now be adapted for the Welsh Regimental lettering. I have already set up the whole of this lettering in full size, but I am not entirely happy with the result. I may have to bring the full size drawings and hang them on the wall in the chapel to make the final adjustments."

The work was set in place by July 1971. This great panel of gilded lettering by Roper uses letters to create an overall art work, abstracting elements and showing letters in their artistic original 'forms and shapes' something many people forget about when they become literate and only see the symbolic meaning, loosing the form, in itself another language.

The David Chapel contains more examples of calligraphy than any other part of the Cathedral with three Roll of Honour books recording the fallen of the Welch Regiment and its successor the Royal Regiment of Wales. They stand in cabinets against the west wall of the chapel and flank a mural memorial by Ieuan Rees to those members of the Welch Regiment who fell in the Korean War. There is also a memorial to the members of the 614 RAF Auxiliary Squadron who fell in the Second World War on an inscribed slate panel, which is a good example of Pace's design.

In the processional way there are some relics: gargoyles from the Jasper Tower and a large stone urn, from John Wood's 'Italianate Temple' built inside the Cathedral during the eighteenth century.

The Processional Cross is of particular note. Charles Nicholson, writing to the Dean in 1935, said "I enclose a revised design for the Processional Cross. As you suggested I have put St Teilo in the middle kneeling... holding the Cathedral up in his hands. I am anxious to avoid any suggestion of St Teilo taking the place of the proper figure for a cross and for this reason have suggested an oval plaque rather than a figure in a 'vesica piscis' which form is traditionally used to frame a figure of our Lord.

Conclusion

The two major restorations of the nineteenth and twentieth centuries brought significant works of art to the Cathedral. In both restorations, the architects

Relics from the Cathedral in the processional way

commissioned leading artists of the day to produce objects that would enhance religious worship. The working relationships were very productive, exemplified by Prichard and Seddon bringing in the Pre-Raphaelites; and by Pace's connection with Frank Roper. In both cases these partnerships also shaped other churches throughout South Wales, which bear their distinctive stamp.

These architects regarded the entire Cathedral as a complete work that incorporated the visual and applied arts. Pace's principles were expounded in his 'Notes on the Restoration' (1949) in which he explained his philosophy of the Cathedral's rebuilding:

> Everything in the building and its fittings and furnishings is designed or controlled by the Architect so that all play their appointed parts in the creation of a Cathedral which is greater than the mere sum of its parts;
>
> Every part to be a Work of Art in itself, but to lose itself in the whole so that the Cathedral is not a mere collection of Works of Art as in a museum or art gallery. The aim has been to create a Cathedral which is a complete offering to God in which every individual has given of his uttermost yet has utterly effaced himself.

This philosophy is expressed in everything Pace designed, from vestments and altar frontals to ironwork and joinery, and in the lines of the pulpitum supporting Epstein's 'Christ in Majesty'. Pace saw the building as an organic whole, working both as a structure and as a space enriched by significant details. This is why his vision gives Llandaff its appeal as a rare example of twentieth century religious architecture where the careful attention to design permeates the interior. In this, Pace could be regarded as a late exponent of the Arts and Crafts concept of involving craftsmen, a concept that was entirely supported by his Victorian forebears Prichard and Seddon. Thus the wheel came full circle from one restoration to the next.

The Stained Glass of Llandaff Cathedral

The vicissitudes through which Llandaff Cathedral has passed over the centuries have left us with very little information about any window glass that existed here prior to the nineteenth century restoration. Even much of the glass that was the product of that great rebuilding was to suffer grievously during the Second World War.

By the 1930s almost all the windows of the Cathedral, with the exception of those in the clerestory, were filled with stained glass and they were largely responsible for the interior being somewhat gloomy. More than half of this glass was to be lost when the Cathedral was bombed on 2nd January 1941. Most, but not all, thanks to the good offices of The Friends of Llandaff Cathedral who had held an Emergency Public Meeting on 12th September 1940 to seek funding for the removal and storage of the best of the glass. One hundred and thirty donors to that appeal made it possible, within three short months, for no fewer than twelve windows to be saved for eventual reinstallation in the restored Cathedral. The debt which the Cathedral owes to its Friends for this act alone is incalculable.

As the post 1840 glass is described below, the losses will be noted.

Medieval Glass

William Clarke, of the famous Llandaff family of builders, stone carvers and Church furnishers, told J.E. Ollivant that

> The only fragments of stained glass which I ever found at the Cathedral were buried in the cill of the East Window of the Lady Chapel behind the old Reredos. They were fragments of painted drapery very thick, almost a quarter of an inch thick.

There was no indication of the age of this glass.

The only written description of the design of any medieval glass at Llandaff is provided by Richard Symonds in his 'Diary of the Marches of the Royal Army during the Great Civil War'. This was published in The Camden Society Proceedings, Volume 74, 1859. In his diary Symonds describes three windows in the Cathedral as well as several of the tombs and statues which he found here.

July/August 1645
Landaffe Cathedral, com Glamorgan.

> North window of the Ladies Chapel. Very old, twise and very large.
> Or, three chevrons gules (CLARE)."fifteen ynches".
> A chappel where they have Welch prayers only."

Having described the Mathew tomb in the north wall, he moved into what is now the Dyfrig Chapel, noted the tomb of David Mathew, and then records:

> In the east window of that chappel:
> Quarterly, 1 and 4, BEAUCHAMP; 2 and 3, WARWICK.

Later, he reached what is now the Teilo Chapel and recorded:

> In a chappel, east end of the south yle of the quire:
> East window aloft; over the altar, large and old:
> ENGLAND
> Gules, a lion rampant guardant or.
> Gules, ten bezant, 4,3,2 and 1 (ZOUCHE) (CLARE)

It is by no means certain that the window he described was in the south aisle, as he went on without a break to describe the Assumption painting on the "bishop's seate" – the window might equally well be above the high altar.

It is clear that all the glass he saw was armorial in content. His brief and somewhat confused words represent all that is known about window glass in Llandaff prior to 1800.

Nineteenth Century Restoration

When John Prichard started the major restoration of the Cathedral in the 1830s no stained glass had survived from earlier centuries. In the early years of the eighteenth century the tracery of the Lady Chapel east window had been partially blocked up with masonry to enclose a small wooden window frame. It was here that Prichard started his reconstruction by opening out this window and replacing the wooden frame with geometrical tracery based on the design of the windows of the Chapter House of York Minster. Into this new tracery was placed the glass executed by Thomas Willement – who was Heraldic Artist to George IV and Artist in Stained Glass to Queen Victoria.

This window, most of which was clear, had armorial glass in the circular sections with the Arms of Precentor Douglas (who had given the initial impulse to the restoration), Bishop Copleston, Chancellor J.M. Traherne and of Dean Bruce Knight, during whose short tenure of office the great restoration got under way. This window, like many more in the building was lost on 2nd January 1941.

The window space above the high altar, now housing the 'Supper at Emmaus' glass by Piper, was filled by 1859 by glass attributed to Michael O'Connor which had been given by J.H. Markland of Bath who was Dean Conybeare's son-in-law. Our Lord was depicted in the centre light flanked in the other lights by Saints Peter and Paul, the principal patron saints of the Cathedral. This window was lost in 1941.

The involvement of the Pre-Raphaelite Brotherhood made a major contribution to the beautifying of the Cathedral as part of the nineteenth century

Window east of the Chapter House in the south wall: Designs by Ford Madox Brown, Edward Burne-Jones and William Morris: In memory of Evan David

restoration. Five windows were to figure amongst the legacy of this association all of which were saved from destruction in 1941 by the Friends initiative in having them removed and stored. These windows were made by Morris, Marshall, Faulkner & Co. between 1866 and 1874 using designs by Ford Madox Brown, Edward Burne-Jones and William Morris himself.

The first window to be ordered from the Morris Company was given in 1866 by John Prichard and his sisters in memory of their parents and is the east window of the south aisle. The restoration of the Cathedral was as yet incomplete when this window was installed. The centre light by William Morris depicts Christ as King, full face, crowned and robed, with an orb in His left hand and His right hand raised in benediction. The left hand light contains the figure of St Elizabeth and the boy John by Ford Madox Brown (design no.37a; Bradford Cathedral, 1863), whilst the right hand light shows Zacharias in a white and gold cope lined with red over mauve and with a censer in his left hand(William Morris design no.172). The two quatrefoils above are also by Morris whilst the original glass for the trefoil at the top has been lost and replaced with a typical example of George Pace leaded light design.

The next Morris window to appear at Llandaff is that which is in the south aisle immediately east of the Chapter House (see page 173). This five light window was installed in 1867 and includes the inscription:

> TO THE GLORY OF GOD AND IN MEMORY OF EVAN DAVID
> BORN MARCH 9TH 1789 DIED NOV 15TH 1862 ALSO OF ANNE
> HIS WIFE BORN JULY 29TH 1789 DIED SEPT 22ND 1867

Evan David who, together with his wife, is buried just outside this window, had lived at Fairwater House – now demolished, was Churchwarden of the Parish of Llandaff, Chairman of the Board of Guardians and a Justice of the Peace.

Reading from left to right, the figures depicted are: St Matthew, carrying his emblem of an Angel (Ford Madox Brown); St Mark, with a winged Lion. (Edward Burne-Jones); Christ on the Cross (Burne-Jones); St Luke, with a winged Ox (William Morris); St John, with an Eagle (Ford Madox Brown).

The window in the North Aisle adjacent to the Mathew Tomb and the pulpit was the next Morris window to come to Llandaff in the following year and was another memorial to a diocesan officer:

> TO THE MEMORY OF EDWARD STEPHENS ESQ FOR MANY
> YEARS DEPUTY REGISTRAR OF THIS DIOCESE HE DIED THE
> 2ND DECEMBER 1861 AGED 71 YEARS

The left hand light (Burne-Jones) depicts St John the Baptist with, on his staff, a scroll reading 'Ecce Agnus Dei' (Behold the Lamb of God). Below St John

Moses carrying the tablets of the
Commandments, by Burne-Jones

is a half-length figure of an angel with an organ. (William Morris).

The centre light shows Moses carrying the tablets of the Law (above) above the figure of an angel, by William Morris, playing a dulcimer. In accordance with convention, Moses is depicted with horns. This arose due to an error in translation of part of Chapter 34 of the Book of Exodus in which we are told that as Moses came down from Mount Sinai "the skin of his face shone". The Hebrew for 'shining' is capable of two interpretations and in the Vulgate the 'horns' version was used.

The right hand light depicts St Paul in a blue cloak lined with pale gold, over white patterned with gold by Burne-Jones. William Morris again provided the design for the half-length angel playing a pipe below St Paul.

In 1869 the window which is now immediately west of the Chapter House in the south aisle was installed, but not in its present position. Prior to its removal for safe keeping in 1940 it was placed two bays further west, but with the building of the pulpitum during the post war restoration, the architect, George Pace, decreed that the opening adjacent to the pulpitum should be filled with plain glass to give maximum natural light to the nave altar. Thus, this Morris window had to be relocated. It carries the inscription:

IN MEMORY OF ISABELLA MARY DAUGHTER OF JOHN
LUDFORD AND EMMA CATHERINE WHITE LATE OF DOWLAIS
PUT UP A.D.1869 BY THE KINDNESS OF THE CHILDS UNCLE
W.H. FORMAN ESQ LATE OF PENYDARREN IRON WORKS

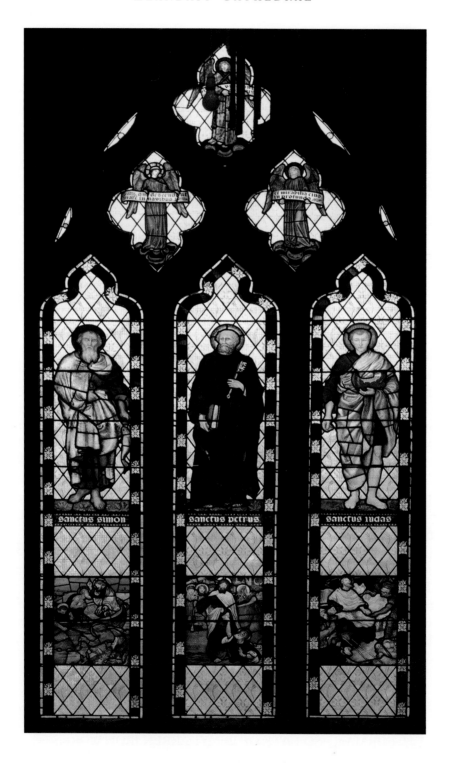

The left hand light shows the figure of David (Burne-Jones) with beneath it 'Nativity', also by Burne-Jones (p. 177). The centre light represents St Stephen, by Burne-Jones with, below it, 'Presentation in the Temple' by William Morris. Burne-Jones was paid £10 for 'Samuel', which is the main subject of the right hand light. It is coupled with 'Christ Blessing Children' by Burne-Jones. The three angelic figures playing the dulcimer, cymbals and harp in the tracery are to designs by William Morris.

The final Morris window was installed in 1874 in the opening immediately north of the Pulpitum, and is probably the most accomplished of the set of five windows here (p. 176). The left hand light (by Ford Madox Brown) shows St Simon as a full length figure viewed full face, with a fish in his left hand. Below is 'The miraculous draught of fishes' (also by Ford Madox Brown) showing two disciples with Christ in a boat, above another disciple in a second boat in the right foreground with a net stretched between the two boats. The centre light contains St Peter holding a golden key (Burne-Jones) with, below, 'Christ walking on the water' (Ford Madox Brown). St Jude is the main figure in the right hand light (Ford Madox Brown) shown full length and carrying a ship. The scene below represents St Paul's shipwreck and is also by Ford Madox Brown. The three full length angels in the tracery are from designs by William Morris.

Five further windows survived the bombing of January 1941 having been removed for safe keeping only weeks before. The oldest of these is in the north aisle immediately behind the organ case (see page 179). It was given in 1883

TO THE GLORY OF GOD AND IN LOVING MEMORY OF MARY ANN THE BELOVED WIFE OF JAMES HARVEY INSOLE, LLANDAFF

This glass is by William Francis Dixon (1848-1929) who was a pupil of Clayton & Bell, before setting up business on his own account in 1872. He moved to Munich in 1894 where he worked as a designer for the firm of Mayer, eventually dying there in 1929. The window is almost Art Nouveau in character showing the influence of Beardsley.

The left hand light shows Ruth gleaning in Boaz' field, above a smaller panel depicting the distribution of bread to the poor, with the texts 'Blessed are the poor in spirit' and 'Blessed are they which do hunger' (an unfortunate shortening of the quotation by the omission of the words 'and thirst after righteousness' one feels!). At the top of this light is an angel bearing a cross. Curiously, Ruth seems to have an extra toe on her right foot!

The centre light has, at the top, an angel bearing a crown (one part of which appears to have been replaced at some time with newer glass, as does part of the wheat-field in the left hand light). Below the crown is the figure of Dorcas, who appears in the Acts of the Apostles (Ch.ix.v.36) as a woman "full of good works

The Dixon window showing Ruth, Dorcas and Anna

and almsdeeds" who was raised from the dead by St Peter. In Victorian times the Dorcas Society of church ladies was active in the making and provision of clothes for the poor. The panel below shows three women with a dying companion – presumably Dorcas – with the text "Blessed are they that mourn for they shall be comforted".

The right hand light has an angel with an anchor at the top above the figure of Anna, a prophetess who was present when the Child Jesus was presented in the Temple (Luke Ch.ii.v.36). The panel below shows children being taught, with the texts "Blessed are the peacemakers children of God" and "Blessed are the pure in heart" above and below.

In 1890 James Insole married Marion Louise Carey at St.George's Hanover Square. He died in January 1901 at the age of 79, and in 1906 his widow gave the window which is in the south aisle next but one west from the Chapter House in his memory. By design or coincidence it is directly across the Cathedral from the Dixon window which commemorates his first wife.

The subject of this window is the Crucifixion with Christ flanked by His Mother and St John, but an extra allegorical dimension is added by the inclusion, at the foot of the Cross, of the figures of Eve and the Serpent recalling the account of the Fall in chapter 3 of Genesis. In the background is the City of Jerusalem and in the quatrefoils at the head of the window the sun and moon are darkened as described in St Luke Ch.xxiii.

The glass is the work of James Silvester Sparrow (1862-1929) and it is worth quoting what Martin Harrison has to say about this artist in his book *Victorian Stained Glass*:

> ...his stained glass is always very dark and dense, with a brooding fin-de-siècle atmosphere to it – he liked to refer to himself immodestly as 'The Wagner of Stained Glass'. The density of his windows was partially due to his fondness for "plating" glass, that is, sandwiching together two pieces of glass of different colours in the same (very wide) leads, a method much frowned upon by the purist craftsmen but which certainly enabled Sparrow to achieve some stunning effects.

The window which is now in the south aisle immediately east of the south door is a memorial to three members of the Thomas family of Llwyn Madoc in Breconshire. It is by Burlison & Grylls and was installed in 1909 in the window space directly across the Cathedral which now opens into the St David Chapel. During the post-war restoration the architect, George Pace, wishing to keep that window clear, relocated this glass to its present position. Unfortunately, by so doing, he destroyed the link between the memorial glass and the related wall memorial by John Prichard and Henry Armstead which was below it. There is a further twist to the history of this particular memorial window: it was itself a

The crucifixion window by Sparrow in the north aisle

replacement for an earlier window in the same opening in the north aisle, in memory of Henry Thomas, which was apparently the work of Michael O'Connor and which was alleged to have 'faded'. Miss Clara Thomas, who arranged for the substitution of the new glass for the old, removed the old glass from the Cathedral and its fate is unknown.

As might be expected for a family which had numerous links with the legal profession, this window abounds with allusions to the law and the administration of justice. The two regal figures which flank Christ carry, on the left, a book and a sheathed sword and, on the right, a book and an orb. The small winged angels in the three top quatrefoils bear a trumpet, a sword and the Scales of Justice.

The remaining two pre-war windows are both in the Dyfrig Chapel, the first being the east window given by Sir William Thomas Lewis, Bart. in memory of his wife. He submitted two designs for the Chapter's consideration early in 1910 and, with minor amendments, the design by C. Powell of Highgate was accepted, manufactured and installed by the end of July in the same year.

The window takes as its theme the traditional Celtic Saints of South Wales. In the left hand light the figure of St Teilo, one of the three Celtic patron saints of this Cathedral, is shown robed as a bishop and carrying a model of his church on his left hand. In his right hand he holds his episcopal crozier and the golden bell which legend has it that he received as a gift in Jerusalem whilst there on pilgrimage with St David and St Padarn. The small scene at the foot of this light depicts Teilo as a monk discussing the plans of his college church; the Arms in the lower left hand corner are those of Sir William Lewis. The centre light shows St Tydfil. Elvan, in company with Medwy, were the two messengers who, according to legend, were dispatched to Pope Eleutherius in AD 156 by King Lucius who was seeking to become a Christian. St Elvan, robed as a bishop, appears in the right hand light of this window above a picture of his baptism and ordination by Eleutherius. Medwy rates inclusion only in the small upper light, second from the left.

St Dyfrig, widely held to be the first Bishop of Llandaff, another patron saint of this Cathedral to whom this chapel is dedicated, also appears in one of the upper lights to the right of Medwy. Tradition holds that Dyfan and Fagan who occupy the two remaining upper lights were also active in spreading Christianity in the area which we now know as Glamorgan. At the head of the window are two small panels with crossed keys to indicate St Peter and the crossed swords, St Paul, the principal Patrons of this Cathedral since Norman times.

The adjacent window in the north wall of this chapel continues the Celtic theme, this time with Kings. This glass was also made by C. Powell of Highgate. The proposal to place this window came from the Hon. Mrs Green, wife of Archdeacon Green (who in later life was to be Archbishop of Wales). Mrs Green was a daughter of Sir William Lewis in whose memory this window was installed. The window was dedicated on 6th December 1920 and, together with its companion in this chapel, was removed for safe keeping in 1940.

Two other windows survived the bombing, both in the north wall of the Lady Chapel and by Geoffrey Fuller Webb. These two windows will be dealt with when all the glass in that Chapel, most of which is post-war, is reviewed as a complete scheme.

Wartime Losses

Although the programme of removal saved twelve of the windows, at least twenty more of the Cathedral's stained glass windows were destroyed on the night of the bombing in 1941. No detailed photographs exist of any of them and explicit written descriptions exist for very few.

Perhaps the most substantial loss of glass was that of the four lancets which grace the west front of the Cathedral – four, because the upper light which now opens into the nave roof space, was visible from within the building prior to the reintroduction of a nave ceiling during the post-war restoration.

Strangely, for glass in such a dominant position, these four panels were not all designed by the same hand or installed at the same time. The two centre lights were the first to appear and their dedication on July 1st 1899, and their design, was reported at length in the Llandaff *Diocesan Magazine* of September 1899.

The design of the large central light, the gift of Mr Clark of Talygarn in memory of Dean Conybeare, represented as its main subject our Lord, seated in glory and robed as Priest and King, ruling over the world, with His right hand extended in the attitude of invitation, whilst His left hand held the regal orb, surmounted by the Cross, as the symbol of universal sovereignty. He was seated on the great white throne, whilst behind Him was figured the rainbow, as symbolical of divine reconciliation with Mankind. Above were two angels in the attitude of adoration, whilst at the top was shown the Holy Spirit as a Dove.

Below were other angels, the one holding a sword, and the other a trumpet. In the lowest panel Dean Conybeare is represented in a kneeling posture at a desk upon which is a book opened before him at Psalm 1, verse 1, whilst a suitable inscription in his memory completes the picture. This light was made by Mr P Powell, of London.

The upper light, the gift of Sir Edward Hill of Rookwood, represented the Angel of the Everlasting Gospel, as described in the Book of Revelation, proclaiming from mid-heaven the divine message to the whole world. Mr J.P. Seddon, of London, was the artist of the upper light.

It was not until December of 1900 that the remaining two lancets of the west front were to receive their stained glass. The light on the north side was installed

*A rare image of the west window from the pre-war
period*

in memory of the late Dean Williams, who completed the restoration of the
Cathedral. It represented Nehemiah superintending the building of the walls of
Jerusalem. He was shown giving instructions to the chief workmen, some of
whom were standing by with their arms at hand. Both below and above this
panel were large figures of angels, in the former case holding with outstretched
arms a scroll bearing the following text: "For the builders, every one had his
sword girded by his side, and so builded. And he that sounded the trumpet was
by me."

The other angel held a model of the church to symbolise the special work of
the late Dean, as being connected with the restoration of the Cathedral, and the
church building of the Diocese. This window is the gift of Mr Seddon, the
Cathedral Architect.

The window on the south side was a memorial raised by public subscription
to the honour of the late Mr Jonas Watson, of Llandaff, and the picture in its
panel was illustrative of the text in Ezra Ch.viii v.36:

And they delivered the King's commissions unto the King's lieutenants, and to the governors on this side of the river: and they furthered the people and the house of God.

Similar angels to those described in the other light appeared above and below this panel and both were surmounted by rich canopy work, and surrounded by ornamental scroll work, etc. Both these windows were from the designs of Mr J.P. Seddon, and were drawn and executed by Mr H.G. Murray, artist, of London.

Beneath the Jasper Tower, lighting what is now the Illtyd Chapel, was a window given in 1920 by Mrs Insole in memory of her husband George Frederick Insole. The glass did not include any inscription but Dean David Jones in one of his invaluable notebooks recorded that there was a brass plate below the cill reading:

TO THE GLORY OF GOD IN LOVING MEMORY OF
GEORGE FREDERICK INSOLE
BORN NOVEMBER 18 1847 DIED FEBRUARY 11 1917

A description of the glass, together with an illustration, appeared in *The Architect* on 21st January 1921, which reads as follows:

We give here a reproduction of a fine example of the Stained-glass Worker's craft in the window recently unveiled in Llandaff Cathedral: This large stained-glass window – by Mr Felix Joubert of Chelsea, who in both his design and colour scheme here has been under the influence of the art of the 'cinquecento' – has been erected to the late George Frederick Insole by his widow.

The central subject here represents the Saviour in the moment of His Passion, standing with bound hands and an expression of resigned sadness, while the cloak, of rich ruby diapered with the pomegranate, is falling from his bared shoulders. Before Him is a parapet with carved columns; and on his either side are the kneeling figures, to right and left, of St George of England in medieval armour, and St David of Wales in the robes of an Archbishop wearing the mitre and holding his pastoral staff: Behind these figures are grouped adoring Angels, and the landscape background, with stone-pines and Cyprus trees outlined against the sky, shows again the attraction of the Italian primitives, noticeably of the fresco paintings of Benozzo Gozzoli.

One feels that the design of this window must have been influenced in no small degree by the death in action at Arras on 12th April 1918 of Captain George Claude Latham Insole MC., at the age of 30. It is also significant that a

A drawing for the Joubert window

wall memorial to Captain Insole was placed on the north wall of what is now the Illtyd Chapel. This was also by Joubert and was in the form of a winged angel holding Captain Insole's inverted sword. The figure and the sword are lost but the inscribed bronze plate which was affixed below is currently held in the Cathedral Archive.

The window in the south wall of the St Teilo Chapel was given in 1864 by Mrs Purchase of Ynysgored. The theme of this glass was 'The Miracles of Our Lord' and was manufactured by Lavers & Barraud from a design by John Seddon. It seems from entries in the Chapter Act Book that Mrs Purchase had originally wished to place the glass in one of the other south windows to which the Chapter regretted that "they cannot comply with Mrs Purchase's request as to the alteration of the window as the aisle windows of the Cathedral will eventually require reconstructing and it may be desirable when painted glass is used in these windows that some continuous design be adopted." It seems that this expressed hope of producing a cohesive window scheme for the aisles failed to materialise.

R.J. King, writing in his *Handbook to the Cathedrals of Wales*, indicates that the window immediately west of the Chapter House, in the south aisle in the opening now occupied by the Morris window depicting David, St Stephen and Samuel, was by Clayton & Bell. An entry dated 16th September 1861 recorded that... "permission be given to Sir John D. Harding to put a painted Glass window in the Cathedral in memory of his late father who for thirteen years represented the Clergy as Proctor in Convocation". This window was executed by Clayton & Bell under Mr Seddon's superintendence and from his design which he admitted was not successful. There is a small and not very clear colour sketch for one panel of this window in the collection of Seddon drawings in the Victoria and Albert Museum. This glass was originally in the opening immediately south of the Pulpitum arch.

Records confirm that the remaining window openings in the south aisle also held stained glass but such information as remains fails to pin down the actual location of the two for which any description survives. J.E. Ollivant, son of Bishop Ollivant, in a footnote to an unpublished paper on the Cathedral now in the Cathedral Archive, notes that there was "one by Lavers & Barrault not very pleasing given by the Conybeare family", whilst a report of a break-in to the Cathedral in July 1893 says that... "the window through which a burglarious entry was made into the Cathedral was placed in memory of the late Mrs William Bruce by Canon Bruce of Brynderwen by whom the cost of its restoration would be borne." This was probably one of the two windows below the Prichard Tower.

Twentieth Century Glass

The involvement of Geoffrey Fuller Webb with the Lady Chapel at Llandaff, starting in 1909 and ending only with his death in January 1954, deserves a booklet of its own, and even in this account of his windows at Llandaff we must look to more than the glass if we are to fully appreciate Webb's contribution to the appearance of the Cathedral at the end of the twentieth century. Fortunately two windows that he had completed prior to the Second World War were among those that were removed for safe keeping.

The son of E.A. Webb FSA and nephew of Sir Aston Webb PRA, PRIBA, Geoffrey was born in 1879 and was educated at Rugby and Westminster Art School. His introduction to stained glass was in the studio of C.E. Kempe, but after a short partnership with Herbert Bryans he set up his own studio in East Grinstead. He was widely read, an accomplished Herald, a devout Roman

Left: The Annunciation; and expulsion from Eden.
Right: The Virgin Mary greets Elizabeth; and Zacharias in the Temple.

Catholic with a profound knowledge of the scriptures and of the legends of the saints.

In 1908 the Archdeacon of Llandaff offered to pay for the re-furbishment of the walls and ceiling of the Lady Chapel, and in consultation with F.R. Kempson, the Cathedral Architect, the Dean and Chapter engaged Geoffrey Webb to design and execute the decoration of the walls and ceiling of the chapel.

Left: The presentation in the Temple; and Adoration of the Magi.
Right: The flight into Egypt; and The first miracle at Cana.

The contract with Webb for the work was signed in April 1909 with a specified completion date of November in the same year.

Webb subsequently produced for the Dean and Chapter, in agreement with Kempson, a design scheme for the six side windows of this chapel and discussed a design for glass in its east window. He later revised this scheme in a letter to the Dean on January 20th 1926 in response to an invitation to design and install a memorial window to Mrs Elize Nixon in the westernmost opening of the Lady Chapel north wall. That window was complete within nine months. The main subject of the window is the Annunciation of the Archangel Gabriel to the Blessed Virgin Mary. Beneath them is a circle running through the two lights representing the expulsion of Adam and Eve from Eden. The position of the two angels is also intended to be symbolic. In the Annunciation picture the Archangel approaches up the Chapel facing towards the Altar. In the Expulsion from Eden, the Angel drives Adam and Eve westwards, away from the east. In the top circle is a half figure of the Prophet Isaiah holding a scroll with the words 'Ecce Virgo Concipiet' (behold a virgin shall conceive). The memorial inscription and the heraldry of the donor, Baron Merthyr, appear in the base.

The central window in the north wall of the Lady Chapel was the next to appear. The two main figures represent the Blessed Virgin on the left in blue who is being greeted by St Elizabeth. Above the head of the Blessed Virgin is a scroll bearing the words from Luke Ch.i v.46 *Magnificat anima mea Dominum* (My soul doth magnify the Lord) and above St.Elizabeth another with the words *Benedicta tu inter mulieres* (Blessed art thou among women). At the foot of these two figures are four little angels playing modern musical instruments, violin and cello on the left, clarinet and flute on the right.

Below this is a picture which shows the Archangel Gabriel appearing to St Elizabeth's husband, the Priest Zacharias, before the Altar of Incense. The Archangel Gabriel has one finger to his lips and the other points to Zacharias indicating that he is to be dumb. At the base of the window is the memorial inscription which is flanked by two military badges, on the Dexter side that of the Welch Regiment, and on the Sinister, the Scots Guards.

At the head of each light are two heraldic achievements, on the Dexter side the arms of the Baronetage of Forrest, a shield which bears, argent on a mount in base vert three oak trees proper, with an oak tree for crest rising from the helm, and the motto below *Vivant dum virent*. On the Sinister side the shield of W.R.H. Forrest's college, Eton, supported by two angels. Above the two lights is a circular piece of tracery containing a half figure of the Prophet Jeremiah holding a scroll bearing the words of his prophecy *Suscitabo David germen justam* (I will raise unto David a righteous branch). Both of these windows by Webb were amongst those which were taken out in 1940 and which were replaced in their original positions during the post-war restoration.

Over the years prior to 1941 several attempts were made to place other memorial glass in the east window but they came to nothing and Willement's glass was not amongst that which was removed prior to the bombing and consequently was totally lost.

Soon after his installation as Dean in July 1948 Glyn Simon, together with Sir Charles Nicholson the Cathedral's Architect, took the decision to implement a scheme, first mooted in 1936, to relocate the Rossetti Triptych, which formed the reredos to the high altar, thus leaving the great Norman arch unimpeded and allowing the whole length of the Cathedral to be open to view. This posed a problem which Dean Simon set out in a letter dated 12 January 1949 to Webb:

> As you have put in two stained glass windows in the Lady Chapel, I wonder whether you would be prepared to meet me and discuss possible schemes for a east window there and also for windows on the south side opposite the two you have put in on the north side.
>
> The main necessity in the east window is that as it is unlikely that we shall have a high reredos behind the High Altar,... whatever stained glass there is there should have the effect of blocking or deadening the extremely bright light that will be coming through this window, and make it impossible for worshippers to see what is going on at the High Altar. It occurs to me that a possible subject for this window might be the Triumph of the Saints with Our Lady as the central figure, supported by St Peter and St Paul with St Teilo and St Dochwy.

Webb replied with alacrity on 14 January welcoming the invitation and suggesting

> ...one other subject which comes to mind, because Mr Kempson [the then Cathedral Architect] discussed it with me in 1910. It is the Tree of Jesse...

A Jesse tree is a representation of Christ's family tree, tracing the royal roots of Jesus from Jesse, who was the father of King David. Dean Simon acquiesced with Webb's suggestion and a Jesse window it became. This east window had not been part of Webb's grand design of 1926 probably because it was still filled with Willement's nineteenth century glass, but he now designed and installed a window fully in keeping with the spirit of that scheme. Fortunately, Dean Simon was able to secure funding for this, the largest of the Cathedral's windows, from the family of Sir William and Lady Reardon Smith in their memory.

In the 1951 Annual Report of The Friends Dean Simon wrote the following footnote about Jesse windows, and described the proposed

> ...heraldry in our new window is as follows: In the heads of the main lights, looking from north to south, Llandaff (on a metropolitical cross to commemorate the archiepiscopal status of its Bishop when the window was put in), Glamorgan, Reardon Smith, and Monmouth. Above are the arms of Prichard and Ollivant.

All of Webb's windows are full of information and symbolism, returning to the traditional use of stained glass as a teaching aid. This east window, which depicts the traditional figures to be found in such glass, is no exception, and

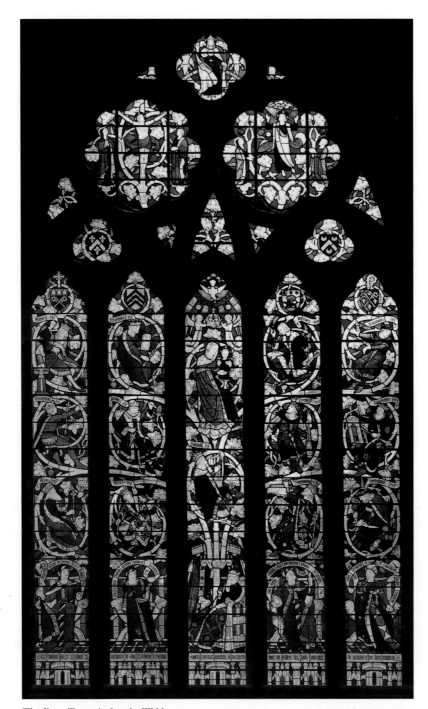

The Jesse Tree window by Webb

Details from the Jesse Tree window

again we are fortunate in having, in the Cathedral Archive, the artist's own written description to call upon:

> The TREE OF JESSE with the list of Kings from the first chapter of St.Matthew's Gospel, omitting Manasses and Amon after Hezekiah.

Jesse appears at the bottom of the central light of this window and is flanked by four Old Testament prophets who foretold the coming of a Messiah; from left to right, Isaiah, Jeremiah, Ezechiel and Daniel. Above Jesse in the central light is David, the psalmist, playing his harp whilst looking upward to the Christ Child who stands on his mother's knee. In the four side lights are twelve Old Testaments kings, with the just and good kings looking toward the Christ Child whilst the others turn or look away. They are Solomon, Rehoboam, Abijah, Asa, Jehosaphat, Jehoram, Uzziah, Jotham, Ahaz, Hezekiah, Josiah and Jehoiachin. Two circular lights at the top of the window show the Crucifixion and the Ascension.

Two further windows by Geoffrey Webb followed on the south side of the Lady Chapel. Given by the Llandaff Diocesan Mothers' Union, they were dedicated on 20 May 1953 and conform once again to Webb's 1926 scheme. By this time however, war damage had taken its toll of the ceiling decoration, with substantial areas of plaster having been dislodged and it is doubtful if Webb, by now a sick man, saw the south side windows installed. At the time of his death on 20 January 1954, he was working on designs for the two easternmost windows of the Lady Chapel which, departing from his master plan, were to have contained heraldic glass. Once again the artist's descriptions of the two Mothers' Union windows are in the Cathedral Archive.

Firstly the centre of the three south wall windows. The main subject is the Presentation of Our Lord in the Temple. This is represented by two large figures, each 5 feet high, of Our Lady in the left light and Simeon in the right light holding in his arms the Holy Child. Below this subject is a scene, drawn to a smaller scale, of the three Magi in the left light offering their gifts to the Holy Child, who is standing on the knee of His mother. One of the Magi points to a star resting above the roof of the house which frames the picture.

In the heads of the two lights above the main picture of The Presentation are two shields. In the left light is the shield of the Mothers' Union and at the head of the right light is a shield taken from a medieval device which refers to the words of Simeon "Yea a sword shall pierce through thine own soul also".

The other Mothers' Union window in the south wall of the Lady Chapel has as its theme the flight into Egypt of the Holy Family. St Joseph holding his bag of carpenters' tools in his right hand and his staff in his left, walks beside a donkey on which Our Lady, holding the Christ Child, is seated. The subject with the smaller figures in the base of this window is the miracle at the marriage at Cana in Galilee. In this window, as in all his windows in Llandaff, Webb has hidden his rebus (punning trademark) in the form of a small and insignificant spider's web.

When the time came in 1958 to restore the Lady Chapel, the decision was made to whiten the walls and ceiling – with the exception of the ceiling bosses – obliterating what remained of Webb's decorative work. It was not until 1988 that, thanks to a generous bequest, it was possible to commission the restoration of the 1909 wall and ceiling designs. Sufficient of that work remained under the whitening to allow Peter Larkworthy to accurately reproduce nearly all of Webb's creation. Some decoration on the upper part of the east wall has been omitted as has the Latin wording of the Magnificat which used to form the dado band above the wall designs. Thus, what now exists represents the summation of Geoffrey Webb's grand design of 1926, a sight he sadly did not live to see.

The window grouping directly above the high altar is undoubtedly the most striking glass in Llandaff Cathedral. Designed by John Piper and executed by Patrick Reyntiens, it was installed in September 1959 as a replacement for the window by Michael O'Connor described above, dating from 1859 and which perished at the time of the bombing in 1941.

It takes as its subject 'The Supper at Emmaus' and Piper's handling and interpretation of that theme were well expounded by Professor W. Moelwyn Merchant in an address which was reproduced in the 27th Annual Report of The Friends of Llandaff Cathedral, and his words cannot be bettered.

> 'The Supper at Emmaus' has clear propriety as the subject of the window which presides over the main altar of the Cathedral. In the roundel above the main theme, there is a formal suggestion of the figures walking to Emmaus; the central design had a more difficult problem to solve; to unite, across the strong verticals of the window which divide it into three panels a single subject of intense emotion, as the disciples "knew Him in the breaking of bread." Christ occupies the whole of the centre panel, His hand raised in a gesture which is at once blessing and consecration; the two disciples fill the side panels, their gestures conveying their wonder and recognition, and in the depths of the intense light and colour we may see the chalice and its wine. We shall not expect the figures to be representational, even to the extent that paint or carved stone can 'represent'. This is the form man may well have taken if God had chosen to create him not out of flesh and blood but out of this stranger material of glass, brittle, angular, but beautiful in form and colour. This is a metamorphosis the creative artist alone dare attempt, and this window is a humble triumph of creation.

One of the great joys of this window is the way in which, on a sunny morning, it casts great pools of brilliantly coloured light on to the stone floor of the Choir.

John Piper's window above the high altar

Acquired Glass

The Cathedral possesses four collections of glass that were acquired from various sources for incorporation in the restored building.

The Chapter House has eleven windows on its two floors, at least six of which were filled with stained glass from the late 1860s, all of which were destroyed in 1941, and about which nothing is known. The present ground floor windows, although filled largely with plain leaded glass, now include a sequence of seven small roundels of painted glass depicting the events of Holy Week. They are thought to be of Swiss or German origin dating from the early nineteenth century, and were given to the Cathedral by Mr and Mrs Hoskens in 1951. To make sense of the series, these roundels need to be examined starting to one's right as one enters the Chapter House and moving in anti-clockwise. The first window contains only clear leaded glass whilst the second window in the west wall holds a single roundel depicting Christ's entry into Jerusalem. The right hand window in the south wall has two roundels, the lower one showing the Last Supper and the upper one illustrating Christ's appearance before Herod. The other window in the south wall again has two roundels, the lower one depicting the road to Calvary and the upper the Crucifixion. Both windows in the east wall hold one roundel, the right hand one showing Christ's body anointed for burial and the left hand window illustrating the Ascension. It seems likely, given the apparent gaps in the narrative, these seven roundels were once part of a larger series.

In 1955 the Friends of Llandaff Cathedral acquired seven small panels of early seventeenth century glass depicting plants, animals and birds which had come from Hale Hall in Lancashire. These they had installed in the second window from the west in the south aisle as a memorial to the Very Reverend David John Jones who had been Dean between 1931 and 1948, and who had been responsible for the foundation of the Friends in 1933. Nothing further is at present known about this glass.

Above the caskets which hold the Welch Regiment's Rolls of Honour in the David Chapel are eight panels of what is thought to be sixteenth century French glass. This glass was given for incorporation into the new Welch Regimental Chapel by Lady Florence Bradney, Miss Evelyn Clarke and Miss Margaret Prothero in memory of Miss Prothero's two brothers Captain Mike Lewis Prothero and Colonel Arthur George Prothero. Each panel is 31 inches high and 22.5 inches wide, five of the panels containing single figures depicting Moses, David, Isaiah, Jeremiah and Baruch whilst the remaining panels are more fragmentary and represent portions of groups of figures.

In the upper room of the Prebendal House, in one of the north wall windows, is an oval panel which contains the Arms of Dean William Daniel Conybeare which was given to the Cathedral by Sir Cennydd Traherne.

Conclusion

Strange as it may seem, it is the windows which have no coloured glass which George Pace used to greatest effect in his restoration of the war damaged Cathedral. It is his placing of clear glass at strategic points which brings to the building the feeling of lightness and spaciousness which was so lacking in the pre-war Cathedral.

Epstein's figure of the Majestas is able to look out into the world beyond the walls through the plain west lancets and the nave altar in the space below the pulpitum is flooded with light from the south. The high altar gains light from both north and south as does also the sanctuary of the Lady Chapel.

This was all part of a very deliberate plan on the part of the Architect, involving as it did the relocation of some of the glass which had been saved, and future generations must guard with care this hard won balance of light which so enhances the appearance of the interior of the building.

The Bells of Llandaff Cathedral

The *Book of Llandaff* relates Teilo's pilgrimage, in company with David and Padarn, to Jerusalem where he was raised to the episcopate and presented with a bell that possessed sweetness of tone "exceeding every organ" and wonderful properties to both heal and judge. Presumably this bell would have somewhat resembled a cow bell in size and shape, but of all the various illustrations of Teilo's bell which can be found in the Cathedral only that on one of the two Churchwarden's staves, designed by George Pace, is of that form. The bell that Teilo carries in the east window of the Dyfrig chapel owes more to the designers of school handbells than to Celtic art, whilst Frank Roper's panel at the Teilo tomb shows a bell of such a size that it would have needed the combined strength of all three saints to have lifted it, much less carry it from Jerusalem to Llandaff! The fourth illustration, which is on the font designed by Alan Durst, is presumably intended to depict an early tower bell.

In Browne Willis' description of Llandaff Cathedral in 1717, there is a reference to a supposed exchange of bells between Llandaff and Exeter in 1484, and to the ruins of the medieval bell tower that still overlook the Cathedral:

> At about forty yards distant from this (south-west) tower South-West from the church, stood heretofore an old tower, which, as appears by the ruins was 42 foot square; the door which stood to the south of the Church is 13 foot high and seven foot broad. In it as tis reported, there formerly hung a very large bell call'd St Peter's Bell; which being taken down by Jasper Duke of Bedford, was conveyed to Exeter, and there exchanged for five bells which were hung up in Jasper's Tower.

Unfortunately there is no documentary evidence to support this tradition either at Llandaff or at Exeter although a version of the story was certainly current in Exeter during the late eighteenth century.

The first written evidence of bells at Llandaff, dating from about 1554, is amongst the records of church goods and properties appropriated at the time of the suppression of the monasteries. There is reference to a Sanctus bell of double silver gilt and to "ropes for six bells" being removed from Llandaff Cathedral. Among the complaints listed in this document is the statement "that there be two of the bells broken and decayed". This is only some seventy-five years after the building of the Jasper Tower, which housed the bells in 1485. By 1670 another document asserted that Llandaff then had five bells.

On page 69 of Browne Willis's survey of 1719 there is reference to William

The ruins of the medieval bell tower

Murray, Bishop of Llandaff 1627-1640, as follows:

> In the second year of his promotion (to the See of Llandaff) it was that the three least bells – one or two of which are now cracked were cast, there being on every one of them this inscription "Anno Secondo Translationis Guilielmi Murray Episcopi landaven 1629 I.P."

The initials I.P. refer to the bellfounder John Pennington who was operating in Exeter. Thus here might be the possible source of the tradition regarding the exchange of bells in the fifteenth century referred to above. Browne Willis continues:

> Of the five bells hanging in the Cathedral of Landaff 3 if not 4 were new cast [ie Recast] in the time of Bishop William Murray Anno 1629. On the fourth there is no inscription and on the fifth or biggest this:-

The new bells, cast in 1992, ranged across the nave, awaiting their hallowing by the Bishop

> "Franc.Davies Lord Bishop Edward Gamage Archdeacon, Let my sound
> move thee to God's Glory R.A.F.B.1672".

The initials R.A.F.B. do not denote any of the known bell founders of the time
and their significance remains unknown – donor or donors perhaps?

The Chapter Act Book records that, at their meeting on 27th June 1696, the
Chapter

> Ordered that the Great Bell which lately fell down in the steeple of The
> Cathedral be set up and fixed in its place as formerly and the clock be put
> to strike thereupon.

The clock is first mentioned in 1695 when William Hammond was paid seven
shillings for work on the bell wheel, the clock and the tower. It was superceded
by the present mechanism in the nineteenth century, and was presented to the
National Museum of Wales after the Second World War. It now in the museum's
reserve collection.

By 1707, according to Browne Willis, the smallest bell together with another
of the bells which were cast in 1629 by I.P. were both cracked. At its Petertide
meeting in 1727 the Chapter ordered its Proctor General "to get the little bell
which is crazed to be new cast". This was duly done, and the accounts for 1728

record the removal, casting by Evan Evans II and William Evans of Chepstow, and its return to Llandaff. Evan Evans set up business in 1686 as a bell founder in Chepstow, casting bells for a number of South Wales churches:

For taking down the little bell and mending the Door of the Pro:Genll's room	00.00.08
For weighing the bell and carrying it to Cardiff	00.02.00
For Casting the Bell	05.05.08
For weighing & porterage of ye new bell from Chepstow Hither.	00.04.06
To Walter Williams for hanging ye little bell and Mending ye wheel of ye great bell.	01.10.04
A rope for ye little bell	00.03.01½
Edwd. William for a chain to ye little bell and their Journey.	00.04.00

The inscription on this newly recast bell was: "INTER OMNES PAX E.E. W.E. 1727."

This bell was to survive in the Jasper Tower until 1890 when it was given to the newly built church of All Saints in Llandaff Yard (now known as Llandaff North). Unfortunately, on the night of January 2nd 1941, this church also suffered during the blitz that so grievously damaged the Cathedral. All Saints was gutted by fire and its bell melted.

In 1736 it was the largest of the five bells that suffered damage as Thomas Davies, the Registrar and Chapter Clerk, described in a letter:

Last Fryday as our sexton was tolling the first time for Evening Prayer, our great bell cracked; soe that now we have no whole bell (but a little one): the loss thereof is much lamented by the neighbourhood because it was a bell of a fine note and was heard at a great distance.

On 28th June 1738 the Chapter

Ordered their Proctor General to cause the Great Bell… wch is now crazed to be new cast… and that it may be made into such a Tenor as may cover a peal of 5 or 6 bells.

Bearing in mind the poor response that the Chapter were encountering in their efforts to fund the restoration of the Cathedral itself, it is remarkable that they were clearly envisaging a continuing programme of bell restoration and that some form of change-ringing was in view. The recasting was undertaken by William Evans of Chepstow at a total cost of £24.6s.2d – which included generous payments for "Ale for the labourers"!

Alas! This new bell – or its hanging – gave trouble from the outset and regular sums appear in the accounts for remedial work. Cathedral finances became ever tighter as attempts were made to repair the fabric and in 1758, at their Petertide meeting, the Chapter "ordered that the cracked Bells in Jasper's Tower be taken down and sold and the money arising from the sale applied to the repairs to the Fabrick". It took some five years before the Chapter received £176.10.2½ from the sale of some two and a half tons of bell metal.

In 1777 the Chapter ordered another recast of this bell, but it was another five years before a contract was entered into with the Rudhall foundry in Gloucester for the work to proceed. The bell was taken down in September 1782 and returned to the tower in early March of the following year. The total cost of recasting and rehanging was £69.03.11 of which £1.14.05 was spent on ale! It would seem that, in the light of the problems that had arisen with the previous recasting, Mr Rudhall was made to wait for 10% of his money! This bell survived, albeit retuned and rehung (as we shall see) in 1879 and 1953, until its metal was recast in 1992 to form the present Tenor bell. Its 1782 inscription was preserved in facsimile on the 1992 Tenor.

For a period of nearly a century the Cathedral continued to possess only two bells, the small one cast by Evans in 1727 and the Rudhall bell of 1782, but as the nineteenth century progressed a restored Cathedral arose. Dean Thomas Williams (Dean 1857-1877) had been in touch with bellfounders and when the question of bells was raised at the celebrations that accompanied the opening of the restored Cathedral, he said that the "the Bells would come in the course of time".

Dean Williams died in 1877 and the idea was quickly born of launching an appeal to provide a peal of bells as his memorial. A committee was formed and approaches were made to several bellfoundries but in the event it was only the Mears & Stainbank (Whitechapel) Bellfoundry and Taylors of Loughborough who reached the stage of submitting firm and costed proposals. The proposition was that the Rudhall bell would be incorporated in a new peal of eight bells but that the small bell would not, being retained in the tower. Scheme 1 was for a peal with a tenor bell of about 30 cwt using the Rudhall bell as the seventh, whilst scheme 2 was for a lighter peal using the existing bell, which weighed about 23½ cwt and was tuned to F, as the tenor bell.

On 7th May 1878 the Chapter decided that the existing bell should be the Tenor of the new peal and that Messrs Mears and Stainbank should be invited to submit a firm tender for the work. In August of the same year the Chapter Clerk was ordered to draw up a contract with the foundry and the new bells were dedicated on 15th April 1879. The tenor bell had been retuned, and therefore made lighter. The details of the bells were as follows:-

Bell	Weight	Diameter	Note
Treble	6cwt 1qr 4lb	2ft 6½ in	E-Flat

Inscription
> MEARS & STAINBANK, FOUNDERS, LONDON, 1879.
> IN GLORIAM DEI ET IN PIAM MEMORIAM
> THOMAE WILLIAMS A.M. HUJUSCE
> ECCLESIAE CATHEDRALIS DECANI.
> AMICI PONI CURAVERUNT 1877.

2	6cwt 3qr 10lb	2ft 7½ in	D

Inscription
> MEARS & STAINBANK, FOUNDERS, LONDON, 1879.
> ATTENDITE POPULI 1877.

3	7cwt 2qr 3lb	2ft 9½ in	C

Inscription
> MEARS & STAINBANK, FOUNDERS, LONDON, 1879.
> SURGITE VOS QUI PROCUL ESTIS 1877.

4	8cwt 3qr 8lb	2ft 11½ in	B-Flat

Inscription
> MEARS & STAINBANK, FOUNDERS, LONDON, 1879.
> VIGITATE ET ORATE 1877.

5	10cwt 1qr 2llb	3ft 2½ in	A-Flat

Inscription
> MEARS & STAINBANK, FOUNDERS, LONDON, 1879.
> SURSUM CORDA 1877.

6	12cwt 2qr 4lb	3ft 4½ in	G

Inscription
> MEARS & STAINBANK, FOUNDERS, LONDON, 1879.
> JUBILATE DEO OMNIS TERRA
> SERVITE DOMINO IN LAETITIA 1877

7	16cwt 3qr 3lb	3ft 8½ in	F

Inscription
> MEARS & STAINBANK, FOUNDERS, LONDON, 1879
> CANTATE DOMINO CANTICUM NOVUM 1877.

Tenor	23cwt – approx.	4ft 1½ in	E-Flat

Inscription
> ME VOCANTE DOMINUS : VOCAT DE NOVO CONFLARI FECIT
> GERVASIUS POWELL L:L:B PROCTOR GENERALIS ANNO
> SALUTIS 1782
> ET CONSECRATIONIS RICARDI WATSON DOMINI EPISCOPI
> PRIMO

[Note the punctuation error in the first line]

Dean Williams was succeeded in June 1877 by Henry Lynch-Blosse but Dean Blosse died suddenly, in office, in February 1879. A new tower clock and carillon were installed in his memory in 1880. Both mechanisms were hand wound daily by the sexton.

In August 1919 the Dean reported to the Chapter that Mr John T. Duncan, of The Avenue, Llandaff, wished to add two bells and to pay for the whole peal to be put in proper order. Mears and Stainbank had quoted a sum of £252:3:4 for the new bells with a further £121 for repair work. This offer was gratefully accepted and by the November of that year the work was in progress and the service of dedication took place on 21st February 1920. The additional bells were mounted in a steel frame above the trebles of the old eight which remained in their oak frame. This was not an ideal arrangement as the ropes of the new bells were long and did not fall straight into the ringing chamber, making these new bells difficult to handle.

The details of the new bells were:

Treble	5cwt 6lb	G

Inscription

BEATUS POPULUS. CUJUS DOMINUS DEUS EJUS
AD PACEM CELEBRANDAM
DONO DEDIT
JOHANNES THOMAS DUNCAN,
LLANDAVIENSIS.
A.D. MDCCCCXIX
M & S LONDINI, FECERUNT

2	5cwt 3qr 17lb	F

Inscription

DOMINUS BENEDICET POPULO SUO IN PACE.
AD GRATIAS AGENDAS DEO,
QUI NOS ADJUVAVIT,
D.D.
JOHANNES THOMAS DUNCAN
CAROLO EDVARDO THOMA GRIFFITH
HUJUS ECCLESIAE CATHEDRALIS DECANO
A.D. MDCCCCXIX
M & S LONDINI, FECERUNT.

In 1937, there were misgivings about the state of the bells and Messrs Gillett and Johnston produced a scathing report that detailed defects in both the oak bell-frame and in many of the fittings as well as with the tuning and hanging of the two treble bells. Costings for what they considered necessary repairs were also included, but the outbreak of war in 1939 seems to have ruled out any serious consideration of the matter. Order No 1042 of 1940 Control of Noise (Defence) Order prohibited the sounding of any Church bell except to indicate that an enemy force were landing or attempting to land. So the Cathedral bells fell silent.

The war damage to the Cathedral in 1941 had no major effect on the Jasper Tower and its bells except for the breaking of the windows and the exposure of the clock and bells to several years of neglect. It was 1950 before consideration was given to the renovation of bells, clock and carillon and their state was not deemed to have been directly attributable to war damage! Initially the Friends of Llandaff Cathedral offered to bear the cost of their restoration but by July 1951 Dean Simon was able to report that the 53rd (Welsh) Division had agreed that the money to be spent on a memorial to the Division might be used to defray the cost of rehanging and maintenance of the bells as well as for the furnishing of a Memorial Chapel (the St Illtyd Chapel) beneath the tower. Reports with estimates of cost had been sought from the three principal bell foundries in the autumn of 1950 and in April 1951 the Dean was reporting to Chapter that he had had replies from both John Taylor and Co. and Messrs Mears and Stainbank. No record can be traced of any response from Gillett and Johnston.

In July 1951 the Chapter Act Book records that

> The estimates for the work to be done in connection with the rehanging of the Cathedral bells was considered, Mr Pace [the Cathedral Architect] was consulted upon the matter and was of the opinion that the lowest tender, that of Messrs Mears and Stainbank should be accepted. This was agreed.

The bells were removed to Whitechapel bell-foundry in January 1952, returned to Llandaff in February 1953 and were ready for ringing on 11th March 1953. The first occasion for which they were formally rung was the Coronation Day of Queen Elizabeth II.

The Victorian bells at rest in the cathedral grounds, prior to being taken to Whitechapel, January 1952

While at Whitechapel the bells had their canons removed, they had been retuned – the Tenor strike note had been raised from E-Flat to E – and 'one eighth turned' so that the clappers would strike on unworn parts of the bells.

The revised weights and tuning of the bells was as follows:-

Bell	Cwt	qr	lb	Note
Treble	5	0	14	G-Sharp
2	5	3	23	F-Sharp
3	6	0	0	E
4	6	1	2	D-Sharp
5	7	0	2	C-Sharp
6	8	0	19	B
7	9	2	16	A
8	11	3	0	G-Sharp
9	15	1	0	F-Sharp
Tenor	20	1	0	E

The clock was converted to be automatically electrically wound.

With a marked revival in the life of the Cathedral following its restoration, the bells were in regular and frequent use and maintenance was heavy. The difficulties in ringing the two lightest bells had not been addressed during the rehanging and this problem became increasingly acute, particularly as more young people were coming forward for training as bellringers. Problems with the oak frame were also developing which made the handling of the heavier bells unpredictable.

In January 1988 the Cathedral Ringers, at their Annual General Meeting, put it to the Dean, The Very Revd. Alun Davies, that the future of the bell installation should reviewed with the aim of undertaking a programme of remedial work before the bells became unringable or the band dispersed because of frustration. The Dean replied by asking for a detailed report which he could lay before the Cathedral Chapter.

Armed with very thorough and detailed reports from both Whitechapel Bellfoundry and Messrs Taylor, which agreed closely in their assessments, the ringers compiled a document which laid out the problems and the various options that were available. This recommended that the very least which should be done was the rehanging of the bells in a new metal frame in two tiers placed lower in the tower and that this frame should cater for future augmentation of the peal to twelve bells. It also recommended that this work should be completed within ten years. The report was submitted to Chapter in October 1988.

Following some preliminary discussions, the Tower Captain and the Tower Keeper were invited to make a formal presentation of their case to the Cathedral Finance Committee. This drew searching questions and a further meeting before the matter eventually went before the Cathedral Chapter. A small project group

The bells return to Llandaff from Whitechapel, February 1953

of ringers was immediately formed, to be quickly strengthened by the appointment of the Chapter Clerk as Chairman and the addition of representatives of
both the Cathedral Chapter and the Parish of Llandaff. Out of this committee
sprang a Technical Sub-committee chaired by the Tower Captain which was
charged with dealing with all the practical aspects of the projected work.

The Finance Committee indicated that a sum of £10,000 would be available
from their funds whilst the Friends of Llandaff Cathedral seemed likely to
contribute £20,000. The ringers suggested that by direct giving they would find
– including reclaimed tax from covenants – £12,000 and the Committee undertook to raise a further £10,000 from a variety of fund raising activities. The
Cathedral Ringers also undertook to dismantle the existing bells and frame, to
prepare the tower structure to receive the new bell-frames and to assist with the
hanging of the new bells.

In 1993 both the Llandaff Diocesan Mothers' Union and the Llandaff and
Monmouth Diocesan Association of Church Bell Ringers were to celebrate their
respective centenaries and both organisations readily agreed to sponsor one bell
each, suitably inscribed, to commemorate the occasion. A turning point in the
fund raising occurred when a bequest to the Friends, which was to be used
specifically for new work, was steered in the direction of the bells. This bequest
from the Estates of two sisters was worth over £20,000 and allowed the project
to be extended to the casting of a ring of twelve bells.

Whilst this fund raising was proceeding, the technical committee studied the proposals of the two major bell-foundries and paid an all-day visit to two brand new twelve bell installations, one from each foundry, talking at length to the local bands at St Martin-in-the-Fields in London and Leighton Buzzard, as well as ringing at each tower. The technical committee recommended that the Chapter should award the contract to the Whitechapel Bellfoundry for the work to be undertaken in 1992, in time for the centenary celebration and for the visit of the Central Council of Church Bell Ringers to Cardiff for their annual meeting in 1993.

The lay members of the committee had, in the meantime, been able to arrange for the substantial amount of foundation steelwork to be given and galvanised. A local churchman offered to assist in transporting the bells to the London foundry and to bring the new frame and bells back to Llandaff. These two gifts in kind represented a major contribution.

Further bells were sponsored by individuals, families and trusts and in April 1992, just before the work was scheduled to start, the Committee were sufficiently confident that funds were materialising well, that they felt justified in asking the foundry to add the flat sixth bell – allowing the ringing of a lighter weight ring of eight bells – to the casting list. A 'price only' item for this bell had been included in the contract at the outset in the hope that it would become possible to fund it.

Easter Sunday evening 1992 saw the last service ringing on the old ten bells (although they were chimed for a wedding on the following morning) and on the Monday morning an almost full turnout of the Cathedral ringers together with friends from other towers and from within Llandaff started the dirty task of stripping the bells of all their fittings ready for the lowering of the bells to commence once a powerful electric chain hoist had been installed. Using three additional manual chain hoists and not inconsiderable expertise the extraction of the bells proved to be a reasonably straightforward exercise. Each bell in turn, starting with the Tenor, was lowered 80 feet onto a pallet and was then moved on a fork-lift truck to a temporary parking spot in the north aisle of the Cathedral where the Cathedral congregation had a chance to see the bells at close hand for the first time in over a century.

This phase of the work was completed without incident by the end of the Wednesday and the removal of the bell frame followed. As this was being dismantled it became clear that several of the lower frame members, in areas previously hidden from view, had suffered substantial damage from beetle (deceased), woodworm and rot. Thus within the first week the tower had been cleared of everything except three floors, the clock and the carillon mechanism. The bells were winched up a specially constructed ramp through the west door and left for London on April 30.

Casting the tenor bell, above, and the 6, left

The foundry allocated two days for the casting of the new thirteen bells – which were to incorporate the metal of the old ten – the odd numbered bells being cast on 21 May 1992 and the remainder, including the flat sixth, on 2 July. On both occasions various donors were able to witness the casting of their particular bells and the Dean of Llandaff watched the casting of the new tenor bell. Each of the new bells is named for a Celtic saint with the three heaviest bearing the names of the Cathedral's patrons Teilo, Dyfrig and Euddogwy whilst the sixth, given by the Llandaff and Monmouth Diocesan Ringers, is named Gwynllyw (Woolos) for the patron saint of Llandaff's sister Cathedral in the Diocese of Monmouth.

Whilst this work was going forward at the bellfoundry, a group of stalwarts spent several evenings each week throughout the summer cutting out the 24 holes in the tower walls into which the steel foundation beams for the bell-frame would fit. Concrete support pads on which the steel foundation beams were to rest were then cast in each of these holes.

It had been planned to re-use the existing bellchamber floor by merely lowering it some 15 feet on to two steel joists which had been built in for the purpose, but once again major defects in all of the 12" by 14" oak supporting beams and the boarding of the old floor led to this plan being abandoned. At short notice a new floor was designed and constructed by the ringers, using timber from the Brunel Workshops in Swindon, in time to form the working platform from which the installation of the foundation steelwork could be undertaken in safety.

The steelwork for the upper level frame, together with its four bells (3, 5, 6 flat and 8) arrived on 9 October and the installation of the steelwork commenced at once. The steelwork for the lower level frame reached Llandaff on 27 October followed a day later by the nine remaining bells; once again a ramp through the West Door allowed ready movement of all this material into the Cathedral.

This lower frame was installed by the volunteer gang in two days and after the level and alignment of both frames had been checked by Phil Jakeman, the bellhanger from Whitechapel Foundry, all the frame foundation beams were grouted in by 6 November. Each of the beams had fitted snugly into their recesses and all were exactly horizontal – a tribute to the 'setting out' undertaken by the ringers.

On Saturday 21 November, at Cathedral Evensong, the Lord Bishop hallowed and named each bell as they stood ranged across the nave below the pulpitum. Monday the 23 November saw the commencement of the task of raising the bells into the tower and once again all went according to plan so that by lunchtime on the following day all the bells were in place. The fitting work was next and the bells were ready for their first trial ring by the Cathedral Band on Thursday 3 December. Minor works and adjustments took another week, but all was ready with the tower swept and garnished for the formal dedication of the

*The peal awaits hallowing and installation.,
above. Teilo is lifted into the bell tower, left*

work during Cathedral Evensong on Sunday 13 December at which Alan Hughes of the Whitechapel foundry formally handed the installation over to the Dean and the new bells rang out – officially – for the first time in the presence of a large congregation of ringers led by the President of the Central Council of Church Bell Ringers, and of parishioners and friends.

In 1988 it had been suggested that the work should be done within ten years – it was complete in four. It had cost £117,000 and had been paid for. The Cathedral Ringers had shown total commitment throughout and had been aided in the project by ringers from no less than ten other towers so that the voluntary work-force had numbered 60 people many of whom revealed – or acquired – a remarkable range of talents.

Detailed information about what was done to the bells in earlier times is often lost but this latest restoration of the Cathedral bells was documented and recorded in the greatest detail. Audio recordings were made of the last quarter peal rung on the old bells and the first quarter peal on the new. The activities of the Bell Restoration Committee and its technical committee were carefully minuted. Each phase of the work was carefully photographed but, most significantly, the progress of the work in all its aspects was recorded on video-tape –

The ringers in action

some fifteen hours of it – which now forms a part of the Cathedral Archive.

DETAILS OF THE BELLS CAST IN 1992

Treble BRIDGET B Flat 4cwt 3qr 1lb
The gift of Llandaff Diocesan Mothers' Union in its Centenary Year

2 TATHAN A Flat 5cwt 0qr 5lb
In Memory of Charles Edmund Bowen

3 ELLTEYRN G 5cwt 1qr 3lb
The Gift of the Baldwin Family

4 ELFAN F 5cwt 3qr 9lb
The Gift of The Ringing Exercise

5 TYDFIL E Flat 6cwt 1qr 26lb
The Gift of Captain Norman Lloyd Edwards,
Lord Lieutenant and Former Chapter Clerk

6 GWYNLLYW D 6cwt 2qr 9lb
The Gift of the Llandaff and Monmouth Diocesan
Association of Church Bell Ringers in its Centenary year

Flat 6 DEWI D Flat 7cwt 0qr 1lb
The Gift of the Llandaff Cathedral Guild of Change
Ringers, past and present

7 SAMSON C 7cwt 0qr 23lb
In Memory of George Gibson

8 CADOC B Flat 8cwt 2qr 14lb
The Gift of Arthur and Iris Sansom

9 ILLTYD A Flat 10cwt 0qr 16lb
In Memory of Sybil Eleanor Hatch

10 EUDDOGWY G 12cwt 0qr 0lb
In Memory of Alice May Hatch

11 DYFRIG F 16cwt 3qr 19lb
The Gift of the Friends of Llandaff Cathedral

Tenor TEILO E Flat 24cwt 1qr 15lb
(This bell carries the inscription of the former Tenor bell
which was last recast in 1782.)

Music at Llandaff Cathedral

O nostra templa, nostra sedes,	O holy towers, O happy bowers!
Landava! collis, vallis, sedes!	Llandaff, thy hill, thy vale, are ours!
Te laeti resonabimus,	Thee we hail with glad acclaim,
Grati te celebrabimus!	Joyful, grateful, sing thy name!
Quid si scholas vetustiores	What though more reverend seats of lore
Terunt pedes frequentiores?	Can show, of scholars, larger store?
Te laeti resonabimus,	Thee we hail with glad acclaim,
Grati te celebrabimus!	Joyful, grateful, sing thy name!
O noster amnis, O perennis	O ancient river, babbling near,
Jucunda veris vox Britannis!	With music sweet to Briton's ear!
Te laeti resonabimus,	Thee we hail with glad acclaim,
Grati te celebrabimus!	Joyful, grateful, sing thy name!
Te tempus omne cariorem	Time shall but win thee greater love,
Videbit et beatiorem!	And larger blessings from above!
Te lacti resonabimus,	Thee we hail with glad acclaim,
Grati te celebrabimus!	Joyful, grateful, sing thy name!

The words of *Carmen Landavense* written by Dean Vaughan as a paean of praise of his vision for the music of Llandaff and the re-founding of the Choir School in 1880.

The origins of music in Llandaff are lost in the mists of time, perhaps over a thousand years or more, but the tradition was not been maintained continuously owing to the chequered history of the Cathedral. Certainly the medieval Cathedral possessed a choir of similar composition to other secular cathedrals. There is some evidence of the existence of a school here as early as the ninth century but like so much at Llandaff it flickered out during the Reformation. Choristers and priests would have sung plainsong masses, which became increasingly complex as the range of musical compositions increased until the development of polyphony in the Renaissance brought about a wholly new musical style.

From the time of the Reformation, Latin church music gave way to English services to accompany the new Prayer Book. These new theological imperatives changed choral music significantly, although a brilliant generation of Elizabethan composers from Byrd onwards found a distinctive new musical direction. The major cathedrals and colleges retained significant choirs up to the English Civil War. The Puritans were of course strongly opposed to sacred music and forbade it in church, but in the years after the Restoration the major choirs returned. The decades after 1660 were again graced by major church composers such as Henry Purcell.

In 1691, Llandaff's penurious situation meant that economies had to be made to keep the Cathedral running. In desperation the Dean and Chapter disbanded the entire choral foundation including their statutory four choristers and dismissed the organist. The organ itself was found in pieces at the turn of the eighteenth century by Browne Willis. It was decided instead that the school-master who ran the National School should sing gradual psalms with his students, accompanied on available instruments.

No steps were taken throughout the Georgian period to resume choral services, the choral endowment being used to finance John Wood's 'Italian Temple'. John Byng, travelling through Llandaff later in the eighteenth century, in fury called it "a modern building like a ballroom with venetian windows." He noted caustically that to keep anything at all going, two Vicars-choral were supposed to reside but there was no habitable residence for them. As a consequence, Byng found there to be hardly any services: "All in neglect and dishonourable to religion". Byng, later to become the fifth Viscount Torrington, kept a series of pithy travel journals from his visits to various cathedrals and recorded his impressions of the services and their music. Evidently there was little music to speak of at Llandaff.

This situation continued until the mid-nineteenth century when John Prichard began his restoration of the Cathedral's Gothic structure. Even as the architecture recovered its former glory, however, the music was still extremely poor. At Bishop Ollivant's enthronement in 1850 they had the National School master heading the procession. He gave out the Psalm, which was sung by about a dozen of his scholars accompanied by a bass viol, being the only instrument then in the possession of the Cathedral.

In the restored Cathedral in 1864 there was Sung Matins at 10a.m. and Evensong at 5p.m. Extracts from Minor Canon Fishbourne's description of the choir at this time were published in the 36th Report of the Friends of Llandaff Cathedral. However Llandaff had to 'borrow' choirs from English cathedrals such as Gloucester for major events until their own choral foundation had been re-established.

This was the state of the Cathedral's music when Dean Vaughan came to

The choir during the 1950s, in temporary stalls

Llandaff in 1879. His installation was a great occasion. By appointing Vaughan the Bishop had brought a whiff of outside air, a breath of sophistication to the Cathedral and he was determined that this installation should be a great function. There was a full choir and the Cathedral was packed with a large congregation eager to see the great man who had come from the metropolis. Vaughan, a great scholar and preacher who was a former headmaster of Harrow and Master of the Temple, re-founded the Cathedral School, the only surviving choir school in Wales.

On a brief visit before his installation Dean Vaughan met the Minor Canon and enquired about the state of Cathedral music. At his first Chapter meeting he raised the question of a residential Cathedral school, but on a larger scale than Minor Canon Fishbourne had suggested – he wanted between thirty or forty boys as he did not approve of small boarding schools. A day school already existed at this time but Vaughan's ambitions were for something more in line with foundations at the English cathedrals.

The Chapter approved the foundation of a choir school in the old Deanery on the Green. In the new Victorian establishment, the Cathedral choristers were

Choristers in the 1950s admire the cockerel before it was placed atop the spire

all boarders with Choral scholarships. The foundation of the school was ideally suited to Dean Vaughan's energies. Because Vaughan had been left with little to do due to the steady work of two former Deans with the fabric, he could now turn from the stones to the Cathedral services and staff. He described the Cathedral School as "my pet child, my chief interest, next to my men – the Doves always came first," (quoted in the *Western Mail* 16th October 1897).

The late Victorian era was a time when the choral services were prepared with great dignity, care, attention and detail, and the modern Cathedral choral tradition was built up throughout the Anglican Communion as far afield as Australia and New Zealand. At Llandaff, Dean Vaughan laid the foundation that was built upon by successive Deans, Organists and Choirmasters in Llandaff to this present day.

Today the Cathedral Choristers are all day boys with scholarships. The school moved from its old premises on the Green to the former Bishop's Palace during October 1958. It now occupies the Georgian building and has six hundred pupils, of whom about a quarter are girls.

The Victorian Nave, looking west, with the organ prominent on the right

The Organs of Llandaff

The recent history of the organs of Llandaff dates back to 1861 when an instrument was installed by Gray and Davidson at the time of the restoration of the building, which for a century and a half had been in ruins. The instrument cost £1,000. All traces of former organs had long disappeared.

An organ had been given to the cathedral after the Restoration of 1660 by Lady Kemeys of Cefn Mably, but when Browne Willis described Llandaff in

George Pace's 1958 organ case

1717 only some broken pipes remained. Browne Willis wrote in 1718 "The organ and organist had breathed their last about thirty years before"!

At the turn of the twentieth century the Gray and Davidson organ was sold to Usk Parish Church, where it remains to this day, having been recently restored by Nicholson's of Malvern. Its colourful Victorian decoration and horizontal trumpets remain very distinctive.

Llandaff's next organ was designed in 1898 by Hope Jones. It was the first organ in south Wales to embody the use of electro-pneumatic action but whereas its predecessor had a specification including a full diapason chorus on both great and swell divisions (with mixtures of four and three ranks respectively) the new instrument also possessed no stop above 4 foot pitch on three manuals and was typical of the degenerative nature of the British organ during this period.

Some years later, probably 1914, Norman and Beard added a solo organ and made a few alterations, bringing the number of speaking stops to thirty-four but still without mixtures and mutations. The instrument was extensively rebuilt in 1938 by Hill, Norman and Beard, with the addition of some upper work on the great and swell but no improvement to the pedal division.

In January 1941 when the landmine fell in the churchyard only the Lady Chapel and Sanctuary remained usuable. For five years music was provided by a manual Mustel organ blown by an operating pedal. Then a two manual organ by Hill (from the Roman Catholic Church at Eastcote) was moved there. Today, the Bates chamber organ of 1800, reconditioned and improved in 1960 by Henry Willis, is now used for worship in the Lady Chapel.

When the nave was restored in 1957, Hill, Norman and Beard rebuilt the main organ and installed a positive division. This was situated to striking visual effect in the cylindrical case atop George Pace's parabolic arch supporting the Epstein Majestas. Pace had conceived this innovation as a means of leading congregational singing (in a similar way to cathedrals with centrally-mounted organs above the Choir) but its specification was quite unsuitable for this purpose, just as its position was unsuitable for its proper use as a positive organ, which should have been in the main case.

In 1977 there was representation to the Chapter for a new organ to rectify this situation, or at least a rebuild to remedy the worst stops. Cecil Clutton was the advisor and four notable builders came to inspect the organ. Instead the Chapter decided to introduce solid state action and repair the wind supply. It was this solid state system that was damaged in the lightening strike of 2007.

A new organ is now installed, designed by Nicholson (see page 222). It involved a wholesale rebuilding of the entire postwar organ and its casework, with an entirely new set of pipes installed in the south aisle on the site of Pace's former organ loft to give the instrument an unparalleled range. The work was completed in time for the Easter services in 2010. There are 4103 pipes and 62 speaking stops. When the planned Solo organ and three more pedal stops are added, the total will be 4870 pipes and 77 stops making this the largest new organ for a British cathedral since that in Coventry Cathedral in 1962. The case was designed by Simon Platt based on his knowledge of Spanish cathedral organs.

Above and opposite, the striking new organ, installed in 2010

The Parish Choir of 1914

The Choirs at Llandaff

Daily music has been performed to a very high standard in the Cathedral as you would expect. Christian worship has always made great use of music to enhance and enrich its power. The choral music at Llandaff engages with the emotions and lifts the words to a great height. Music is not only an aid to worship but also a positive act of worship itself, performed by the accomplished choir on behalf of the congregation.

In 2010, the Cathedral has five choirs: the Consort which consists of the girls, men and women; the Cathedral Parish Choir; and the Merbecke Choir – a voluntary choir made up of members of the Cathedral congregation who sing when the Cathedral choir are on holiday.

The reason for having a separate Parish Choir is that the Cathedral also functions as the parish church for Llandaff. A choir for these services has existed since at least the late 1800s and was maintained as a traditional all-male group until girls and women were admitted around 2004. It has always provided a high standard of amateur choral singing.

There was a time when the 11a.m. service on the first Sunday of the month was a Choral Eucharist and on other Sundays a Choral Matins. This changed in the 1980s when the 11a.m. service became a Sung Eucharist. This means that many wonderful settings of the Matins canticles are no longer used in the

Cathedral repertoire other than the occasional Te Deum and Jubilate.

In the Eucharist there are a wide range of settings from Victoria, Byrd, Palestrina, the Latin masses by Haydn, Mozart and Schubert together with settings by composers as varied as Stanford, Darke, Vaughan Williams, Jackson, Mathias, Wills, Ireland, Caesar Berkeley, Britten, Simon Preston and Herbert Sumsion.

During the course of a year about ninety settings of the evening Canticles are sung and there is a repertoire of about three hundred anthems in regular use in addition to settings of the Responses. There about two hundred and sixty sung services in a year.

Since 2000 the Cathedral Choir have sung Evensong in many parishes throughout the Diocese. Their international tours have included visits to Singapore, Italy, Prague and Paris.

The Llandaff Choral Society

All cathedral choirs face significant problems of size when called upon to attempt large scale works or perform on special occasions. So it was in 1937 that the Llandaff organist and choirmaster Dr Harry Gabb suggested forming a 'Special Choir' to cope with such eventualities. The Cathedral Chapter nominated a committee of seven and arranged the finances. The inaugural concert was given on the 17th December 1937 with 56 singers.

When the Special Choir was formed, the Cathedral organ was almost unplayable and the choir concentrated on unaccompanied works. In 1938 the organ was rebuilt and more adventurous works were performed such as the Wesley Anthems. In 1939 the Red Cross authority asked every cathedral in the British Isles to give a concert in aid of their funds. The choir was enlarged through newspaper articles inviting any experienced singers who could attend all six rehearsals to come along to Llandaff to rehearse and perform the Brahms Requiem. Eventually the choir numbered 150 good and enthusiastic singers. The concert was such a success that it was repeated in St Germans and St Catherine's in central Cardiff. The proceeds donated to the Red Cross from the Llandaff performances were greater than any those given by any other cathedral.

At an emergency meeting of the Chapter in January 1940, under the extremities of war, only essential business was transacted and the choir operations suspended 'indefinitely' and prayers offered for safety and peace. Those present could not have foreseen that when the choir could meet again much of the Cathedral would lie in ruins.

In 1946 the choir was reformed and although the Cathedral was virtually unusable, the choir was keen to expand under the Dr Butcher's direction. There were some difficulties in that much music was not available, for publishers had allowed certain works to go out of print during the war; and the Lady Chapel, the only part of the Cathedral then in use, was not large enough for the choir. Additional performances were therefore given in Cardiff churches such as St John's, St Germans and sometimes St Catherine's.

As parts of the Cathedral remained unusable for up to ten years, performances in the other churches increased. The pattern of giving concerts at various churches was, however, continued in one form or another for the next thirty years.

Much work remained to be done on the building including the restoration of the organ and the choir's concert began financially benefiting the Cathedral Restoration Appeal in various ways.

It was therefore a double blow to the choir when the young Thomas Hallford, a conductor and musician of vision and energy, died suddenly. A proposed Restoration Appeal concert was hurriedly changed and Dr. Gabb returned from St Paul's Cathedral to conduct the performance.

The Llandaff Choral Society developed under the leadership of Eric Coningsby, Kenneth Turner, Eric Fletcher, Robert Joyce, Michael Smith, Avril Harding and the present conductor Dominic Neville. There was a growing basic repertoire of choral works including contemporary and Welsh composers, especially during the Robert Joyce period. Joyce, remembering his time with them, writes:

> I was with the Society for fifteen years from 1958-1973. I have still happy memories of the Monday evening rehearsals in the Prebendal House and all the devoted hard work put in to ensure rewarding performances. In particular, I remember the sense of partnership which developed between Tony Lewis, Deputy Conductor and Accompanist. His musicianship and sense of humour had much to do with the enjoyable atmosphere at rehearsals and the success of concerts.

The repertoire of the Society is wide ranging. All the standard choral works have featured in the Society's repertoire over the years: Bach, Beethoven, Handel, Hummel, Mendelssohn, Rossini, Schubert and Vivaldi; and the works of recent composers such as Britten, Elgar, Faure, Vaughan Williams. David Fanshawe's African Sanctus was one of the most colourful performances ever witnessed in the Cathedral.

The Society has also given world premiere performances of works by modern Welsh composers: Alan Hoddinott, Daniel Jones, William Mathias, Arwel Hughes, Grace Williams and David Nevens. For instance, 1972 marked the fiftieth anniversary of the founding of Urdd Gobaith Cymru by the late Sir Ifan ab Owen Edwards and in celebration they commissioned two new works.

One of these, 'Ieuenctid y dydd' by Alan Hoddinott to words by Sir Thomas Parry Williams, had its premiere on the 5th June, sung by the Cardiff Aelwyd Choir with the BBC Welsh Symphony Orchestra.

Avril Harding was the first woman to hold the post of Conductor and the Monteverdi Vespers was a performance not to be forgotten. Accompanists over the years have included V. Anthony Lewis, Colin Yeoman, David Geoffrey Thomas, Morley Lewis and the present incumbent John Cheer.

The Llandaff Festival

The Llandaff Festival was a very important part of Cathedral life from 1958-1986. It brought a tremendous number of people to the Cathedral from the City, the Diocese and from far and wide for a very cultured week of music, art and drama in the wonderful setting that Llandaff has to offer.

As the Cathedral neared completion in 1958, the Special Choir and Friends of the Cathedral suggested a Festival in celebration. The idea of the Festival sprang in the first instance from the Friends of the Cathedral to mark their Silver Jubilee in some suitable way and the conception of a Festival of Music and Drama commended itself from the beginning. Despite the risks, for the public support for concerts of this kind is often unpredictable, the Friends Council went ahead with the plans and set up the Festival Committee.

The Festival was under the leadership of Dean Thomas. He was a visionary who said:

> I see the Cathedral as a centre of activities from which life should radiate to the Diocese at large. So far as the cultural life is concerned there is a place for the Cathedral to be a centre of art in all its forms. It should encourage art and musical festivals and has a specific contribution to make with such things as Mystery Plays!

Due to the respect and influence he held in the Diocese and the City, the Festival was supported by the Welsh Arts Council, the City of Cardiff and Glamorgan County Council.

The first Artistic Director was Christopher Cory, a man of immense dedication, with wide musical contacts and the early success of the Festival owed much to him until his untimely death in 1981. Other directors were Hugh Tregelles Williams, Roy Bohana and George Guest of St John's College, Cambridge.

The lack of a proper concert hall in Cardiff made it all the more important that Llandaff should encourage the musical life of the City until the building of St. David's Hall in the City centre. The Llandaff Festival certainly did this to fill serious gaps in the musical life of the Principality's capital city.

The BBC Welsh Symphony Orchestra in concert at the Llandaff Festival

Significantly, the first Festival in 1958 was known as the Llandaff Cathedral Festival of Music and the programmes were designed to suit the venue. The opening recital on the restored organ was given by Jeanne Demessieux, was eagerly awaited and the virtuoso programme ended with an improvisation of a theme submitted by Archdeacon Gwynno James on the hymn tune Gwalchmai or 'King of Glory King of Peace'.

There were performances of Handel's dramatic oratorios 'Esther' and 'Jephtha' by Llandaff Special Choir, as the choral society was known at that time, and Cherubini's Requiem by Treorchy Male Voice Choir.

The festival had a very fine record of commissions by Welsh composers: Alun Hoddinott's 'Race of Adam', William Mathias' 'St Teilo' and Arwel Hughes' 'St Francis', Daniel Jones' oratorio 'St Peter', Grace Williams's *Missa Cambrensis* as well as symphonies from Daniel Jones, William Mathias' Harp Concerto and a larger number of shorter works. There were also many larger orchestral works with fine orchestras, chamber music and piano recitals from renowned international soloists and conductors.

The Festival grew in reputation until the death in 1981 of its first Artistic Director, Christopher Cory. By this time Cardiff's cultural scene had been transformed by the advent of the St David's Hall, which provided a previously unavailable concert venue for South Glamorgan. The festival struggled to find a new identity in the face of persistent issues and dwindling audiences. The trouble was that the Llandaff Festival was trying to operate on a similar scale to St. David's Hall, with lots of events packed into a short space of time, and this format no longer worked. A further problem was the commitment and purpose on the part of the large festival council. Recognising this, in 1987 Dean Alun Davies resigned as Chairman and Mr David Lambert as Company Secretary. The Festival was subsequently wound down.

Though the Festival was discontinued, the Cathedral had in its possession one of the finest pianos in Wales. Many eminent pianists have played the Steinway in concertos and recitals. The piano was chosen by Miss Moura Lympany who performed at the Festival many times.

In 2008, a fundraising appeal was begun for a new organ at Llandaff at a cost of £1.5 million. As Canon at Llandaff, I had the idea to recapture the momentum of this great festival of the past as part of our fundraising initiative. With the help of a very enthusiastic committee we re-launched the Llandaff Festival for one week in June 2008.

The concerts on Monday to Friday were free as the artists were giving their time and talent to the Organ Appeal and a retiring collection was taken at each concert. We were fortunate that we had a good partnership with the Royal Welsh College of Music and Drama who responded to the festival with great enthusiasm. The programmes included a Lieder recital; the Brass Ensemble of the Royal

The St Teilo play, performed at the 1963 Landaff Festival

Welsh College of Music and Drama; an organ recital by Huw Tregelles Williams; a piano recital with students from the Royal Welsh College; a performance by the Llandaff Cathedral Choral Society; and the Festival Service of Thanksgiving with a champagne and canapés lunch which followed. The Festival made over £11,000 towards the organ appeal and gave many young musicians the opportunity to perform in a marvellous building.

The 2009 Festival surpassed all expectations, raising the grand sum of £31,000 towards the organ appeal. Perhaps the Llandaff Festival will return as an annual or semi-annual fixture in Cardiff's cultural calendar.

Coda: Llandaff Cathedral Music Today

Today, the Cathedral's music is more popular than ever before, as much with regular worshippers as with the casual visitor. What is on offer, and how it is presented, has a magnetic appeal for them and is an essential ingredient in their worship. It follows that the expectations of the listeners are high and they derive much inspiration and spiritual benefit from the music.

Even if in cathedrals the role of the congregation is lessened in terms of vocal participation, compared to parish worship, it is possible and desirable for many to participate silently. This appeals as a means of escaping from the noise which characterises so much contemporary worship. Not everyone wishes to sing and, in any event, the cathedral repertoire was conceived purely for choirs to perform. A highly-skilled choir singing on behalf of a congregation is able to mediate and contemplate through music, enriching their spiritual life as a result.

The Cathedral continues to fulfil an important function as a centre for musical activity in the Diocese and city. The round of Cathedral worship at Llandaff goes on keeping alive the age-old tradition of Cathedral music that is peculiar to Britain and the envy of the musical world. The Cathedral Choristers under Richard Moorhouse strive for as high a standard as possible, in the hope that just occasionally, in the words of John Milton, they may "bring all heaven before our eyes."

Bibliography

'Acts of the Bishops of Llandaff, Books i–iv.' *Llandaff Records*, vol. ii–iv, 1908–12

Annual Report of the Friends of Llandaff Cathedral,1931, 1964, etc.

Debra Bardo and Madeleine Gray, 'The Power and the Glory: The Medieval Tombs of Llandaff Cathedral' *Welsh Journal of Religious History*, 2 2007

Enid Bird, *Organists and Organs of the Welsh Cathedrals in the Twentieth Century*, 1992

David Bateman, *History of Llandaff Cathedral*, new edn. (Cardiff) 1958

Roger Lee Brown, *The Letter Books of Edward Copleston, 1828-1849*, 2003

Browne Willis, *A Survey of the Cathedral Church of Llandaff*, 1719

Donald Buttress, 'Llandaff Cathedral in the Eighteenth & Nineteen Centuries', *Journal of the Historical Society of the Church in Wales*, 1966

W.R Compton-Davies, *Historical & pictorial glimpses of Llandaff Cathedral*, 1896

David Crouch (ed.), *Llandaff episcopal acta, 1140-1287* (South Wales Record Society) 1988

Michael Darby, *John Pollard Seddon*, 1983

Chrystal Davies, 'They looked at Llandaff' and 'Bishop Hugh Lloyd and the Battle of St Fagans' *Occasional Papers No.7*, Llandaff Society, 1992

E.T. Davies, 'John Wood's Italianate temple' *Publications of the Historical Society of the Church in Wales*, 6 (1956)

John Reuben Davies, *The Book of Llandaf and the Norman Church in Wales* (Studies in Celtic History, 21). (Woodbridge: Boydell Press) 2003.

John Reuben Davies, 'The Book of Llandaf: a twelfth-century perspective' *Anglo-Norman Studies*, 21 1998

Wendy Davies, *The Llandaff Charters*, 1979

Wendy Davies, *An Early Welsh Microcosm* (Royal Historical Society Studies in History) 1978

R.W.D. Fenn, 'St Teilo and the Llandaff Tradition', Friends Festival Lecture 1968

E.A. Freeman, *Remarks on the Architecture of Llandaff Cathedral: With an Essay towards a History of the Fabric* (London) 1850

Stephen Gardiner, *Epstein: Artist against the Establishment*, 1993

C. Given-Wilson, *The Chronicle of Adam of Usk 1377-1422* (Clarendon Press) 1997

W. de Gray Birch, *Memorials of the see and cathedral of Llandaff: derived from the Liber landavensis, original documents in the British Museum, H.M. Record Office, the Margam muniments*, Neath, 1912

Madeleine Gray, 'The medieval bishops' effigies at Llandaff Cathedral', *Archaeologia Cambrensis* vol. 153, 2004

Madeleine Gray, 'The diocese of Llandaff in 1563', *Journal of Welsh Religious History 2*, 1994

William Greenway, 'The election of John of Monmouth, bishop of Llandaff, 1287-97', *Morgannwg*, 5 1962

John R. Guy (ed.), *The Diocese of Llandaff in 1763*, 1991

G.E. Halliday, *Llandaff church plate* (London) 1901

Martin Harrison, *Victorian Stained Glass*, 1980

Philip Henderson, *William Morris: His Life Work and Friends*, (London: Thames & Hudson) 1976

John Hilling, *Llandaf past and present* (Barry) 1978.

L.J. Hopkin James, *The Soul of a Cathedral* (Cardiff) 1930

J. H. James, *A history and survey of the cathedral church of SS. Peter, Paul, Dubritius, Teilo, and*

Oudoceus, Llandaff, (Cardiff) 1898, Revised 1929

N.A. James & J.M. Lewis 'Speed revisited: a reconstruction of the road map of Llandaff in 1610', *Occasional Papers No.3*, Llandaff Society, 1987

Owain Jones, *Glyn Simon, his life and opinions*, 1980

Owain W. Jones, *Saint Michael's College, Llandaff 1892-1992*, 1992

John R Kenyon & Diane Williams, *Cardiff: Architecture and Archaeology in the Medieval Diocese of Llandaff* (*BAA Conference Transaction Series*, Maney Publishing) 2006

R.J. King, Handbook to the cathedrals of Wales: Llandaff, St. David's, St. Asaph, Bangor 1873

B.M. Lodwick, '"Poor Landaff" during the episcopate of John Tyler, 1706-1724', *Morgannwg*, 49 2005

E.W. Lovegrove, *The Cathedral Church of Llandaff*, 1934

Fiona MacCarthy, *William Morris, A Life for our times*, 1994

John H. Matthews (ed.), *Cardiff Records*, Vol. I-VI (Cardiff), 1911

Rice Merrick (ed. Brian Ll James), *Morganiae Archaiographia: A book of Glamorganshire antiquities South Wales Record Society* (Barry Island) 1983,

E.J. Newell, *Diocesan History of Llandaff*, 1902

John Newman (ed.), *The Buildings of Wales – Glamorgan*, 1995

F.J. North, *The Stones of Llandaff Cathedral* 1957

A. Ollivant, *Some account of the condition of the fabric of Llandaff cathedral : from 1575 to its reopening in 1857; with extracts from the act books of the Cathedral* (London) 1857

Peter Pace, *The Architecture of George Pace*, 1990

Fiona Pearson, *Goscombe John at the National Museum of Wales* 1979

M.J. Pearson, 'Introduction: The Welsh Cathedrals 1066-1300", *Fasti Ecclesiae Anglicanae 1066-1300* volume 9

M.J. Pearson, *The Welsh Cathedrals (Bangor, Llandaff, St Asaph, St Davids)* 2003

John Perkins, *The building stones of Cardiff.* Geological trail guides (University College Cardiff Press) 1984

T.B. Pugh, *Glamorgan County History* Vol. III 'The Middle Ages: The Marcher Lordships of Glamorgan and Morgannwg and Gower and Kilvey from the Norman Conquest to the Act of Union of England and Wales', 1971

Jeremy Knight, 'From Villa to Monastery: Llandough in Context', *Medieval Archaeology*, 49 (Maney) 2005

Lambert Rees, *Timothy Rees of Mirfield and Llandaff*, 1945

A.C. Sewter, *The stained glass of William Morris and his circle* (New Haven: Yale) 1974

Evelyn Silber & Terry F. Friedman, *Jacob Epstein: Sculpture and Drawings,* 1984

W. A. Strange, 'The rise and fall of a saint's community: Llandeilo Fawr, 600-1200', *The Journal of Welsh Religious History*, new series 2 (2002)

Lawrence Thomas, *The Reformation in the Old Diocese of Llandaff*, 1930

Herbert Thompson, *Llandaff Cathedral – An Amateur's Study*, 1924

Malcolm Thurlby, *Romanesque Architecture and Sculpture in Wales* (Logaston Press) 2006

David Walker (ed), *A History of the Church in Wales,* 1976

Roger White: *Britannia Prima* (The History Press, Cirencester) 2007

Glanmor Williams, *Wales and the Reformation*, 1997

E.W. Williamson, 'The inimitable chancellor Bogo de Clarc', *Publications of the Historical Society of the Church in Wales*, 1 (1947)

Bishops, Deans and Organists of Llandaff

BISHOPS

982-993	Marcluith	c.1557-1560	vacant for 3 years
993-1022	Bledri	1560-1575	Hugh Jones
1022-1059	Joseph	1575-1591	William Blethyn
1059-1107	Herewald	1591-1594	Gervase Babington
1107-1134	Urban	1594-1601	William Morgan
vacant for 6 years		1601-1618	Fraser Godwin
1140-1148	Uhtred	1618-1619	George Carleton
1148-1183	Nicholas ap Gwrgant	1619-1627	Theophilus Field
1186-1191	William de Saltmarsh	1627-1639	William Murray
1193-1218	Henry de Abergavenny	1639-c.1644	Morgan Owen
1219-1229	William de Goldcliff	1644-1660	vacant during Commonwealth
1230-1240	Elias de Radnor		
1240-1244	William de Christchurch	1660-1667	Hugh Lloyd
1245-1253	William de Burgh	1667-1675	Francis Davies
1253-1256	John de la Ware	1675-1679	William Lloyd
1257-1266	William de Radnor	1679-1707	William Beaw
1266-1287	William de Braose	1707-1724	John Tyler
1287-1297	Philip de Staunton or vacant	1724-1728	Robert Clavering
1297-1323	John de Monmouth	1728-1738	John Harris
1323-1323	Alexander de Monmouth	1738-1740	Matthias Mawson
1323-1347	John de Egglescliffe	1740-1748	John Gilbert
1347-1361	John Paschal	1748-1754	Edward Cresset
1361-1382	Rodger Cradock	1754-1761	Richard Newcome
1383-1385	Thomas Rushook	1761-1769	John Ewer
1385-1389	William Bottlesham	1769-1769	Jonathan Shipley
1390-1393	Edmund Bromfeld	1769-1782	Hon. Shute Barrington
1394-1395	Robert Tideman of Winchcombe	1782-1816	Richard Watson
		1816-1819	Herbert March
1395-1396	Andrew Barret	1819-1826	William Van Mildert
1396-1398	John Burghill	1826-1827	Charles Richard Sumner
1398-1407	Thomas Peverel	1827-1849	Edward Copleston
1408-1423	John de la Zouche	1849-1882	Alfred Ollivant
1425-1440	John Wells	1883-1905	Richard Lewis
1440-1458	Nicholas Ashby	1905-1931	Joshua Pritchard Hughes
1458-1476	John Hunden	1931-1939	Timothy Rees
1476-1478	John Smith	1939-1957	John Morgan
1478-1496	John Marshall	1957-1971	William Glyn Hughes Simon
1496-1499	John Ingleby	1971-1975	Eryl Stephen Thomas
1500-1516	Miles Salley	1976-1985	John Worthington Poole Hughes
1517-1537	George de Athequa		
1537-1545	Robert Holgate	1985-1999	Roy Thomas Davies
1545-c.1557	Anthony Kitchin	1999-	Dr Barry Cennydd Morgan

DEANS

1840-1843	John Probyn
1843-1845	William Bruce Knight
1845-1857	William Daniel Conybeare
1857-1877	Thomas Williams
1877-1879	Henry Lynch-Blosse
1879-1897	Charles John Vaughan
1897-1913	William Harrison Davey
1913-1926	Charles Edward Thomas Griffith
1926-1929	Frederick William Worsley
1929-1931	Frank Garfield Hodder Williams
1931-1948	David John Jones
1948-1954	William Glyn Hughes Simon
1954-1968	Eryl Stephen Thomas
1968-1971	Gordon Lewis Phillips
1971-1977	John Frederick Williams
1977-1993	Alun Radcliffe Davies
1993-1999	John Rogers (Retired)
2000-	John Thomas Lewis

ORGANISTS

1861	John Bernard Wilkes
1866	Francis Edward Gladstone
1870	Theodore Edward Aylward
1876	Charles Lee Williams
1882	Hugh Brooksbank
1894	George Galloway Beale
1937	William Henry Gabb
1946	Albert Vernon Butcher
1949	Thomas Hallford
1950	Eric Arthur Coningsby
1955	Charles Kenneth Turner
1957	Eric Howard Fletcher
1958	Robert Henry Joyce
1974	Michael John Smith
2000	Richard Moorhouse

Image Acknowledgements

The publisher is grateful to the following for permission to reproduce the images in this book:

David Abbott: 201, 212; *The Architect*: 186; *The Builder*: 83; the Cathedral archives: 8, 11, 19, 30, 53, 44, 48, 61, 65, 67, 68, 70, 72, 73, 79, 82, 84, 87, 95, 96, 97, 98, 99, 121, 129, 145, 184, 217, 218, 219, 224; *The Daily Herald*: 90, 91, 94; J.H. James: Endpapers, 24, 32, 34, 36; Nevil James: 13, 58, 81, 105, 106, 110, 124, 133, 150, 179, 206, 208, 210; Delme Jenkins: 102, 104; National Library of Wales: 15; Nick Lambert: 41, 222, 223; Stanley J. Milner: 29, 85; R.J.L. Smith: 26, 37, 40, 115, 118, 119, 125, 127, 130, 134, 139, 143, 148, 149, 152, 153, 155, 159, 160, 162, 165, 166, 169, 173, 175, 176, 177, 181, 188, 189, 192, 193, 196, 200; Stanley Travers: 28, 42, 103, 107, 108, 109, 111, 112, 120, 123, 137, 140, 146, 164, 168, 220, 228, 230; John Vesey: 213

Index

?LADY RIPLEY

Abergavenny Abbey 45
Adam of Usk 39
Armstead, Henry Hugh 78, 101, 119, 128-9, 131, 132, 163, 165; memorial to Henry Thomas 163, 180

BBC Welsh Symphony Orchestra 227, *228*
Bishopston 11
Bliss, Sir Arthur 113
Book of Llandaff q.v. *Liber Landavensis* 14-7, 20, 199
Boxholm, John 45
Brandon, David 71
Bristol Cathedral 30, 59
Brown, Ford Madox 120, 126, 157, 173, 174-8
Brozavic, Jan 130
Bruce, Henry, Lord Aberdare 120, 154
Buckler, John 38
Burges, William 119, 121
Burne-Jones, Edward 126-7, 157, 173, 174-8; 'Six Days of Creation' 117, 126-7, *127*, 147
Byng, John 216

Pope Calixtus II 23
Caradog ap Gruffudd 21
Cardiff Friary 45
Carey, Marion Louise 180
Carter, John 38
Castell Coch 22, 121
Charles I 47
Charles, Rollo 153
Chepstow Priory 25
Christ Chuch Cathedral, Dublin 33
Christian, Iwan 9
Churches: *All Saints, Llandaff* 202; *St Catharine's, Baglan* 80; *St Catherine's, Hoarwithy* 80; *St Catherine's, Cardiff* 225; *St Germans, Cardiff* 225; *St John's, Cardiff* 21, 64; *St John Evangelist, Canton* 80, 120; *Llangwm Uchaf* 80; *St Margaret's, Aberdare* 154; *Malty Parish Church* 164; *St Mary's, Cardiff* 21; *St Mary's, Tenby* 161; *St Mary's, Usk* 78; *St Mary's, Wootton* 27; *Nazareth House, Cardiff* 80; *St Peter's, Newchurch* 80, *St Tewdric's, Mathern* 41; *Usk Parish Church* 220
de Clare, Bogo 38
Clarke, Guy 89
Clarke, Edward 78-79, 123, 128-9, 160, 163, 165
Clarke, William 129, 131, 135, 171
Clarke, Wyndham 130
Cole, Rev William 64
Conybeare, Crawford 75
Conybeare, Henry 76

Conybeare, John C. 72
Cornforth, Fanny 157
Cranmer, Thomas 46
Crichton-Stuart, John, 2nd Marquess of Bute 163
Crichton-Stuart, John Patrick, Third Marquess of Bute 77, 119, 121, 131

David, Evan 173-4
Davies, Robert 1
Demessieux, Jeanne 229
Dixon, William Francis 178
Dore Abbey 33
Duncan, John T. 204
Durham Cathedral 167-8
Durst, Adam Lidiart 101; font 112, 136-8, *137*, 199

Edinburgh Cathedral 136
Edward I 38
Edward IV 62, 163
Edward VI 43, 46
Elizabeth I 46
Elizabeth II 113
Ely Cathedral 77
Epstein, Jacob 101, 122, 138-45: 'Christ in Majesty' 110, 117, 120, 135, 138-45, 170
Evans, Col. Lionel 167
Ewenny Priory 22, 25, 27
Excell, John 130

Ferry, Benjamin 77
fitz Hamon, Robert 21, 23
Forrest, W.R.H. 190
Fowler, Charles B. 83
Fra Angelico 120
Freeman, E.A. 31, 69
Friends of Llandaff Cathedral 66, 86, 87, 148, 158, 167, 171, 174, 191, 195, 197, 206, 208, 216, 227

Gill, Charles 89
Glastonbury Abbey 31, 33
Gloucester Cathedral 25, 76

Halliday, George 9
Harding, Sir John D. 187
Henry II 22, 27, 33, 124
Henry VIII 43, 46
Herbert, William 43
Hereford, Cathedral 25; Diocese of 22, 27
Hoddinot, Alun: 'Ieunectid y dydd' 227; 'Race of Adam' 229
Holman Hunt, William 128
Hughes, Arthur 120

Hughes, Arwel: 'St Francis' 229
Hughes, Timothy 157

Insole, George 82, 185
Insole, George Claude 185
Insole, James 180

James, J.H.: *A History and Survey of the Cathedrl Church of SS Peter, Paul, Dubritius, Teilo and Oudoceus Llandaff* 7
James I 47
Jenkins, Delme *108*
King John 31, 159
John, William Goscombe 117, 130-3, 135; 'Canon James Buckley' (medallion) 132; 'Canon James Buckley' (statue) 133, *133*; Great War Memorial' 131; 'Bishop Joshua Hughes' (medallion) 133; 'Bishop Richard Lewis' (bronze) 132; 'St David' 131; 'Dean Charles Vaughan' 132;
Jones, Daniel: 'St Peter' 229
Joubert, Felix 185-6

Kaye, Geoffrey 167, *168*
Kemeys, Lady Anne 219
Lambert, David 229
Larkworthy, Peter 85, 116, 158, 195
Laud, William 47
Lear, Edward 120
Lewis, Sir William Baron Methyr 182, 190
Lhuyd, Edward 21, 49
Liber Landavensis q.v. *Book of Llandaff* 14-17, 20, 23, 25
The Life of Teilo 16, 23
Lincoln Cathedral 84
Llancarfan, monastery at 10, 17, 18, 20, 21
Llancarfan Cartulary 16

Llandaff Cathedral
ARCHITECTURAL FEATURES
Archdeacon's Castle 30; *Bishop's Castle* 9, 12, 22, 29-30, *40; belltower* 30, 41, 199, *200; Bishop's throne* 57, 77, 78, 121, 163, 165; *Cathedral clock* 201, 204; *Chapter House* 33, 56-57, 73, 76, 89, *104*, 104, 175, 197; *Italianate Temple* 9, 49, 66-69, *67, 68,* 72, 75, 78, 109, 151, 169, 216; *Jasper Tower* 9, 35, 40, 54, 66, 76, 89, 91, 113, 158, 161, 169, 199, 200, 205; *north and south doors* 29-31, *30; northern tower* 31, 54; *Prebendal House* 89, 9, 100, 103, 132, 197, 226; *processional way* 35, 69, 169; *south west tower* 49, 54, 64, 121, 128; *southern tower* 31, 35, 49, 54, 76; *spire* 35, 77, *106,* 107-8, *108; Teilo Cross* 14; *St Teilo's Door* 55, 84, 100; *Teilo Shrine* 25, 27, 38; *Urban arch* 29, 49, 57, 60, 74, 81, 93, 95, *96,* 96, 100, 101, 113, 154, 158, 164, 191; *west front* 29, 31, 33, *34,* 35, 54, 55, 117

ART (see also individual artists)
'Falling Asleep of the Blessed Mary', 125-6, *125; 'Madonna and Child'* (school of Murillo) 153-4, *153; Marshall throne* 40, 57, 151-3, *152,* 172; *Medieval Majestas* 124-5, *124; pillar cross* 19-20; *processional cross* 169
BELLS 199-214; *bell ringers* 207, 213; *St Peter's Bell* 199; *Teilo's bell* 199
CATHEDRAL CLERGY *Archdeacons:* David Davies 85; Frederic Edmondes 83; Edward Gamage 201; Charles Green 182; Gwynno James 229; John, Smyth 45, 46; *Bishops:* George de Athequa 43, 45; Gervaise Babbington 47; William Beaw 49; William Blethin 45, 46-7; William de Breuse 38, 158-9; Edmund Bromfield 160; Edward Copleston 69, 71, 74, 163, 172; Francis Davies 48, 201; John Harris 66-7; Henry of Abergavenny 31, 159; Herewald 20, 21, 22; Robert Holgate 43, 45; John Hughes 132; Anthony Kitchin 43, 45, 46; Hugh Jones 45, 46; John of Monmouth 38-40; Joseph 18, 21; Richard Lewis 163; Hugh Lloyd 48; William Lloyd 49; John Marshall 40, 43, 57; John Morgan 136; William Morgan 47, 129; William Murray 200; Alfred Ollivant 74, 80, 108 119; 120-1, 128, 132, 152, 163, 171, 216: *Account of the Condition of the Fabric from 1575 to the present time* 78; Morgan Owen 48; John Paschall 38; Charles Sumner 112; William of Radnor 161; Timothy Rees 87, 136; Urban 14, 20, 21, 22-30, 35; William de Braose 35, 38; William Goldcliff 31; William Saltmarsh 29, 30; *Canons:* William Bruce 187; E.T. Davies 66; Edward Fishbourne 80, 216, 217; Henry Morgan 46; *Curate:* Bob Evans 142; *Deans:* William Bruce Knight 69, 71, 72, 114, 172; James Rice Buckley 132, *133;* William Conybeare 72-3, 74-6, 114, 173, 183, 197; Alun Davies 145, 207, 229; David J. Jones 85-6, 88-92, 100, 101, 114, 122, 147, 185, 197; Henry Lynch-Blosse 204; Glyn Simon 100, 105, 114, 122, 126, 138, 141, 142, 164, 178, 190, 191, 206; Eryl Thomas 105, *107, 108,* 108, 114, 122, 144, 147, 167, 227; Charles Vaughan 215, 216-17, 218; Thomas Williams 76, 79, 114, 203; Frank Williams 184; F.W. Worsley 84; *Precentor:* Henry Douglas 71, 172
CATHEDRAL OFFICERS *Architects:* Donald Buttress 85, 115-6, 126, 158, 163; Robert Heaton 114, 115; Frederick R. Kempson 83-84, 151, 191; Sir Charles Nicholson 38, 85, 86, 88, 89, 92-101, 108, 114, 122, 135, 147, 158, 169, 190; George Pace 60, 62, 69, 82, 101-4, *103,* 108-10, 112, 113, 114, 122, 126, 128, 138-41, 144, 146, 147, 148-9, 151, 153, 158, 164-5, 167-68, 169, 174, 175, 180, 198, 199, 206, 221; John Prichard 9-10, 33, 38, 59, 60, 71, *72,* 74-81, 96-

7, 100, 101, 104, 114, 116, 119, 121, 128, 131, 147, 165, 169, 172, 174, 180, 216; Seddon John Pollard 59, 75-80, 82, 101, 113, 114, 119, 120-1, 136, 154, 158, 166, 169, 183, 184, 185, 186; *Verger*. Bob White 88

CHAPELS *(St) David Chapel* 35, 54, 55, 60, 125, 126, 128, 132, as regimental chapel 98, 100, 103, 104, 108-9, 114, *115*, 117-8 , 166-9, 197; *St Dyfrig Chapel* 59, 62, 96, 114, 126, 151, 161, 163, 164, 172, 182; *St Illtyd Chapel* 113, 116, 158; *Lady Chapel* 35-8, *36-37*, 49, 54, 59, 60, 62, 63, 64, 69, 71, 72, 74, 77, 83-4, *84*, 85, 88, 92, 93, 102, 112, 113, 116, 122, 135, 147, 151, 158, 161, 171, 183, 187-90, 198, 226; *Mathew Chapel* 59, 96; *Teilo Chapel* 86, 116, 172

WINDOWS 171-98; *loss during World War 2* 171, 183-7; *medieval glass* 171-2; *removal for World War 2* 87, 171, 188; *Mothers' Union windows* 194-95; *Pre-Raphaelite* 101; *Chapter House* windows 197; *Dixon window* 178-80, *179; Evan David window 173*, 174-5; *Lady Chapel: 188, 189*, 187-90; east window 171, 172, 182; north window 172; Tree of Jesse 38, 191-94, *192, 193*; Prebedal House windows 197; *St David Chapel* 167; *St Dyfrig Chapel* east window 172, 199; *St Teilo Chapel* east window 172; *west front windows* 183-85, *184*, 185-6, 206

HISTORY 9-10; *bombed* 87-95, *90, 91, 94, 96; and Civil War* 48, 54, 57, 118, 171-2, 216; *'emergency cathedral'* 93, *95*, 104, 226; *expansion* 14-28, 31; *first church, 'little minster'* 18, 27; *foundation* 14, 16; *impact of Industrial Revolution* 50, 119; *neglect in 15th-17th centuries* 40-9, 54, 63, 74; *19th century restoration* 59, 60, 71-82, 100, 101, 109, 113, 119, 169, 173-4; *Norman cathedral* 20, 23, 25-30; *patron saints* 14, 128, 182, 211; *possible transfer of see to Cardiff* 64, *possible unification with Bristol* 69; *postwar restoration* 93-116, 169; *and the Reformation* 38, 43-7, 54, 118, 151, 215-16

MUSIC 215-31; *pre-victorian music* 215-6; Llandaff Festival 227-30, *228, 230;* Directors: Roy Bohana 227; Christopher Cory 227, 228; George Guest 227; Hugh Tregelles Williams 227, 230; *Choral* Accompanists: John Cheer 227; Colin Lewis 227; Morley Lewis 227; David Thomas 227; Colin Yeoman 227; Conductors: Eric Coningsby 226; Eric, Fletcher 226; Harry Gabb 225, 226; Thomas Hallford 226; Avril Harding 226, 227; Robert Joyce 226; Richard Moorhouse 231; Dominic Neville 226; Michael Smith 226; Kenneth Turner 226; current choirs 224-5; choir 49; choir school 215; Llandaff Choral Society 225-27; Director: Albert Butcher 225; *Organ* 17the century organ 216, 219-20; 19th century organ 78, 80, 82-3, 219-20; Hope

Jones organ 82, 99-100, 221, 225; pulpitum organ 110-11, 221, 229; 21st century organ 221, *222-3,* 229; organists 49, organ loft 18C 57; Lady Chapel organ 221;

TOMBS Bishop de Breuse 158; St Dyfrig 25, 160, *160*; Bishop Henry of Abergavenny 159, *159;* Bishop Marshall 60, *61*, 62, 161; Sir Christopher Mathew 54, 62, 63, 151, 161-62, *162*; Sir David Mathew 62-3, 163, 172; Sir William Mathew *42*, 55, 62, 80, 161, 162, 172, 174; St Teilo 43-45, 46, 118, 160, 163, 199

Cathedral School 12, 56, 80, 89, 131, 132, 152, 217-8

Llandaff (village) 9-10, 21, 30, 31, 43, 47, 55, 83, 166

Llandaff Court 12, 19

Llandaff Green *11*, 12, 22, 41

Llandaff Diocesan Mothers' Union 194, 208

Llanddewi Ystradenni 21

Llandeilo Fawr, monastery at 16-17, 20

Llandough, monastery at 12, 13, 17, 18-20, 21; early cross at 13, 19-20; Irbic cross at 20

Llanthony Priory 33

Llantwit Major, monastery at 12, 13, 17, 18

Lord, Joseph 52

Lympany, Moura 229

Malmesbury Abbey 27

Margam Abbey 22, 25, 45

Margam Annals 21

Markland, J.H. 173

Queen Mary 43, 46

Mathern 11, 17; Bishop's Palace 39, 41, 43, 46, 47, 49, 152

Mathew family 30, 41, 45, 161; Sir Christopher 55; Sir David Mathew 62-3, 162, 163; Lady Elizabeth Mathew 63; Huw Mathew 55, 162; Lady Jenette Mathew 42, 55; Miles Mathew 43; Sir William Mathew 42, 55, 162

Mathias, William: Harp Concerto 229; 'St Teilo' 229, *230*

McCracken, Robert J. 145

Memling, Hans 156

Merrick, Rice 47

Milo ap Griffith 120, 144; Pre-Raphaelite figures 120, *120*, 144; statue of John Batchelor 144

Mitchell, Lionel 166-7

Morgan, John 101, 110, 142

Morris, Jane 127, 157

Morris, William 126, 157, 173, 174-8

Munro, Alexander 121

Murillo, Bartolome Esteban 154

Murray, H.G. 185

National Library of Wales 15-16, 59

National Museum of Wales 131, 153, 201

Neath Abbey 45
Newport Friary 45
Nobis, Bishop of St Teilo 20
Norman presence in Wales 10-11, 14, 21-2;
castles: Caerphilly 22, Cardiff 11, 21, 22, 25, 27,
119, 120, 121, 126, Chepstow 25, Kidwelly 27
Norman, Herbert 90, 92

O'Connor, Michael 173, 182, 195
Ollivant, J.E. 187
Opie, John 120
Ouseley, Sir Frederick Gore 78
Owain Glyndwr 39, 41

Parker, Matthew 45, 46
Pearson, John L. 83
Piper, John 101, 113, 122; window 172, 195, *196*
Powell, Charles 182
Powell, P. 183
Prichard, Rev Richard 71

Rathbone, Harold 127
Rees, Ieuan 114; memorial of bombing 164;
memorial to William Morgan 163-4; memorial to
Glyn Simon 164; memorial to Welsh Regiment
168; memorial to 614 Squadron 168
Reith, John 92
Reyntiens, Patrick 101, 113, 195
Riverside Church, New York 144-5
Roger, Bishop of Salisbury 27
Roman presence in South Wales 10-13, 18
Roper, Frank 86, 102, 117, 122, 127, 146-50,
168, 169; 'Flowers of Mary' 86, *148*, 148;
Passiontide lecterns 122, *146*, 147; figure of St
Francis 150; St Teilo frieze 148-9, *149, 150,* 199
Rossetti, Dante Gabriel 119, 120, 122, 126, 127;
'The Seed of David' 79, 86, 87, 98, 101, 113,
116, 117, 120, 122, 123, 154-8, *155,* 191
Rossetti, William 157
Royal Welsh College of Music and Drama 229
Rushton, T.J. 101
Ruskin, John 119, 120, 127
Ryan, Sally 144, 145

St Albans Abbey 94, 97
St Davids, Cathedral 30, 31, 33, 150, 159;
Diocese of 27
St Dogmael's Abbey 161
St Michael's College 100, 106, 132
St Woolos Cathedral 80
Saints: *St Cadoc* 16, 17, 18; *St David* 199; *St
Dochau* 17, 18; *St Dyfrig* 17, 18, 22, 25, 27, 54,
138; *St Euddogwy* 17, 20; *St Gwynllyw* 17; *St
Illtud* 13, 17, 18; *St Padarn* 199; *St Paul* 14; *St
Peter* 14; *St Teilo* 14-16, 20, 39, 138, 199; *St
Tewdrig* 17

Salisbury Cathedral 35
Sarum Cathedral 27
Scott, George Gilbert 77
Scott, Sally 126
Seddon, Thomas 75, 119, 121, 154
Seldon, John 15
Siddal, Elizabeth 127, 157
Sims, Ronald 114
Southwark Cathedral 59
Sparrow, James Silvester 180-1
Speed, John map (1610) 43, *48*
Spencer, Stanley 101, 109, 122, 141, 147
Stock-Hill, Col. Edward 79, 129, 183
Stokes, Harry 130
Swinburne, Algernon Charles 157
Symonds, Richard: 'Diary of the Marches of the
Royal Army during the Great Civil War' 171-2

Teilo Gospels 20
Temple-Morris, Peter 92
Tewkesbury Abbey 21
Thomas, Henry 128, 180-2
Thomas, John Evan 121; memorial to Edward
Copleston 163; memorial to John Nicholl 163
Thomas, William 121
Tintern Abbey 9, 45
Traherne, John Montgomery 71, 172
Truro Cathedral 83, 136
Treorchy Male Voice Choir 229
Tudor, Jasper, Duke of Bedford 41

Walker, Arthur George 135; 'Virgin and Child'
88, 122, *134,* 147
Webb, Geoffrey 38, 83, 102, 116, 151, 183, 187-
94
Webb, Philip 126
Welch Regiment 88, 98, 103, 166-9
Wells Cathedral 31, 33, 84, 161
Westminster Abbey 35
Wilberforce, Samuel 75, 81
William the Conqueror 21
William Rufus 21
Williams, Grace: 'Missa Cambrensis' 229
Williams, Thomas 77, 78
Willemont, Thomas 71, 172, 190, 191
Willis, Browne 43, 49, 52-65, 80, 94, 95, 96,
199, 201, 216, 219-20
Winchelsey, Robert, 38
Winchester Cathedral 97
Wood, John 9, 49, 60, 66-69, 78, 151, 169, 216
Woolner, Thomas 80, 89, 101, 119, 121
Wyatt, Thomas Henry 59, 71, 75, 114
Wyon, Allan Gairdner 136; 'Rees Memorial' 136

York Minster 38, 71, 172

Pedestrian prose.

Poor editing.

Almost useless index

Some unnecessarily poor pics. e.g. p200, 159, 201,